GCSE Edexcel

Chemistry

Looking for the best way to prepare for Edexcel GCSE Chemistry?
This brilliant CGP book covers everything you need for exam success!

It's bursting with realistic exam-style questions on every topic.
All the core practicals are covered too and there are plenty of targeted analysis questions to test those tricky AO3 skills.

On top of expertly written questions on each topic, we've also included mixed questions, just like you'll face in the real exam. You'll find fully-worked answers at the back, so what are you waiting for — hurry up and get stuck in!

Exam Practice Workbook

Contents

☑ Use the tick boxes to check off the topics you've completed.

Topic 8 — Fuels and Earth Science

Topic 9 — Separate Chemistry 2

Mixed Questions

You can find some useful information about What to Expect in the Exams and other exam tips at cgpbooks.co.uk/GCSEChem-Edex/exams

Published by CGP

Editors:
Rob Hayman, Paul Jordin, Sarah Pattison.

Contributors:
Ian Davis, Chris Workman.

With thanks to Sharon Keeley-Holden for the proofreading.

With thanks to Jan Greenway for the copyright research.

Page 3 contains public sector information published by the Health and Safety Executive and licensed under the Open Government Licence.
http://www.nationalarchives.gov.uk/doc/open-government-licence/version/3/

Page 103 contains public sector information licensed under the Open Government Licence v3.0.
http://www.nationalarchives.gov.uk/doc/open-government-licence/version/3/

Data to construct a graph on page 103: Satellite sea level observations - NASA's Goddard Space Flight Center

Data for the global temperature anomaly and CO_2 concentration in the table on page 104: NOAA National Centers for Environmental information, Climate at a Glance: Global Time Series, published October 2022, retrieved on October 31, 2022 from https://www.ncdc.noaa.gov/cag/.

ISBN: 978 1 83774 004 8

Clipart from Corel®
Illustrations by: Sandy Gardner Artist, email sandy@sandygardner.co.uk
Printed by Elanders Ltd, Newcastle upon Tyne

Based on the classic CGP style created by Richard Parsons.

How to Use This Book

- Hold the book upright, approximately 50 cm from your face, ensuring that the text looks like this, not siɥʇ. Alternatively, place the book on a horizontal surface (e.g. a table or desk) and sit adjacent to the book, at a distance which doesn't make the text too small to read.
- In case of emergency, press the two halves of the book together firmly in order to close.
- Before attempting to use this book, familiarise yourself with the following safety information:

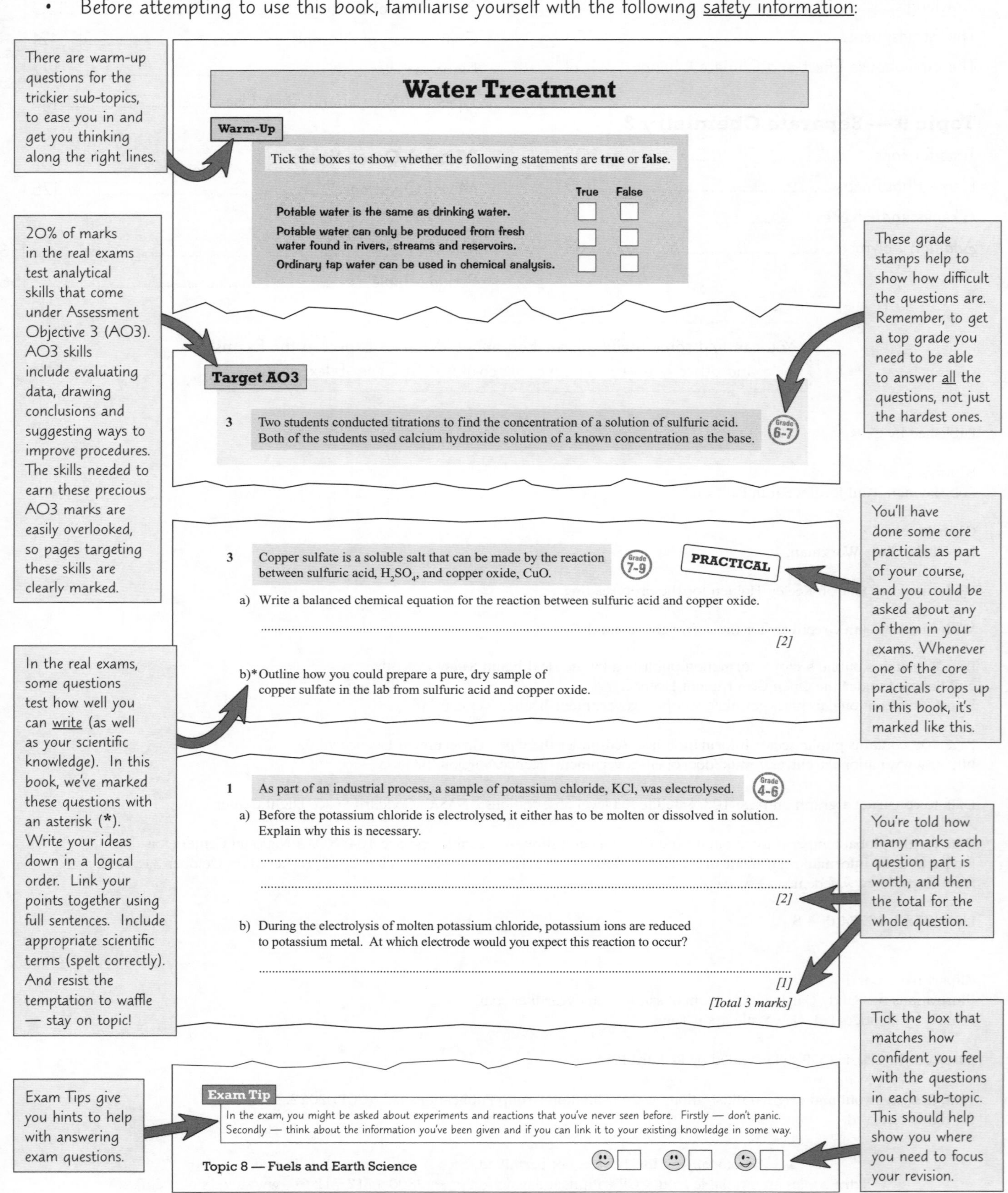

Chemical Equations

1 Hydrogen gas is used as a reactant in the Haber Process. It can be made using the following reaction. Grade 4-6

$$CH_4 + H_2O \rightarrow CO + 3H_2$$

Which of the following word equations correctly describes this reaction? Tick **one** box.

☐ **A** methane + water → carbon dioxide + hydrogen

☐ **B** ethane + water → carbon dioxide + hydrogen

☐ **C** methane + water → carbon monoxide + hydrogen

☐ **D** methane + water → carbon + oxygen + hydrogen

[Total 1 mark]

2 Calcium carbonate chips were reacted with nitric acid at room temperature. The products of the reaction were water, a gas and a salt solution. Grade 4-6

Complete the reaction equation by adding state symbols to describe the reaction.

$CaCO_3$(...........) + $2HNO_3$(...........) → $Ca(NO_3)_2$(...........) + H_2O (...........) + CO_2(...........)

[Total 2 marks]

3 Sodium metal can react with oxygen molecules in the air to form sodium oxide (Na_2O). Grade 4-6

Write a balanced equation for this reaction.

....

[Total 2 marks]

4 In a chemical reaction, sulfuric acid and aluminium metal react to form hydrogen gas and a salt solution of aluminium sulfate. Grade 6-7

Ben has written this equation for the reaction:

$$Al_{(s)} + H_2SO_{4\,(aq)} \rightarrow Al_2(SO_4)_{3\,(aq)} + H_{2\,(g)}$$

a) Explain what is meant by the symbol '(aq)' in the chemical equation.

....

[1]

b) Ben's equation is not balanced. Write a balanced chemical equation for this reaction.

....

[1]

[Total 2 marks]

5 Nitric acid can be made using ammonia. 

a) The first stage in the manufacture of nitric acid is to oxidise ammonia, NH_3, to nitrogen(II) oxide, NO. Balance the equation for the reaction.

$$\text{.........} \; NH_3 + \text{.........} \; O_2 \rightarrow \text{.........} \; NO + \text{.........} \; H_2O$$

[1]

b) The reaction below shows the final stage in the manufacture of nitric acid. The equation is not balanced correctly. Explain how you can tell.

$$2NO_2 + O_2 + H_2O \rightarrow 2HNO_3$$

....

....

[1]

[Total 2 marks]

6 Silver chloride, AgCl, can be made by reacting silver nitrate, $AgNO_3$, and sodium chloride, NaCl, together in a precipitation reaction. 

$$AgNO_{3\,(aq)} + NaCl_{(aq)} \rightarrow AgCl_{(s)} + NaNO_{3\,(aq)}$$

a) How can you tell from the reaction equation that this is a precipitation reaction?

....

[1]

b) Write a balanced ionic equation for the reaction above.

....

[2]

[Total 3 marks]

7 Balance the following symbol equation to show how sulfur reacts with nitric acid. 

$$S + HNO_3 \rightarrow H_2SO_4 + NO_2 + H_2O$$

....

[Total 1 mark]

8 Zinc reacts with tin sulfate solution in a redox reaction. The full reaction equation is shown below. 

$$Zn_{(s)} + SnSO_{4\,(aq)} \rightarrow ZnSO_{4\,(aq)} + Sn_{(s)}$$

Write the ionic equation for the reaction above.

....

[Total 2 marks]

Hazards and Risk

1 Eric is carrying out an experiment using some hazardous chemicals. One of the chemicals is stored in a flask, marked with the label shown in **Figure 1**.

Grade 4-6

Figure 1

a) Which of the following hazards are associated with the contents of the flask? Tick **one** box.

- [ ] **A** oxidising
- [ ] **B** corrosive
- [ ] **C** harmful
- [ ] **D** highly flammable

[1]

b) Suggest **one** safety precaution that Eric should take when using the chemical from the flask.

....

[1]

[Total 2 marks]

2 A lab technician is cleaning up a lab after an experiment. The experiment involved using chemicals from flasks marked with the label shown in **Figure 2**.

Grade 6-7

Figure 2

With reference to **Figure 2**, explain why the technician needs to be careful when disposing of the chemicals.

....

....

[Total 2 marks]

3* A student is planning an experiment to assess how the rate of a certain reaction changes with concentration. The reaction involves her using chemicals that are marked as harmful and corrosive. It also produces a gas.

Grade 7-9

Construct a risk assessment to outline the hazards associated with the experiment and the safety precautions that the student should take to reduce them.

....

....

....

....

....

....

....

....

[Total 6 marks]

The History of the Atom

Warm-Up

Draw **one** line from each atomic model to the correct description of that model.

Atomic Model	Description
Plum pudding model	A positively charged 'ball' with negatively charged electrons in it.
	A small, positively charged nucleus surrounded by a 'cloud' of negative electrons.
Bohr's model	Electrons in fixed orbits surrounding a small, positively charged nucleus.
Rutherford's nuclear model	Solid spheres with a different sphere for each element.

1 Models of the atom have changed over time. Grade 4-6

Which of the following statements is the best description of what scientists thought an atom was like before the electron was discovered? Tick **one** box.

☐ **A** Tiny solid spheres that can't be divided.

☐ **C** Flat geometric shapes.

☐ **B** Formless 'clouds' of matter.

☐ **D** Discrete packets of energy.

[Total 1 mark]

2 In 1911, Rutherford, Geiger and Marsden carried out the gold foil experiment. They fired positively charged alpha particles at gold foil. They predicted that most of the particles would pass straight through the foil and a few might be deflected slightly. Grade 6-7

a) Describe what actually happened to the alpha particles during the gold foil experiment and explain why it happened.

....

....

....

....

[4]

b) Name the scientist who adapted Rutherford's nuclear model by suggesting that electrons orbit the nucleus at specific distances.

....

[1]

[Total 5 marks]

The Atom

1 **Figure 1** shows the structure of a certain atom. Grade 4-6

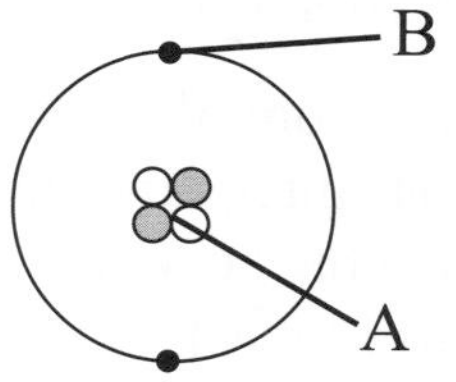

a) Name the region where most of the mass of the atom is concentrated.

....

[1]

B

A

Figure 1

b) What is the name of particle **B**?

....

[1]

c) State the **two** subatomic particles which are present in region **A**.

....

[1]

d) Use the relative charges of the subatomic particles to explain why an atom has no overall charge.

....

....

....

....

[3]

e) The atom shown in **Figure 1** has an atomic number of 2.
What is the name of the element that the atom in **Figure 1** makes up? Tick **one** box.

☐ **A** hydrogen ☐ **B** lithium ☐ **C** helium ☐ **D** beryllium

[1]

[Total 7 marks]

2 A potassium atom can be represented by the nuclear symbol $^{39}_{19}\text{K}$. Grade 4-6

a) What is the mass number of $^{39}_{19}\text{K}$?

....

[1]

b) What is the atomic number of $^{39}_{19}\text{K}$?

....

[1]

c) How many protons, neutrons and electrons does an atom of $^{39}_{19}\text{K}$ have?

protons: .... neutrons: .... electrons: ....

[3]

[Total 5 marks]

Isotopes and Relative Atomic Mass

1 This question is about isotopes. 

a) A neutral atom of sulfur, ^{32}S, has 16 electrons.
Sulfur has three other naturally occurring isotopes, with mass numbers 33, 34 and 36.
Complete the table in **Figure 1**, giving the number of protons, neutrons and electrons for each of the naturally occurring isotopes of sulfur.

Isotope	Number of Protons	Number of Neutrons	Number of Electrons
^{32}S	....	....	16
^{33}S	....	....	....
^{34}S	....	....	....
^{36}S	....	....	....

Figure 1

[3]

b) Atom **X** has a mass number of 51 and an atomic number of 23.
Atom **Y** has a mass number of 51 and an atomic number of 22.
Atom **Z** has a mass number of 52 and an atomic number of 23.

Identify which pair of atoms are isotopes and explain why.

....

....

....

[3]

[Total 6 marks]

2 **Figure 2** shows some information about three isotopes of silicon. 

Name	Atomic Number	Mass Number	Abundance (%)
Silicon-28	14	28	92.2
Silicon-29	14	29	4.70
Silicon-30	14	30	3.10

Figure 2

a) How many neutrons does an atom of silicon-29 contain?

neutrons = ...

[1]

b) Work out the relative atomic mass of silicon.

relative atomic mass = ...

[2]

[Total 3 marks]

3 Bromine has two main isotopes: Br-79 and Br-81. Grade 6-7

a) Give the definition of the term **isotopes**.

....

....

[1]

b) Bromine has an atomic number of 35. Calculate the number of neutrons in both isotopes.

Br-79 : .... neutrons

Br-81 : .... neutrons

[1]

c) The relative isotopic abundances of bromine-79 and bromine-81 are 12.67 and 12.32 respectively. Calculate the relative atomic mass of bromine. Give your answer to 2 significant figures.

relative atomic mass = ...

[2]

[Total 4 marks]

4 The relative atomic mass of every element can be found in the periodic table. Grade 6-7

a) Give the definition of the **relative atomic mass** of an element.

....

....

[2]

b) Explain why some elements have relative atomic masses that are not whole numbers.

....

....

[1]

[Total 3 marks]

5 Gallium can exist as two stable isotopes: Ga-69 and Ga-71. Grade 7-9

Give than 60.1% of gallium atoms are Ga-69 atoms, and the rest are Ga-71 atoms, calculate the relative atomic mass of gallium.

relative atomic mass = ...

[Total 3 marks]

Exam Tip

Don't let isotopes confuse you. Just because they've got different numbers of neutrons, a pair of isotopes will still have the same number of protons, so they're still the same element. Those relative atomic mass calculations aren't too bad either. Remember — if your isotopic abundances are given as percentages, then they should always add up to 100%.

The Periodic Table

1 Chemical elements are arranged in the periodic table. Grade 4-6

a) How are the elements ordered in the modern periodic table?

....

[1]

b) Why do elements in groups have similar chemical properties? Tick **one** box.

- ☐ **A** They have the same number of shells of electrons.
- ☐ **B** They have the same number of outer shell electrons.
- ☐ **C** They all have at least one full inner shell of electrons.
- ☐ **D** The atoms of the elements are similar in size.

[1]

[Total 2 marks]

2 Mendeleev created an early version of the periodic table, in which he arranged the elements according to their atomic masses and their properties. Mendeleev left some gaps in his table. Grade 6-7

a) Explain why Mendeleev left gaps in his table.

....

....

[1]

b) Mendeleev used his table to predict the properties of undiscovered elements that would fit in the gaps he left. One of these was an element in Group 4, which Mendeleev called **eka-silicon**. **Figure 1** shows some properties of the Group 4 elements silicon and tin, plus some predictions about the properties of eka-silicon.

	Silicon (Si)	**Eka-silicon (Ek)**	**Tin (Sn)**
Atomic Mass	28	72	119
Density in g/cm^3	2.3	?	7.3
Appearance	grey/silver non-metal	grey metal	grey metal
Formula of oxide	SiO_2	EkO_2	SnO_2
Formula of chloride	$SiCl_4$	?	$SnCl_4$
Reaction with acid	None	?	Slow

Figure 1

Use the information in **Figure 1** to predict the following properties of eka-silicon:

i) Density: ....

ii) Formula of chloride: ....

iii)Reaction with acid: ....

[3]

[Total 4 marks]

Electronic Configurations

1 The atomic number of neon is 10. Grade 6-7

How many electrons does neon have in its **outer shell**?

☐ **A** 2 ☐ **C** 8

☐ **B** 6 ☐ **D** 10

[Total 1 mark]

2 The atomic number of sulfur is 16. Grade 6-7

a) Write down the electronic structure of sulfur.

....

[1]

b) Draw a diagram to show how the electrons are arranged in a single sulfur atom.

[1]

[Total 2 marks]

3 Magnesium is found in group 2 and period 3 of the periodic table. Grade 6-7

a) Explain how you could use this information to **deduce** the electronic structure of magnesium.

....

....

....

....

....

[3]

b) Give the electronic structure of magnesium.

....

[1]

[Total 4 marks]

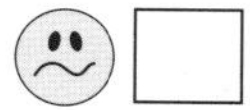  

Ions

Warm-Up

The formulas of the ion formed by four mystery elements are shown below. Draw lines to match each of the ions to the correct description of the element that it was formed from.

A^+	A non-metal from Group 6
D^-	A metal from Group 2
X^{2+}	A metal from Group 1
Z^{2-}	A non-metal from Group 7

1 Ions can have either a positive or a negative charge. Grade 6-7

a) Describe what happens to an atom when it turns into a negative ion.

....

[1]

b) Magnesium is in Group 2 of the periodic table.

i) Predict what charge a magnesium ion will have.

....

[1]

ii) Magnesium has the atomic number 12.
Calculate the number of electrons found in one magnesium ion.

number of electrons = ...

[1]

[Total 3 marks]

2 Potassium can react with oxygen to form the ionic compound potassium oxide. Grade 7-9

a) Which of following shows the correct formula for potassium oxide?

☐ **A** KO ☐ **B** KO_2 ☐ **C** K_2O ☐ **D** K_2O_2

[1]

b) The most common isotope of oxygen has an atomic number of 8 and a mass number of 16.
How many protons, neutrons and electrons would an oxide ion have?

protons = ...

electrons = ...

neutrons = ...

[3]

[Total 4 marks]

Ionic Bonding

1 Ionic bonding is one of the three types of chemical bonds found in compounds. Grade 4-6

a) In which of the following compounds are the particles held together by ionic bonds?
Put a tick in the box next to the compound that you think is ionic.

☐ calcium chloride ☐ carbon dioxide

☐ nitrogen monoxide ☐ phosphorus trichloride

[1]

b) **Figure 1** shows the formation of the ionic compound lithium chloride from its elements, but it is incomplete. Complete **Figure 1** by drawing an arrow to show the transfer of the electron, adding the charges of the ions and completing the chloride ion to show the electrons in its outer shell.

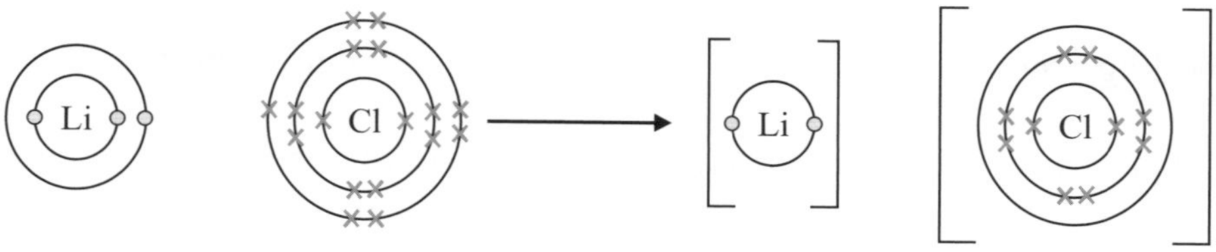

Li Cl → [Li] [Cl]

Figure 1

[3]

c) Name the force that holds the ions together in an ionic bond.

....

[1]

d) Suggest how you can tell from a dot and cross diagram that the particles in a compound are held together by ionic bonds.

....

....

[1]

[Total 6 marks]

2 Calcium fluoride, CaF_2, is an ionic compound. Grade 6-7

Draw a dot and cross diagram to show the bonding in calcium fluoride.
You should include the charges on the ions in your diagram.

[Total 4 marks]

Ionic Compounds

Warm-Up

Circle the correct words or phrases below so that the statement is correct.

In an ionic compound, the particles are held together by weak/strong forces of attraction.

These forces act in all directions/in one particular direction which results in the particles bonding together to form giant lattices/small molecules.

1 This question is about the structure and properties of ionic compounds. Grade 4-6

a) Which of the following properties is **not** typical for an ionic compound?
Tick **one** box.

☐ **A** high boiling point ☐ **C** high melting point

☐ **B** conduct electricity in the liquid state ☐ **D** conduct electricity in the solid state

[1]

b) Name the type of structure that ionic compounds have.

....

[1]

[Total 2 marks]

2 Sodium chloride is an ionic compound. Grade 6-7

a) Describe the structure of a crystal of sodium chloride. You should state:

- What particles are present in the crystal.
- How these particles are arranged.
- What holds the particles together.

....

....

....

....

....

[4]

b) Explain why sodium chloride has a high melting point.

....

....

[2]

[Total 6 marks]

3 Potassium bromide has a lattice structure that is similar to sodium chloride. 

a) Complete **Figure 1** below to show the position and charge of the ions in potassium bromide. Write a symbol in each blank circle to show whether it is a potassium ion or a bromide ion.

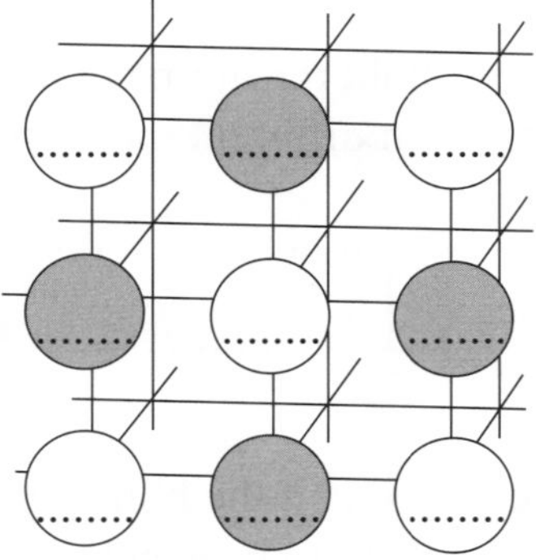

Figure 1

[3]

b) Give **one advantage** and **one disadvantage** of using the type of diagram above to represent the structure of an ionic compound.

Advantage: ....

Disadvantage: ....

[2]

c) State whether potassium bromide is likely to be **soluble** or **insoluble** in water.

....

[1]

[Total 6 marks]

4 **Figure 2** shows some data about the ionic compound lithium chloride. For each of the properties shown, explain how the structure of lithium chloride causes this property. 

Boiling point / °C	Electrical conductivity of solid	Electrical conductivity of solution
1382	Low	High

Figure 2

Boiling point ....

....

....

Electrical conductivity of solid ....

....

Electrical conductivity of solution ....

....

[Total 6 marks]

Exam Tip

Don't panic if you're asked about an ionic compound that you haven't met before. Think about what you do know about ionic compounds, and read the question carefully to make sure you've picked up on any extra information given.

Covalent Bonding

1 This question is about the forces in simple molecular substances. Grade 4-6

a) Compare the strength of the bonds that hold the atoms in a molecule together with the forces that exist between different molecules.

....

....

[2]

b) When a simple molecular substance melts, is it the bonds between atoms or the forces between molecules that are broken?

....

[1]

[Total 3 marks]

2 Silicon has the electronic structure 2.8.4. Grade 6-7

Use this information to predict how many covalent bonds one atom of silicon will form in a simple molecule. Explain your answer.

....

....

....

[Total 2 marks]

3 Nitrogen has the electronic structure 2.5. Chlorine has the electronic structure 2.8.7. Nitrogen trichloride, NCl_3, is a covalent compound. In each molecule of NCl_3, one nitrogen atom is covalently bonded to three chlorine atoms. Grade 6-7

a) Draw a dot and cross diagram to show the bonding in **one molecule** of nitrogen trichloride. You only need to include the outer shell electrons of each atom.

[3]

b) Predict, with reasoning, whether nitrogen trichloride can conduct electricity.

....

....

[1]

[Total 4 marks]

4 Hashim says: "Covalent bonds are very strong, so you need a lot of energy to separate the atoms in a covalent compound. This means simple molecular substances must have high melting and boiling points."

Grade 6-7

Is Hashim correct? Explain your answer.

....

....

....

....

....

....

[Total 3 marks]

5 Methane and poly(ethene) are both substances that are made up of molecules whose atoms are joined together by covalent bonds.

Grade 7-9

a) Briefly describe how the carbon and hydrogen atoms in methane, CH_4, bond to gain stable electronic structures.

....

....

....

....

[4]

b) What type of molecule is poly(ethene)?

....

[1]

c) At room temperature and pressure, methane is a gas, while poly(ethene) is a solid. Suggest why poly(ethene) has a higher boiling point than methane.

....

....

....

....

[4]

[Total 9 marks]

Exam Tip

If you answered these questions correctly, then that's a pretty good sign that you know all about simple molecules and covalent bonding. But don't forget, that's only part of the story — you need to be able to compare simple molecular substances with all the other types of structure covered in this topic, such as ionic structures and giant covalent structures.

Giant Covalent Structures and Fullerenes

1 The diagrams below show two different types of carbon structure.

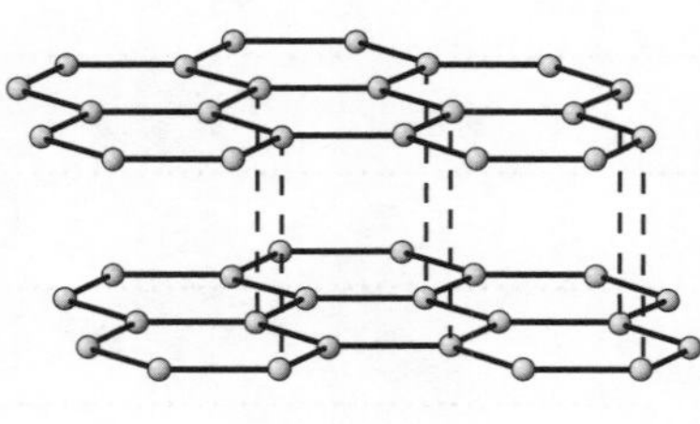

Figure 1

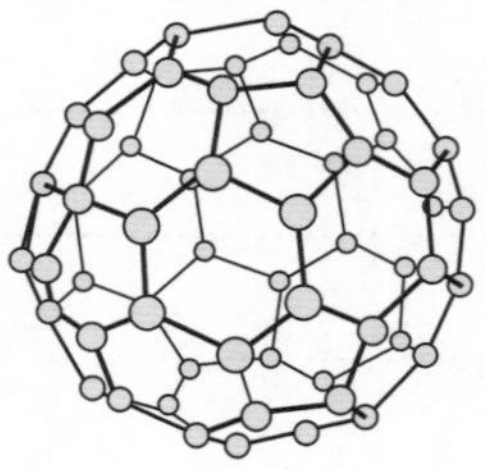

Figure 2

a) Name the two carbon structures shown.

i) **Figure 1**: .... *[1]*

ii) **Figure 2**: .... *[1]*

b) Both of the structures shown are able to conduct electricity.
Explain why this is possible.

....

....

.... *[2]*

c) Which of the two forms of carbon shown would you expect to have a **higher** melting point?
Explain your answer.

....

....

....

.... *[3]*

d) Name **one** other type of carbon structure, and draw a diagram below to show its bonding.

Structure: ....

[2]

[Total 9 marks]

Metallic Bonding

1 This question is about how the structure and bonding of metals affects their properties. 

a) Draw a labelled diagram to show how the metal ions and the electrons that take part in bonding are arranged in a metal.

[3]

b) Explain how the metal ions are held together in this arrangement.

....

....

[2]

c) i) State whether metals generally have high or low boiling points. Explain your answer.

....

....

[2]

ii) A student has samples of two solids, marked **A** and **B**. One is copper, a metallic element, and the other is iodine, a non-metal element. Solid **A** has a melting point of 1085 °C and solid **B** has a melting point of 114 °C. Suggest which of the solids is iodine and explain your answer.

....

....

[1]

d) Explain why metals are good conductors of electricity.

....

....

[2]

e) Explain how the structure of metals means they are able to be bent and shaped.

....

....

....

[2]

[Total 12 marks]

Exam Tip

Metals have some really nifty properties, and being able to explain all the properties of metals requires you to be really familiar with metallic bonding. Remember, it's because of those layers of positive metal ions and that sea of electrons that metals behave the way they do. Make sure you're able to explain the bonding in metals and link it to their properties.

Conservation of Mass

1 A student mixes 3.0 g of silver nitrate solution and 15.8 g of sodium chloride solution together in a flask and seals it with a bung. The following precipitation reaction occurs:

$$AgNO_{3\,(aq)} + NaCl_{(aq)} \rightarrow AgCl_{(s)} + NaNO_{3\,(aq)}$$

Predict the total mass of the contents of the flask after the reaction. Explain your answer.

....

....

....

[Total 2 marks]

2 A student is investigating a reaction between zinc and hydrochloric acid. The reaction produces hydrogen gas and a solution of zinc chloride. The student's experimental set-up is shown in **Figure 1**.

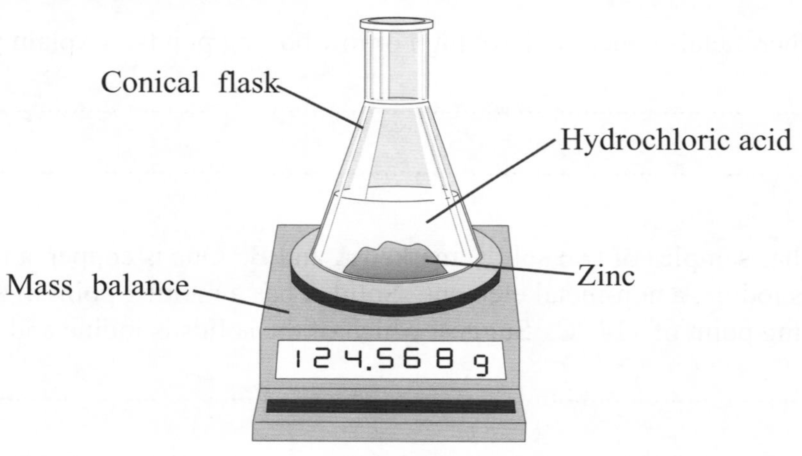

Figure 1

a) How would you expect the mass of the conical flask and its contents to change over the course of the reaction? Explain your answer.

....

....

....

[2]

b) The student repeats the reaction, but this time attaches a gas syringe to the top of the flask. How would you expect the mass of the apparatus and its contents to change over the course of the reaction? Explain your answer.

....

....

....

....

[2]

[Total 4 marks]

Relative Masses and Chemical Formulas

Warm-Up

Match up the following formulas with the correct relative formula mass of the substance.

F_2	38
C_2H_6	40
CaO	30
NaOH	56

1 The compound butane-1,4-diamine has the molecular formula $C_4H_{12}N_2$. Which of the following is the empirical formula of butane-1,4-diamine? Grade 4-6

- [ ] **A** C_2H_5N
- [ ] **B** $C_2H_6N_2$
- [ ] **C** CH_3N
- [ ] **D** C_2H_6N

[Total 1 mark]

2 Decaborane is a compound with the molecular formula $B_{10}H_{14}$. Grade 4-6

What is the empirical formula of decaborane?

empirical formula = ...

[Total 1 mark]

3 **Figure 1** shows the displayed formula of the compound dithionic acid. Grade 4-6

```
        O    O
        ‖    ‖
H—O—S—S—O—H
        ‖    ‖
        O    O
```

Figure 1

a) What is the molecular formula of this compound?
Give your answer in the form $H_aS_bO_c$, where *a*, *b* and *c* are whole numbers.

....

[1]

b) What is the empirical formula of this compound?

empirical formula = ...

[1]

[Total 2 marks]

4 The formula of the compound barium nitrate is $Ba(NO_3)_2$. Grade 6-7

Find the relative formula mass of barium nitrate.

relative formula mass = ...

[2]

5 Oct-1-ene is a compound with the molecular formula C_8H_{16}.
Emmy says the empirical formula of oct-1-ene is C_2H_4. Grade 6-7

Is Emmy correct? Explain your answer.

....

....

....

[Total 1 mark]

6 An oxide of an element, X, has the formula X_2O_3.
The relative formula mass of X_2O_3 is 160. Grade 7-9

Calculate the relative atomic mass of element X.

relative atomic mass = ...

[Total 3 marks]

7 Compound Q has the empirical formula C_2HF.
The relative formula mass of compound Q is 132.

What is the molecular formula of compound Q?

molecular formula = ...

[Total 3 marks]

Moles and Concentration

1 What is the approximate number of atoms in 1 mole of carbon atoms? Grade 4-6

☐ **A** 7.23×10^{23} atoms   ☐ **C** 6.02×10^{-23} atoms

☐ **B** 7.23×10^{24} atoms   ☐ **D** 6.02×10^{23} atoms

[Total 1 mark]

2 A student makes a saline solution by dissolving 36 g of sodium chloride in 0.40 dm^3 of water. What is the concentration of the solution? Grade 4-6

☐ **A** 90 g dm^{-3} ☐ **B** 14.4 g dm^{-3} ☐ **C** 14 400 g dm^{-3} ☐ **D** 0.090 g dm^{-3}

[Total 1 mark]

3 A pharmacist is synthesising aspirin, $C_9H_8O_4$, as part of a drugs trial. After the experiment, the pharmacist calculates that she has made 12.4 moles of aspirin. What mass of aspirin has the pharmacist made? Grade 4-6

The relative atomic mass, A_r, of C = 12, of H = 1 and of O = 16.

mass = ... g

[Total 2 marks]

4 How many atoms are there in 7 moles of ammonia, NH_3? Give your answer to 3 significant figures. Grade 6-7

.... atoms

[Total 2 marks]

5 A student makes up a volume of a standard solution of copper sulfate with a concentration of 75.0 g dm^{-3}. He does this by dissolving powdered copper sulfate in 220 cm^3 of water. Grade 6-7

Calculate the mass of copper sulfate that was used to make the solution.

mass = ... g

[Total 1 mark]

6 A student dissolves 56 g of potassium chloride in 400 cm^3 of water. Grade 6-7

a) Calculate the concentration of the resultant potassium chloride solution in g dm^{-3}.

concentration = ... g dm^{-3}

[1]

b) The student wants to make a solution with the same concentration using only 300 cm^3 of water. Use your answer from part a) to calculate the mass of potassium chloride that the student will need to add to this volume of water to create a solution with the same concentration.

mass = ... g

[1]

[Total 2 marks]

7 A lab technician is making up some solutions for students to use in some of their classes. Grade 7-9

a) The technician makes a standard solution of sodium hydroxide for a titration experiment. She makes 600 cm^3 of the solution at a concentration of 52 g dm^{-3}.

Calculate the number of moles of sodium hydroxide used to make the solution.
Relative formula mass, M_r, of NaOH = 40

number of moles = ...

[2]

b) i) The technician also makes a standard solution of sodium carbonate. The solution has a concentration of 80.0 g dm^{-3} and was made by adding 36.0 g of sodium carbonate to a volume of water. Calculate the volume of water, in cm^3, that she used to make the solution.

volume of water = ... cm^3

[2]

ii) For a separate experiment, the technician needs a sodium carbonate solution with a concentration of 40.0 g dm^{-3}.
What can she do to her 80.0 g dm^{-3} solution to make it this concentration?

....

[1]

[Total 5 marks]

8 A sample of an unknown element contains 1.204×10^{25} atoms. Grade 7-9

a) How many moles of atoms of the element are in the sample?

number of moles = ...
[1]

b) Given that the atoms have a mean mass of 9.3×10^{-23} g, what is the identity of the element?

....
[2]
[Total 3 marks]

9 A student is investigating an unidentified acid, which is made up of oxygen, sulfur and hydrogen atoms. Grade 7-9

a) Given that 3.5 moles of the acid has a mass of 343 g, what is the relative formula mass of the acid?

relative formula mass = ...
[1]

b) The percentage mass of the acid made up of oxygen atoms is 65%. To the nearest whole number, how many moles of oxygen atoms are in one mole of the acid?

number of moles = ...
[2]

c) In one mole of the acid, there is one mole of sulfur atoms. Deduce the chemical formula of the acid.

chemical formula = ...
[3]
[Total 6 marks]

Calculating Empirical Formulas

1 An oxide of lead contains 2.07 g of lead and 0.16 g of oxygen. What is the empirical formula of the lead oxide?

$A_r(Pb) = 207$, $A_r(O) = 16$

empirical formula = ...

[Total 2 marks]

2 53.66 g of an oxide of copper contains 10.8 g of oxygen by mass. Calculate the empirical formula of the copper oxide.

$A_r(Cu) = 63.5$, $A_r(O) = 16$

empirical formula = ...

[Total 3 marks]

3 83% of the mass of a certain hydrocarbon is made up of carbon atoms. Calculate the empirical formula of the hydrocarbon.

$A_r(C) = 12$, $A_r(H) = 1$

empirical formula = ...

[Total 3 marks]

4 A student carried out an experiment to calculate the empirical formula of an oxide of iron. She burnt 3.808 g of iron until it had all reacted. She found that the weight of the product was 5.440 g.

a) Suggest a piece of equipment that the student could use to carry out the reaction in.

....

[1]

b) Calculate the empirical formula of the iron oxide formed during the experiment.
$A_r(Fe) = 56$, $A_r(O) = 16$

empirical formula = ...

[3]

[Total 4 marks]

Limiting Reactants

Warm-Up

Complete the following sentences by filling in the blanks with the words on the right.

1) If the amount of limiting reactant in a reaction is decreased, then the amount of product made will ....

2) If the amount of limiting reactant in a reaction is increased, then the amount of product made will ....

3) If the amount of an excess reactant is increased, then the amount of product made will ....

not change

decrease

increase

1 James is investigating the reactivity of some metals. As part of his investigation, he places a piece of magnesium metal in a flask containing an excess of hydrochloric acid and monitors the reaction. The reaction produces hydrogen gas and a metal salt solution. Grade 4-6

a) Which of the reactants is the limiting reactant?

....

[1]

b) James repeats the experiment but changes the starting quantities of magnesium and acid. He lets the reaction proceed to completion, and notes that once the reaction has finished, the reaction vessel contains a small amount of grey metal and a clear solution.

In this second experiment, what is the limiting reactant? Explain your answer.

....

....

....

[2]

[Total 3 marks]

2 An industrial process converts the alkene ethene into ethanol, according to the reaction below. Grade 6-7

$$C_2H_4 + H_2O \rightarrow CH_3CH_2OH$$

What mass of ethanol can be made from 53 g of ethene, given that water is in excess?

mass = ... g

[Total 2 marks]

3 The following equation shows the complete combustion of ethane in air. 

$$2C_2H_6 + 7O_2 \rightarrow 4CO_2 + 6H_2O$$

a) In a complete combustion reaction, some ethane reacted with exactly 128 g of oxygen. Calculate the mass of water produced. Give your answer to three significant figures.

mass = ... g

[3]

b) A company burns ethane to generate power for an industrial process.

As part of a carbon-reducing scheme, the company can only produce a maximum 4.4 tonnes of carbon dioxide per day (where 1 tonne = 1 000 000 g). What is the maximum mass, in tonnes, of ethane that the company can burn each day so as not to exceed the limit of carbon dioxide?

mass = ... tonnes

[3]

[Total 6 marks]

4 Urea, $(NH_2)_2CO$, is a compound that can be synthesised industrially using the following reaction. 

$$2NH_3 + CO_2 \rightarrow (NH_2)_2CO + H_2O$$

a) A company makes 120.6 tonnes of urea each day (where 1 tonne = 1 000 000 g). What mass of carbon dioxide, in tonnes, is required to make this mass of urea?

mass = ... tonnes

[3]

b) Usually the reaction happens in an excess of ammonia. However, a leak in a pipe means the mass of ammonia entering the reaction chamber on one day is reduced to 59.5 tonnes.

What is the decrease, in tonnes, in the amount of urea produced on this day?

decrease in mass = ... tonnes

[4]

[Total 7 marks]

Balancing Equations Using Masses

1 Viola reacts 200 g of a metal, **X**, with oxygen. The result of the reaction is 280 g of a single product, which is an oxide of metal **X**.

a) What mass of oxygen was used in the reaction?

mass = ... g

[1]

b) Given that Viola's reaction produced 5 moles of X oxide, write a balanced symbol equation for the reaction of **X** with oxygen.
$A_r(X) = 40$, $A_r(O) = 16$

....

[4]

[Total 5 marks]

2 1.0 g of warm sodium was added to a gas jar containing 1.0 g of chlorine gas (Cl_2). They reacted to form sodium chloride. The equation for the reaction is $2Na + Cl_2 \rightarrow 2NaCl$. Determine which reactant was the **limiting reactant** in this reaction.

A_r (Na) = 23, M_r (Cl_2) = 71

....

[Total 3 marks]

3 A scientist gently heats tin and iodine together. They react to form a single product, which is a metal halide. Given that 3.57 g of tin reacts exactly with 15.24 g of iodine, write a balanced equation for this reaction.

A_r (Sn) = 119, M_r (I_2) = 254, M_r (metal halide) = 627

....

[Total 5 marks]

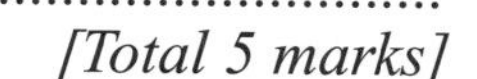

States of Matter

Warm-Up

Identify which of the following statements is **false**. Tick **one** box.

Particles in liquids are free to move past each other but tend to stick together. ☐

Particles of a substance in the liquid state have more energy than particles of the same substance in the solid state. ☐

There is hardly any force of attraction between particles in gases. ☐

Particles in liquids are held in fixed positions by strong forces. ☐

1 Substances can exist in three states of matter: solid, liquid or gas. (Grade 4-6)

a) In which of these three states of matter are the forces of attraction between the particles **strongest**?

....

[1]

b) Name the state of matter illustrated in **Figure 1**.

Figure 1

....

[1]

[Total 2 marks]

2 A student has a sample of a solid substance. She heats it gradually until it turns into a liquid. (Grade 6-7)

Describe the differences between the particles in the substance when it is in the liquid state and when it is in the solid state. Give your answer in terms of the movement of the particles and the amount of energy that they have.

....

....

....

....

....

[Total 3 marks]

 ☐  ☐  ☐

Changes of State

1 The equations below show four processes that use water as a starting material. 

A: $H_2O_{(l)} \rightarrow H_2O_{(s)}$ **B**: $2H_2O_{(l)} + 2Na_{(s)} \rightarrow 2NaOH_{(aq)} + H_{2(g)}$

C: $H_2O_{(l)} \rightarrow + H_2O_{(g)}$ **D**: $2H_2O_{(l)} \rightarrow 2H_{2(g)} + O_{2(g)}$

a) State which equation shows evaporation.

....

[1]

b) State which **two** equations show chemical changes and explain your answer.

....

....

[2]

[Total 3 marks]

2 **Figure 1** shows some properties of four elements. 

Figure 1

Name	Melting point / °C	Boiling point / °C	Appearance		
			solid	liquid	gas
fluorine	–220	–188	colourless	bright yellow	pale yellow
mercury	–39	357	silvery metallic	silvery metallic	n/a
bromine	–7	59	red-brown	red-brown	orange
rubidium	39	688	silvery-white metallic	silvery-white metallic	n/a

During an experiment, samples of each of these four elements were placed in separate test tubes. All four test tubes were then gradually cooled together, from 25 °C to –200 °C.

Describe what you would expect to observe during the experiment as it progressed. In your answer you should describe what you think will happen to each sample.

....

....

....

....

....

....

....

....

[Total 4 marks]

Purity

1 Misty-Marie is doing a chemistry experiment.
The instructions say she needs to use pure water.
Stanley offers her a bottle labelled '100% Pure Spring Water'.

Suggest why Stanley's water is unlikely to be suitable for Misty-Marie's experiment.

[Total 2 marks]

2 Copper can be made extremely pure. The melting points of two samples of copper were measured. Sample **A** had a melting point of 1085 °C and sample **B** melted over the range 900 – 940 °C.

Suggest which of the samples, **A** or **B**, was the **most pure**. Explain your answer.

[Total 2 marks]

3 A scientist is comparing samples of two substances.
One sample is a pure compound, but the other is a mixture.
Both substances are solids at room temperature.

a) The scientist decides to work out which is the pure compound by heating both samples and recording their melting points. Explain how she will be able to tell which is the pure compound, even if she does not know its melting point.

[2]

b) Suggest what apparatus the scientist could use to measure the melting points of the substances in the lab.

[1]

[Total 3 marks]

Separating Mixtures

1 **Figure 1** shows a set of equipment you could use for separating a mixture in the lab.

Figure 1

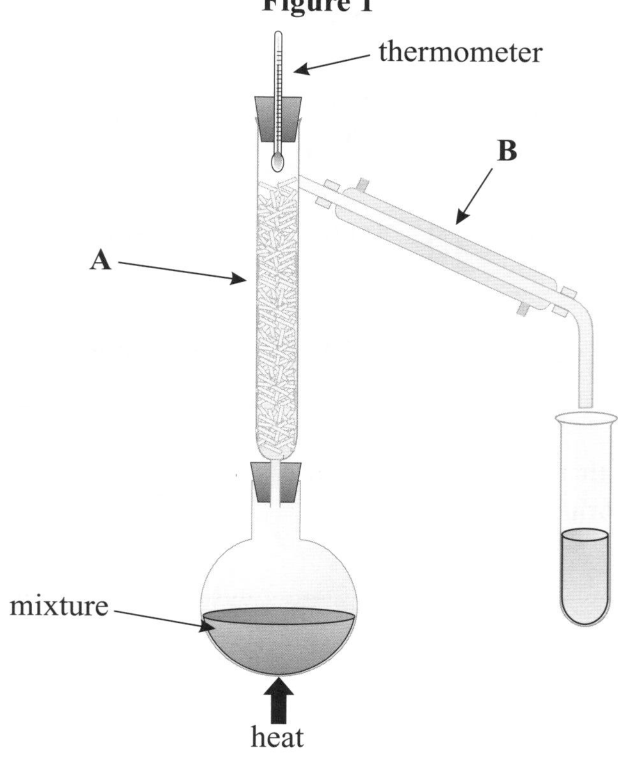

a) Name the pieces of equipment labelled **A** and **B**.

i) **A**: ....

[1]

ii) **B**: ....

[1]

b) i) What is the name of the separation method this equipment would be used for?

....

[1]

ii) Describe what type of mixture you would use this method to separate.

....

....

[2]

iii) Reuben is using this method to separate a mixture.
His mixture contains a substance that is flammable.
Suggest a suitable piece of equipment that he could use to heat the mixture.

....

[1]

[Total 6 marks]

2* A student wants to separate the components of a mixture.
The mixture is a white powder composed of barium sulfate and potassium iodide.
Figure 2 shows some information about the two compounds in the mixture.

Figure 2

Name	Melting point / °C	Boiling point / °C	Appearance at room temperature	Soluble in water?
barium sulfate	1580	1600	white solid	no
potassium iodide	681	1330	white solid	yes

Describe a detailed method that the student could use to obtain pure samples of **both** compounds.

....

....

....

....

....

....

....

....

....

....

....

....

....

....

....

....

....

....

[Total 6 marks]

3 Sodium chloride dissolves in water, but not in ethanol.
Sodium chloride has a melting point of 801 °C and a boiling point of 1413 °C.
Ethanol has a melting point of –114 °C and a boiling point of 78 °C.

a) Suggest a purification method which would separate a mixture of sodium chloride and ethanol, but **not** a mixture of sodium chloride and water. Explain your answer.

[3]

b) Suggest a purification method which would separate a mixture of sodium chloride and water and would **also** separate a mixture of sodium chloride and ethanol. Explain your answer.

[2]

[Total 5 marks]

4 **Figure 3** lists the boiling points of three compounds. Grade 6-7

Figure 3

Name	Formula	Boiling point / °C
cyclopentane	C_5H_{10}	49
cyclohexane	C_6H_{12}	81
ethyl ethanoate	$C_4H_8O_2$	77

Suggest why a mixture of cyclohexane and ethyl ethanoate might be more difficult to separate than a mixture of cyclohexane and cyclopentane.

[Total 2 marks]

Exam Tip

You might find some of these separation techniques cropping up in questions about other practicals — you often need to use one of them at the end of an experiment to separate out a pure sample of the product from the reaction mixture.

Target AO3

5 A student was given a solution containing water, ethanol and the salts bismuth iodide and potassium chloride. Bismuth iodide is soluble in ethanol and potassium chloride is soluble in water. The boiling point of ethanol is 78 °C and both salts have melting points above 400 °C.

Here is the method the student plans to use to produce pure samples of the two salts:

1. Using distillation apparatus, heat the mixture to 120 °C to separate the ethanol from the solution.
2. Pour the remaining mixture through a filter to remove the solid bismuth iodide.
3. Pour the filtrate into an evaporating dish.
4. Gently heat the filtrate until dry potassium chloride crystals are left.

a) Evaluate whether the student's method will work.
Explain your answer.

....

....

....
[1]

b) Explain how the method should be changed to produce separate samples of each salt.

....

....
[2]

c) The student suggests using a Bunsen burner to heat the mixture in step 1.
Suggest a risk of this if the mixture contains a large amount of ethanol.

....
[1]

d) Potassium hydrogencarbonate is another water-soluble salt.
The student planned to produce potassium hydrogencarbonate crystals by heating a sample of potassium hydrogencarbonate solution in an evaporating dish until no more liquid remains.
However, potassium hydrogencarbonate decomposes on heating.
Describe a method that the student could use to ensure they make pure, dry crystals.

....

....

....
[2]

[Total 6 marks]

Exam Tip

You might be given a method in the exam with lots of different steps — the examiner could introduce errors for you to spot in any of them. Read and think about each part of the method carefully to spot any potential problems.

Chromatography

1 Olivia analysed an unknown mixture of liquids using paper chromatography. The solvent she used was ethanol. The chromatogram she produced is shown in **Figure 1**. 

Figure 1

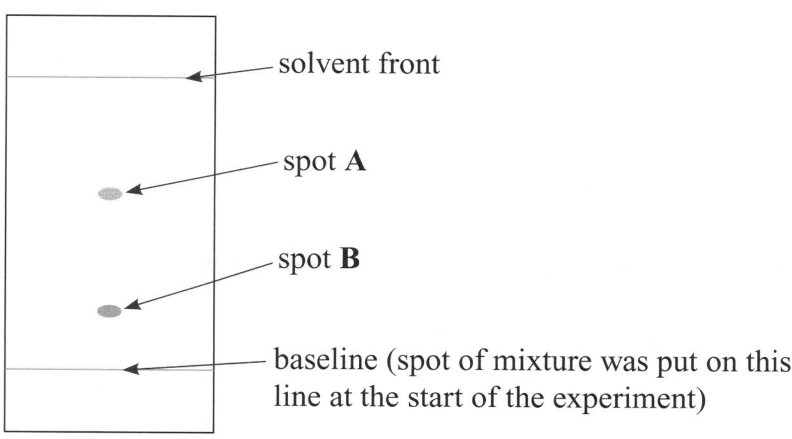

a) Name the mobile phase in Olivia's experiment

....

[1]

b) What does this chromatogram tell you about the number of components in the mixture? Explain your answer.

....

....

[2]

c) Calculate the R_f value of spot **B**. Use a ruler to help you.

$$R_f = \frac{\text{distance travelled by solute}}{\text{distance travelled by solvent}}$$

R_f = ...

[3]

d) Olivia is given a list of five chemicals.
She is told that her mixture is made up of a combination of some of the chemicals on the list.
Explain how Olivia could use pure samples of the chemicals on the list to identify the components of the mixture using paper chromatography.

....

....

....

....

[2]

[Total 8 marks]

2 Lamar wants to analyse the composition of a sample of ink.
The ink is made up of a number of dyes dissolved in a solvent.

Grade 6-7

PRACTICAL

a) The boiling point of the solvent is lower than the boiling point of any of the dyes.

i) Suggest a method Lamar could use to separate the mixture of dyes from the solvent.

....

[1]

ii) Explain how this method can provide data that could help Lamar to identify the solvent.

....

....

[1]

b) Lamar uses paper chromatography to analyse the mixtures of dyes in the ink.
He compares the mixture with five different water soluble dyes, A to E.
After 30 minutes, the chromatogram in **Figure 2** was obtained.

Figure 2

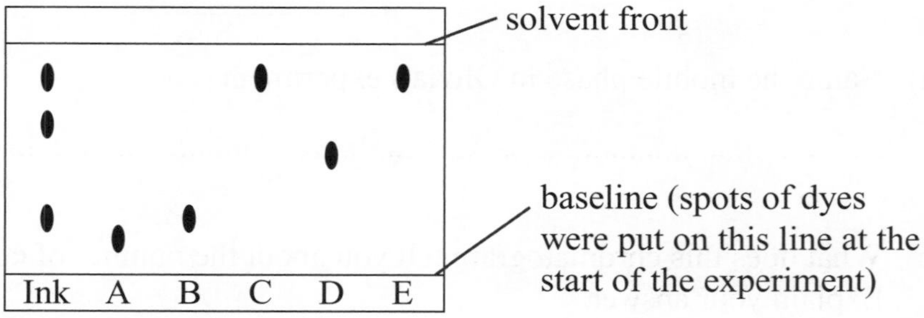

Outline the procedure for setting up and running this experiment.

....

....

....

....

....

....

[5]

c) Explain the results shown on Lamar's chromatogram.

....

....

....

....

....

....

[4]

[Total 11 marks]

Target AO3

3 A student set up a chromatography experiment to investigate a sample of ink which contained a mixture of several different compounds.

a) The chromatogram from the student's experiment is shown in **Figure 3**.

Figure 3

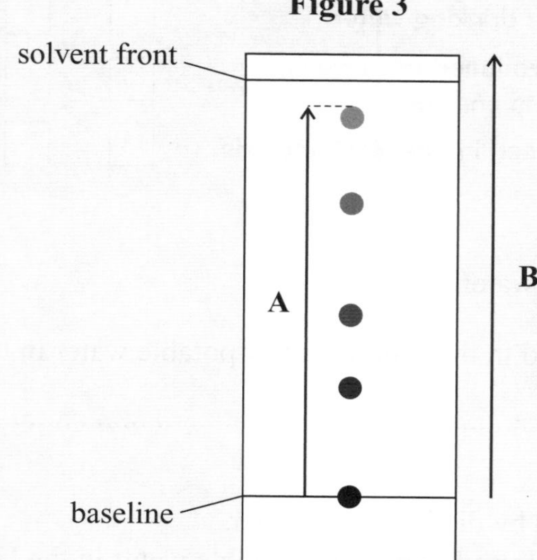

What **two** conclusions could the student make about the compounds in the ink? Explain your answers.

....

....

....

....

[4]

b) The student used distances **A** and **B** to calculate the R_f value for one of the compounds. Explain the **two** mistakes that the student has made and what they should have done instead.

....

....

....

....

[4]

[Total 8 marks]

Exam Tip

If you're asked to suggest possible conclusions about an experiment, be careful that you don't assume something that isn't mentioned. You'll only get marks for conclusions that can be worked out from the information you're given.

Water Treatment

Warm-Up

Tick the boxes to show whether the following statements are **true** or **false**.

	True	False
Potable water is the same as drinking water.	☐	☐
Potable water can only be produced from fresh water found in rivers, streams and reservoirs.	☐	☐
Ordinary tap water can be used in chemical analysis.	☐	☐

1 This question is about potable water. Grade 4-6

a) Name **one** source of water used in the production of potable water in the UK.

....

[1]

b) Potable water can be produced by distilling sea water.
Explain why this method is not used to produce potable water in the UK.

....

....

[2]

[Total 3 marks]

2 A purification plant uses multiple steps to purify water. Grade 6-7

a) When the water arrives at a water purification plant, it is passed through wire meshes and gravel beds to remove large solid impurities. Give the name of this step.

....

[1]

b) Some water purification plants use aluminium sulfate to carry out a sedimentation step.
How does the aluminium sulfate contribute to the purification process?

....

....

[1]

c) The purification process ends with chlorination.
Describe what happens to the water during this process and state why it is carried out.

....

....

[2]

[Total 4 marks]

 ☐  ☐  ☐

Acids and Bases

Warm-Up

Circle the statements below that are **true**.

As H^+ concentration increases, pH decreases.

Acids contain lots of OH^- ions.

Neutral substances have a pH of 8.

Alkalis turn Universal indicator blue/purple.

Acids have pHs of less than 7.

Alkalis are soluble bases.

1 This question is about acids and bases.
Figure 1 shows the pH values of some everyday substances.

Figure 1

Substance	pH
Beer	4
Bicarbonate of soda	9
Milk	7

a) Write the name of the substance in **Figure 1** that is an acid.

....

[1]

b) What colour would you expect to see if phenolphthalein was added to bicarbonate of soda solution?

....

[1]

c) Which ion is produced by an acid in aqueous solution? Tick **one** box.

☐ **A** Cl^-

☐ **B** H^+

☐ **C** OH^-

☐ **D** OH^+

[1]

[Total 3 marks]

2 Which of the following equations shows a neutralisation reaction? Tick **one** box. Grade 4-6

☐ **A** $HNO_3 + LiOH \rightarrow LiNO_3 + H_2O$

☐ **B** $Mg + H_2O \rightarrow MgO + H_2$

☐ **C** $Na_2O + H_2O \rightarrow 2NaOH$

☐ **D** $C_4H_{10} + 6½O_2 \rightarrow 4CO_2 + 5H_2O$

[Total 1 mark]

3 Acids and bases react together in neutralisation reactions. Grade 4-6

a) Write the general word equation for a neutralisation reaction between an acid and a base.

....

[1]

b) In terms of hydrogen ions and hydroxide ions, write an ionic equation for a neutralisation reaction in aqueous solution.

....

[1]

[Total 2 marks]

4 Kevin has samples of three different alkaline solutions. Solution **A** has a pH of 11, solution **B** has a pH of 13 and solution **C** has a pH of 8. State which of Kevin's solutions has the **lowest** concentration of hydroxide ions and explain your answer. Grade 6-7

....

....

....

[Total 2 marks]

5 Haifa is investigating the properties of a sample of dilute hydrochloric acid, HCl. Grade 6-7 PRACTICAL

a) She puts 100 cm^3 of the acid into a flask. Suggest a piece of apparatus that Haifa could use to accurately measure out 100 cm^3 of the acid.

....

[1]

b) Haifa adds a measured mass of powdered calcium hydroxide to the flask. It reacts completely. She takes a sample of the resultant solution and tests its pH using universal indicator paper.

i) Suggest what colour the universal indicator paper will turn when Haifa adds a spot of the solution. Explain your answer.

....

....

[3]

ii) Haifa repeats the same procedure several times. After she adds the fifth lot of calcium hydroxide, she sees a small amount of unreacted solid left at the bottom of the flask. Suggest what colour the universal indicator paper will turn at this point. Explain your answer.

....

....

[3]

[Total 7 marks]

Strong and Weak Acids

1 Tamal has two beakers, each containing a sample of a different acid. The acid in beaker X is **stronger** than the acid in beaker Y. The acid in beaker Y is **more concentrated** than the acid in beaker X.

Which row of the table in **Figure 1** could describe the contents of the two beakers? Tick **one** box.

Figure 1

	Beaker X	Beaker Y
☐ **A**	0.002 mol/dm^3 HCl	4.0 mol/dm^3 CH_3COOH
☐ **B**	4.0 mol/dm^3 HCl	0.002 mol/dm^3 CH_3COOH
☐ **C**	0.002 mol/dm^3 CH_3COOH	4.0 mol/dm^3 HCl
☐ **D**	4.0 mol/dm^3 CH_3COOH	0.002 mol/dm^3 HCl

[Total 1 mark]

2 Methanoic acid, HCOOH, is a **weak acid**. Grade 7-9

a) Explain what is meant by the term 'weak acid'.

....

....

[1]

b) Write a chemical equation to show how methanoic acid acts as a weak acid.

....

[2]

[Total 3 marks]

3 Jackie is carrying out an experiment to measure how the pH of a strong acid is affected by its concentration. Grade 7-9

a) Jackie takes a sample of an acidic solution, A, made by dissolving a solid acid in deionised water. He wants to make his sample of the acid more concentrated. Which of the following things could he do? Tick **one** box.

☐ **A** Add a more dilute solution of the acid to the sample.

☐ **B** Add more water to the sample.

☐ **C** Add more solution the same as A to the sample.

☐ **D** Dissolve more solid acid in the sample.

[1]

b) At a certain dilution, the hydrogen ion concentration is 0.001 mol/dm^3 and the acid has a pH of 3. Jackie increases the concentration of hydrogen ions in the sample to 0.1 mol/dm^3. What is the new pH of the acid?

....

[1]

[Total 2 marks]

Reactions of Acids

1 June reacts a metal and an acid together in a flask. Which of the following describes the products of this reaction? Tick **one** box. Grade 4-6

- ☐ **A** A salt and water.
- ☐ **B** A salt and carbon dioxide gas.
- ☐ **C** A salt, water and carbon dioxide gas.
- ☐ **D** A salt and hydrogen gas.

[Total 1 mark]

2 Complete **Figure 1** to show the chemical formulas of the salts created in the reactions involving the following acids. Grade 6-7

Figure 1

	Hydrochloric acid (HCl)	Nitric acid (HNO_3)	Sulfuric acid (H_2SO_4)
Zinc metal (Zn)	$ZnCl_2$	....	$ZnSO_4$
Calcium carbonate ($CaCO_3$)	$CaCl_2$	$Ca(NO_3)_2$	....
Sodium hydroxide ($NaOH$)	$NaCl$	$NaNO_3$	....
Potassium carbonate (K_2CO_3)	....	KNO_3	K_2SO_4

[Total 4 marks]

3 Pauline mixes zinc carbonate, $ZnCO_3$, with hydrochloric acid, HCl, and notes that the mixture starts to bubble as a gas is given off. Grade 6-7

a) Give the name of the gas that is responsible for the bubbles in the reaction. Describe a test you could perform to identify this gas.

....

....

[3]

b) Write a balanced chemical equation for the reaction between hydrochloric acid and zinc carbonate.

....

[2]

c) What is the name of the salt produced by the reaction?

....

[1]

[Total 6 marks]

Making Insoluble Salts

1 Insoluble salts can be made by precipitation reactions.
Which of the following equations describes a precipitation reaction? Tick **one** box. Grade 4-6

- [ ] **A** $CuO_{(s)} + 2HCl_{(aq)} \rightarrow CuCl_{2\,(aq)} + H_2O_{(l)}$
- [ ] **B** $HCl_{(aq)} + NaOH_{(aq)} \rightarrow NaCl_{(aq)} + H_2O_{(l)}$
- [ ] **C** $2HNO_{3\,(aq)} + ZnCO_{3\,(s)} \rightarrow Zn(NO_3)_{2\,(aq)} + H_2O_{(l)} + CO_{2\,(g)}$
- [ ] **D** $Pb(NO_3)_{2\,(aq)} + 2NaCl_{(aq)} \rightarrow PbCl_{2\,(s)} + 2NaNO_{3\,(aq)}$

[Total 1 mark]

2 Jerry is making a sample of silver chloride, an insoluble salt, by mixing two salt solutions. Grade 6-7

a) Suggest two salt solutions that Jerry could mix to make silver chloride.

....

....

[1]

b) Once Jerry has made the salt, he pours the whole solid and salt solution into a filter funnel, as shown in **Figure 1**.

Figure 1

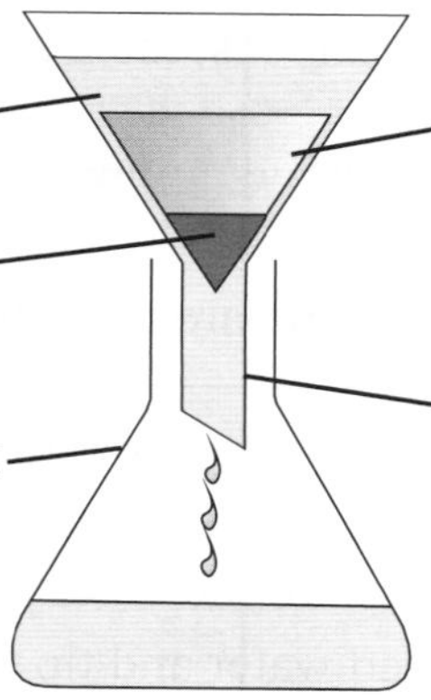

What has Jerry done wrong? Explain how this could affect the mass of solid salt that he collects from the solution.

....

....

....

[2]

c) After Jerry has isolated the salt, he washes it with deionised water.
Explain why he uses deionised water as opposed to tap water.

....

....

[1]

[Total 4 marks]

3 The students in a chemistry class are investigating the properties of calcium salts. (Grade 6-7)

a) They plan to carry out reactions to make calcium nitrate, $Ca(NO_3)_2$, and calcium sulfate, $CaSO_4$.
Before they start, four students predict whether the salts will be soluble or insoluble.
Which prediction is correct? Tick **one** box.

☐ **A** Ashley: "Both calcium salts will be insoluble."

☐ **B** Benni: "Both reactions will make soluble calcium salts."

☐ **C** Chen: "We'll get an insoluble precipitate of calcium sulfate, but calcium nitrate is soluble in water."

☐ **D** Dermot: "Calcium sulfate dissolves in water, but calcium nitrate doesn't, so only calcium nitrate will form as a precipitate."

[1]

b) In a third reaction, the students want to produce the insoluble salt calcium carbonate, $CaCO_3$.
Suggest two soluble salts they could react together to make a precipitate of calcium carbonate.

....

....

[2]

[Total 3 marks]

4 Davina reacts aqueous iron(III) nitrate solution, $Fe(NO_3)_3$, with aqueous sodium hydroxide solution, NaOH, to make an insoluble salt containing iron. (Grade 6-7)

a) Write down the chemical formula of the insoluble salt.

....

[1]

b) Davina used the following method to prepare the salt:

1. Mix the sodium hydroxide solution with the iron(III) nitrate solution in a beaker and stir.
2. Line a filter funnel with filter paper and place it in a conical flask.
   Pour the contents of the beaker into the filter paper.
3. Rinse the beaker with deionised water and tip this into the filter paper.
4. Rinse the contents of the filter paper with deionised water.

i) Explain why Davina rinsed the beaker and added the rinsings to the filter paper.

....

[1]

ii) After completing step 4, Davina wants to dry the solid product. Suggest how she could do this.

....

[1]

iii) Given that Davina used an excess of iron(III) nitrate solution, state which **three** ions will be present in the solution that is left in the conical flask at the end of the experiment.

....

[2]

[Total 5 marks]

Making Soluble Salts

Warm-Up

Nina is making the soluble salt zinc chloride by reacting zinc with hydrochloric acid.
She wants to prepare a pure, dry sample of solid zinc chloride.
The equipment Nina has available is listed below.
Circle the pieces of equipment below that you would expect Nina to use.

filter funnel pipette desiccator fume cupboard thermometer water bath methyl orange indicator conical flask safety glasses burette filter paper condenser fractionating column

1 The following steps are parts of a method you could use to produce a pure, dry sample of the soluble salt magnesium sulfate, $MgSO_4$, from solid magnesium hydroxide and sulfuric acid.

1 Slowly heat the solution to evaporate off some of the water.
2 Filter the solid off and dry it in a desiccator.
3 Filter out the excess solid using a filter funnel and filter paper.
4 Add magnesium hydroxide to a flask containing warm sulfuric acid. Continue adding the magnesium hydroxide until no more reacts (at this point, the excess solid will just sink to the bottom of the flask).
5 Leave the solution to crystallise.

a) Which is the correct order that these steps should be carried out in? Tick **one** box.

- [ ] **A** 4, 1, 3, 2, 5
- [ ] **B** 1, 4, 2, 5, 2
- [ ] **C** 4, 3, 1, 5, 2
- [ ] **D** 3, 1, 2, 5, 4

[1]

b) Write a balanced symbol equation, including state symbols, that describes the reaction between magnesium hydroxide, $Mg(OH)_2$, and sulfuric acid, H_2SO_4.

....

[3]

[Total 4 marks]

2 Andy is making a sample of potassium sulfate by reacting potassium hydroxide, KOH, and sulfuric acid, H_2SO_4, together. Grade 6-7

a) Potassium sulfate is a soluble salt. Explain what is meant by the term soluble in this context.

....

[1]

b) Write a balanced chemical equation for this reaction.

....

[2]

c) Andy uses a titration method to add a potassium hydroxide solution to the acid until he reaches the end point, which is shown by a change in colour of an indicator in the solution. He then crystallises the solution to obtain the salt. Will this produce a pure sample of the salt? Explain your answer.

....

....

[1]

[Total 4 marks]

3 Copper sulfate is a soluble salt that can be made by the reaction between sulfuric acid, H_2SO_4, and copper oxide, CuO. Grade 7-9

PRACTICAL

a) Write a balanced chemical equation for the reaction between sulfuric acid and copper oxide.

....

[2]

b)* Outline how you could prepare a pure, dry sample of copper sulfate in the lab from sulfuric acid and copper oxide.

....

....

....

....

....

....

....

....

....

....

[6]

[Total 8 marks]

Electrolysis

1 As part of an industrial process, a sample of potassium chloride, KCl, was electrolysed. Grade 4-6

a) Before the potassium chloride is electrolysed, it either has to be molten or dissolved in solution. Explain why this is necessary.

....

....

[2]

b) During the electrolysis of molten potassium chloride, potassium ions are reduced to potassium metal. At which electrode would you expect this reaction to occur?

....

[1]

[Total 3 marks]

2 Electrolysis is carried out on a solution of copper chloride, $CuCl_2$, using inert electrodes. Grade 6-7

a) Which of the following ions is **not** present in the solution? Tick **one** box.

☐ **A** H^+ ☐ **B** H_2O^- ☐ **C** Cl^- ☐ **D** Cu^{2+}

[1]

b) What would you expect to see happen at:

i) the anode? ....

ii) the cathode? ....

[2]

[Total 3 marks]

3 A solution of sodium chloride, NaCl, is electrolysed using platinum electrodes. Grade 6-7

a) Platinum electrodes are an example of inert electrodes. Explain what is meant by the term 'inert' when referring to electrodes.

....

[1]

b) The sodium chloride solution contains dissolved sodium chloride and water only. List the ions that are present in solution during the electrolysis of sodium chloride solution using inert electrodes.

....

[2]

c) Write balanced half equations to show the reactions that occur at:

i) the anode ....

ii) the cathode ....

[4]

[Total 7 marks]

4 The half-equation for the reaction at the cathode during an electrolysis experiment is $Pb^{2+} + 2e^- \rightarrow Pb$. The half-equation for the reaction at the anode is $2I^- \rightarrow I_2 + 2e^-$. Grade 6-7

a) Give the definition of the term **electrolyte**.

....

[2]

b) Give the chemical formula of the electrolyte in this experiment, given that it's a molten ionic compound.

....

[1]

[Total 3 marks]

5* A student is investigating the electrolysis of sodium chloride solution using inert electrodes. Describe how you would set up an electrochemical cell to carry out this investigation and predict what you would observe happening at each electrode as the reaction progressed. Grade 6-7

....

....

....

....

....

....

....

....

....

[Total 6 marks]

6 When sodium sulfate solution is electrolysed using inert electrodes, sodium is not discharged at the cathode. Grade 7-9

a) Explain why sodium **is not** discharged at the cathode and state what product **is** discharged instead.

....

....

[3]

b) State which **two** products are discharged at the anode.

....

[2]

c) Suggest an alternative electrolysis experiment that could be carried out that **would** produce sodium metal at the cathode.

....

[2]

[Total 7 marks]

7 Marco is investigating the electrolysis of copper sulfate. He sets up two cells as shown in **Figure 1**. In cell A, Marco uses platinum electrodes. In cell B, he uses pure copper electrodes. The cells are identical in all other respects.

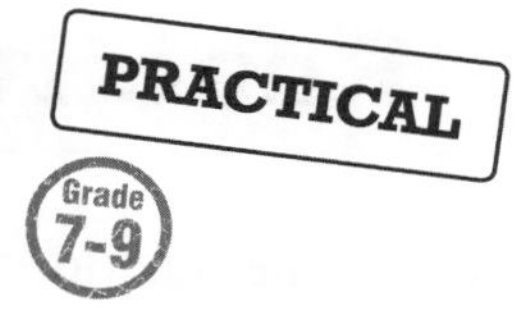

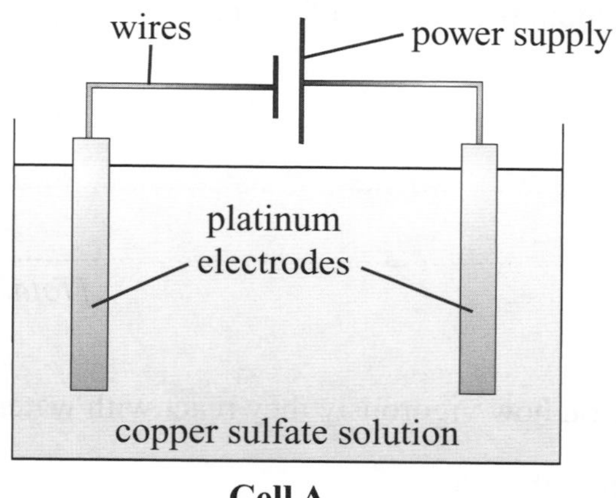

Cell A

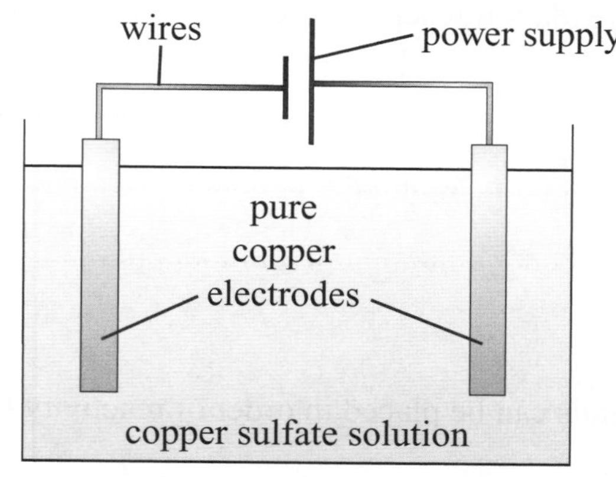

Cell B

Figure 1

a) Both cells are turned on and left for 1 hour. Given that the masses of the two cells were the same at the start of the electrolysis, how would you expect them to compare after 1 hour? Explain your answer. Use appropriate half equations to justify your conclusion.

....

....

....

....

....

....

[6]

b) A similar cell to cell B can be used to purify copper. Give **one** similarity and **one** difference between the cell used to purify copper in industry and cell B.

....

....

[2]

[Total 8 marks]

8 Write half-equations to show what reactions occur at the cathode and the anode when acidified water is electrolysed.

Grade 7-9

Cathode: ....

Anode: ....

[Total 4 marks]

Exam Tip

It's important to remember that when you electrolyse aqueous solutions (rather than molten salts) what products are made will depend on the reactivity of all the ions present in the solution. Make sure you've learnt which ions will be discharged from which solutions. And get plenty of practice at writing half-equations too — they're really important...

Reactivity Series and Reactivity of Metals

1 The reaction that occurs when a metal is burnt in oxygen can be described as an oxidation reaction. Explain why, using ideas about the transfer of oxygen. Grade 4-6

....

....

....

[Total 2 marks]

2 Metals can be placed in order of reactivity based on how vigorously they react with water. Grade 4-6

a) Write a word equation for the reaction of sodium with water.

....

[1]

b) Explain, using ideas about oxidation, why iron reacts much more slowly with cold water than sodium does.

....

....

[1]

[Total 2 marks]

3 Some metals can react with water. Grade 6-7

a) i) Complete the symbol equation below for the reaction of calcium and water. Include state symbols.

$$Ca_{(s)} + 2H_2O_{(l)} \rightarrow \text{.........................} + \text{.........................}$$

[2]

ii) Identify which element is oxidised. Explain your answer in terms of oxygen.

....

....

[2]

iii) Suggest a metal which will react more vigorously with water than calcium. Explain your answer.

....

....

[2]

b) Put the metals sodium, zinc and potassium in order, based on how vigorously you think they would react with water.

Most vigorous .... Least vigorous

[1]

[Total 7 marks]

4 Which of the statements below about metal reactivity is **incorrect**? Tick **one** box. Grade 6-7

- [ ] **A** The easier it is for a metal atom to form a positive ion, the less reactive it will be.
- [ ] **B** The more resistant a metal atom is to oxidation, the less reactive it will be.
- [ ] **C** In a reactivity series, you will find a reactive metal above a less reactive metal.
- [ ] **D** The more reactive a metal is, the faster its reaction with water will be.

[Total 1 mark]

5 Amal performed some experiments to investigate the reactivity of metals. Grade 6-7

a) First, Amal placed pieces of four different metals into dilute hydrochloric acid. **Figure 1** shows what the four experiments looked like after 1 minute.

Figure 1

Use **Figure 1** to put these metals in order of reactivity, starting with the **most reactive**.

....

[1]

b) Next, Amal was given samples of three mystery metals, marked **X, Y** and **Z**. She put small pieces of each of the metals in cold water. If there was no reaction with cold water, she tested the metal to see if it would react with steam. Her results are shown in **Figure 2**.

Metal	Any reaction with cold water?	Any reaction with steam?
X	Reacts vigorously. Hydrogen gas is produced.	
Y	no reaction	Reacts vigorously. Metal is coated with a white solid. Hydrogen gas is produced.
Z	no reaction	no reaction

Figure 2

i) Metal **Y** was zinc. It reacted with the steam to produce hydrogen gas and a white solid. Name the white solid that was produced by this reaction.

....

[1]

ii) One of the other metals Amal was given was sodium. Suggest whether sodium was metal **X** or metal **Z**. Give a reason for your answer.

....

....

[1]

[Total 3 marks]

Displacement Reactions

1 A student carries out a displacement reaction by reacting magnesium with an aqueous solution of iron chloride to produce magnesium chloride and iron. 

$$Mg_{(s)} + FeCl_{2(aq)} \rightarrow MgCl_{2(aq)} + Fe_{(s)}$$

Explain why this displacement reaction is an example of a redox reaction.

....

....

[Total 2 marks]

2 Shaun adds small pieces of some metals to metal salt solutions. He records whether or not any reaction has taken place. His table of results is shown in **Figure 1**. 

	Magnesium	**Silver**	**Aluminium**	**Lead**
Magnesium chloride	no reaction	no reaction	no reaction	no reaction
Silver nitrate	magnesium nitrate and silver formed	no reaction	aluminium nitrate and silver formed	lead nitrate and silver formed
Aluminium chloride	magnesium chloride and aluminium formed	no reaction	no reaction	no reaction
Lead nitrate	magnesium nitrate and lead formed	no reaction	aluminium nitrate and lead formed	no reaction

Figure 1

a) Shaun says "My results show that lead is more reactive than silver."
Do you agree? Explain your answer.

....

....

[1]

b) Construct a balanced symbol equation for the reaction between magnesium and aluminium chloride, $AlCl_3$.

....

[2]

c) Nickel is above lead in the reactivity series. Nickel is a shiny grey metal and nickel nitrate is green in solution. Lead is a dull grey metal and lead nitrate is colourless in solution. Suggest what Shaun would observe if he added nickel to lead nitrate solution.

....

....

....

[2]

[Total 5 marks]

Extracting Metals Using Carbon

1 The method used to extract metals from their ores can be determined using the reactivity series. Part of the reactivity series is shown in **Figure 1**.

Potassium	K	Most Reactive
Calcium	Ca	↓
Aluminium	Al	
Carbon	C	
Zinc	Zn	
Tin	Sn	
Copper	Cu	Least Reactive

Figure 1

a) Give the definition of a metal ore.

....

....

[1]

b) Suggest how copper is extracted from its ore in industry.

....

....

[1]

c) State **one** other metal from **Figure 1** that can be extracted in the same way as copper.

....

[1]

[Total 3 marks]

2 Iron is extracted from its ore, iron oxide (Fe_2O_3), in a blast furnace using carbon. Grade 7-9

a) Write a balanced equation for this reaction.

....

[2]

b) A certain batch of iron ore that contains impurities of zinc oxide and calcium oxide is reacted in a blast furnace. After the reaction is complete, any metal produced by the reaction was removed. Any unreacted ore was left in the reaction vessel.

The iron metal product was tested for purity and was found to contain traces of another metal. Suggest an identity for the other metal. Explain why it is present.

....

....

....

....

[3]

[Total 5 marks]

Other Methods of Extracting Metals

1 Aluminium is a metal that is widely used in construction. It can be extracted from its ore, aluminium oxide.

a) What is the name given to the technique used to extract aluminium from its ore?

[1]

b) As part of the extraction process, aluminium oxide is mixed in cryolite. What is the purpose of mixing the aluminium oxide with cryolite?

[1]

c) Pure aluminium is more expensive to buy than many metals which are extracted from their ores by reduction with carbon. Explain how the extraction process contributes to the higher cost of pure aluminium.

[2]

[Total 4 marks]

2 The increasing demand and the limited supply of metal-rich ores means that scientists are now developing new ways to extract metal from low-grade ores.

a) Describe how phytoextraction is used to extract some metals from their ores.

[4]

b) Give **one** advantage and **one** disadvantage of using phytoextraction to extract metals from their ores.

[2]

c) Name one other biological method of extracting metals from low-grade ores.

[1]

[Total 7 marks]

Recycling

1 This question is on recycling. (Grade 6-7)

a) An alternative to recycling is disposing of waste into landfill.
Give **one** disadvantage associated with using landfill to dispose of waste.

....

[1]

b) Avoiding using landfill is one environmental advantage of recycling. Give **two** other environmental reasons why recycling is considered more sustainable than making new materials.

....

....

[2]

c) Give **two** economic benefits of recycling.

....

....

[2]

[Total 5 marks]

2 Rachel is sorting some rubbish that has accumulated around her house. (Grade 6-7)

a) Rachel has three pieces of rubbish made from three different materials, **A**, **B** and **C**.
Some data about the materials is shown in **Figure 1**.

Material	Availability of resource	Energy to recycle	Energy to extract
A	Abundant	High	Low
B	Limited	Low	High
C	Limited	Medium	High

Figure 1

From the data given, which material in **Figure 1** is the **best** to recycle? Explain your answer.

....

....

....

....

[2]

b) Rachel is able to recycle plastic bottles at her local recycling centre.
Given that many parts of the manufacturing process involve using fractions of crude oil, explain why it is important to recycle plastics.

....

....

[1]

[Total 3 marks]

Life Cycle Assessments

Warm-Up

A company is developing a new product. Identify the factors that they should consider when producing a life cycle assessment. Tick **two** boxes.

Colour of the product ☐ Demand for the product ☐

Recyclability of the product ☐ Attractiveness of the product ☐

Source of raw materials ☐ Profitability of the product ☐

1 A furniture company is designing a new range of chairs for children. They need to decide whether the chairs will be made out of polypropene or timber. Grade 6-7

a) The company carries out a life cycle assessment of both possible products. Describe the purpose of a life cycle assessment.

....

....

[1]

b) Some data about the two materials are shown in **Figure 1**.

Material	Source	Relative Energy Cost to Make/Extract	Cost
Timber	Trees	1	Medium
Poly(propene)	Crude oil	15	Low

Figure 1

Use the data in **Figure 1** to explain which material would be the **best** choice to make the chairs from, in terms of sustainability. Explain your answer.

....

....

....

....

....

[3]

c) Suggest **two** factors, other than those given in **Figure 1**, that the company should consider in their life cycle assessment when deciding whether to make the chairs from timber or polypropene.

....

....

[2]

[Total 6 marks]

2 A garden tool company is considering the environmental costs of producing a rake. Grade 6-7

a) The rake contains components made from iron.
Suggest **two** environmental problems associated with extracting iron from its ore.

....

....

[2]

b) The rake contains parts that cannot be recycled, so the company thinks that it is likely to be disposed of in landfill at the end of its life span.
Give **one** disadvantage of disposing of waste using landfill.

....

[1]

c) The rake is sold in plastic packaging.
Suggest a sustainable way that consumers could dispose of the packaging.

....

[1]

[Total 4 marks]

3 A toy company is carrying out a life cycle assessment of four prototype toys. **Figure 2** displays some of the data from their assessments. Grade 7-9

Toy	CO_2 emissions (kg)	Solvent use (dm^3)	Energy consumption (MJ)
A	16.2	3981	267.84
B	14.8	2672	212.26
C	14.9	3876	159.82
D	12.4	2112	174.56

Figure 2

Using the data in the table, evaluate the relative environmental impact of producing each toy.

....

....

....

....

....

....

....

[Total 4 marks]

Exam Tip

You may be given data and asked to figure out which product has the biggest or smallest environmental impact. It's likely that there won't be an obvious answer at first glance — some products may have really low CO_2 emissions but may pollute lots of water. You'll have to look at all the factors and decide which product is the best or worst overall.

Target AO3

4 **Figure 3** contains life cycle assessment data for two types of soft drink container. 

Figure 3

	Glass Bottles	**Aluminium Cans**
Raw Materials	Sand, soda ash and limestone	Aluminium ore
Manufacturing	• Have to be produced at very high temperatures • Their production releases greenhouse gases	• Require large amounts of electricity to extract aluminium from the ore • Their production releases greenhouse gases
Usage	Can be refilled and reused	Usually only used once
Disposal	Widely recycled and used to produce new glass	Can be continually recycled as a source of aluminium

a) Use information from **Figure 3** to suggest **one** way in which glass bottles are more environmentally friendly than aluminium cans.

....

[1]

b) Aluminium cans can also be produced from recycled aluminium cans.
Evaluate whether the life cycle assessment for aluminium cans produced from recycled cans would be more positive or negative than the life cycle assessment for aluminium cans in **Figure 3**.

....

....

....

[2]

c) Certain glass objects cannot be recycled with the glass bottles.
Explain why this negatively affects the life cycle assessment of the glass bottles.

....

....

[2]

d) Suggest another useful comparison that could be added to the disposal section of these LCAs.

....

....

[1]

[Total 6 marks]

Exam Tip

An important skill in the exam is to consider potential impacts that haven't been given as part of the life cycle assessment. Companies may produce assessments that make their products look great when they are actually environmentally damaging. This is why it's important to consider all the information you can before answering.

Dynamic Equilibrium

Warm-Up

Complete the paragraph below by circling the correct option from the choices.

The Haber Process is <u>an irreversible / a reversible</u> reaction that forms <u>ammonia / sulfuric acid</u> from hydrogen and nitrogen. The nitrogen used in the process is extracted from <u>the air / crude oil</u> and the hydrogen is extracted from <u>the air / natural gas</u>.

The conditions used for the Haber Process are a temperature of <u>200 °C / 450 °C</u>, a pressure of <u>250 atm / 200 atm</u> and in the presence of an <u>iron / aluminium</u> catalyst.

1 Dynamic equilibrium can only be achieved in reversible reactions. Grade 4-6

a) Compare the rates of the forwards and backwards reactions at dynamic equilibrium.
State how this affects the concentrations of reactants and products present at dynamic equilibrium.

....

....

[2]

b) Dynamic equilibrium can only be reached in a closed system.
Explain what is meant by a 'closed system'.

....

....

[1]

c) During a certain reversible reaction, the equilibrium lies to the left. How should the concentration of the reactants be altered in order to increase the rate of product formation?

....

[1]

[Total 4 marks]

2 An aqueous solution of blue copper(II) ions can react with chloride ions to form a yellow copper compound. The ionic equation for this reaction is: $Cu^{2+} + 4Cl^{-} \rightleftharpoons [CuCl_4]^{2-}$ Grade 6-7

a) What does the symbol '$\rightleftharpoons$' mean in this reaction?

....

[1]

b) A solution containing copper(II) ions is mixed with a solution containing chloride ions in a flask. The solution quickly turns green. When observed for a few minutes no further change in colour can be seen. Explain these observations.

....

....

....

[2]

[Total 3 marks]

Le Chatelier's Principle

1 The equilibrium position of a reaction is dependent on the conditions that the reaction is carried out under.

Grade 4-6

a) What does Le Chatelier's Principle say about the effect of changing the conditions of a reversible reaction at equilibrium?

....

[1]

b) State **two** conditions you could change in order to alter the position of equilibrium of a reaction that happens in solution.

....

....

[2]

[Total 3 marks]

2 Methanol can be manufactured industrially from a gas mixture of carbon monoxide and hydrogen in the following reaction: $CO_{(g)} + 2H_{2(g)} \rightleftharpoons CH_3OH_{(g)}$.
This occurs over a Cu-ZnO-Al_2O_3 catalyst, under conditions of 250 °C and 50 –100 atm.
The forward reaction is exothermic.

Grade 6-7

a) Under a certain set of conditions, the equilibrium lies to the right.
Describe what this means, in terms of the concentration of products and reactants.

....

....

[1]

b) Identify which of the following statements is **false**. Tick **one** box.

☐ **A** A decrease in the concentration of CO shifts the position of equilibrium to the left.

☐ **B** Increasing the concentration of H_2 shifts the position of equilibrium to the right.

☐ **C** Increasing the temperature to 470 °C shifts the position of equilibrium to the left.

☐ **D** The Cu-ZnO-Al_2O_3 catalyst shifts the position of equilibrium to the right.

[1]

c) Amara says, to increase the yield of the reaction, they should decrease the pressure of the reaction. Russell disagrees. Which student do you agree with? Explain your answer.

....

....

....

....

[2]

[Total 4 marks]

3 A mixture of iodine monochloride (ICl) and chlorine is sealed in a gas syringe. The gases react in a reversible reaction to form iodine trichloride (ICl_3) and eventually reach an equilibrium. The equation for the reaction is: $ICl_{(g)} + Cl_{2(g)} \rightleftharpoons ICl_{3(s)}$.

Grade 7-9

a) Given that the forward reaction is exothermic, explain how the relative quantities of ICl and ICl_3 would change if the mixture was heated, and all other conditions remained the same.

....

....

....

[2]

b) Explain how the relative quantities of ICl and ICl_3 would change if the plunger were pushed into the syringe, and the temperature remained constant.

....

....

....

[3]

[Total 5 marks]

4 Dinitrogen tetroxide (N_2O_4) is a colourless gas. It decomposes in a reversible reaction to form the brown gas, nitrogen dioxide (NO_2). The reaction equation is: $N_2O_{4(g)} \rightleftharpoons 2NO_{2(g)}$.

Grade 7-9

a) When a sample of N_2O_4 is left to decompose in a sealed tube, a pale brown colour can be seen. If this mixture is heated, the colour becomes a darker brown. Explain this observation and predict whether the forward reaction is exothermic or endothermic.

....

....

....

[3]

b) Explain how you would expect the colour of the equilibrium mixture to change if the pressure of the mixture is decreased, and all other conditions are kept the same.

....

....

....

....

[3]

[Total 6 marks]

Exam Tip

Working out what happens to the position of an equilibrium when you change the conditions can be a bit of a brain twister. Just remember that for any change that's made, the reaction will try to do the opposite. So if you increase the temperature the endothermic reaction will speed up, if you increase the pressure the equilibrium will move to the side where there are fewer moles of gas, and if you increase the concentration of a reactant you'll get more products.

Target AO3

5 A scientist investigated the gas phase reaction between sulfur dioxide and oxygen.
The equation for this reversible reaction is: $2SO_{2(g)} + O_{2\,(g)} \rightleftharpoons 2SO_{3\,(g)}$.
Figure 1 shows how the concentration of sulfur dioxide and sulfur trioxide change with time.

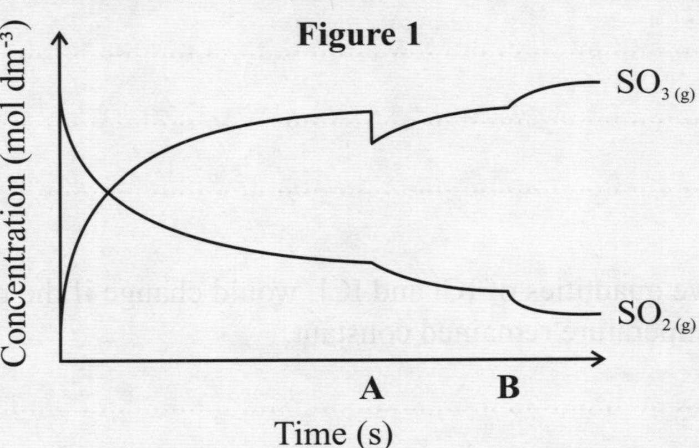

a) Suggest what happened to cause the change in concentration of SO_3 at time **A** and shortly after.

....

....

[2]

b) Increasing the temperature of the reaction causes the amount of SO_3 produced by the reaction to decrease. Use this information to determine whether the forward reaction is endothermic or exothermic, and justify your answer.

....

....

....

[2]

c) State whether the pressure was decreased or increased at time **B**. Explain your answer.

....

....

....

[2]

d) In a separate reaction, SO_3 is added to a container, which is then sealed to form a closed system. Sketch a graph of the concentrations of sulfur dioxide and sulfur trioxide versus time for the reaction, $2SO_{3\,(g)} \rightleftharpoons 2SO_{2\,(g)} + O_{2\,(g)}$, assuming the reaction takes place at a constant low pressure.

[2]

[Total 8 marks]

Concentration (mol dm^{-3})

Time (s)

Exam Tip

As well as asking you to draw graphs, the examiner may ask you to interpret and explain what a graph tells you about a reaction. Make sure you understand how the key changes in the graph relate to the reaction in the question.

Transition Metals

Warm-Up

Circle all of the elements listed below that are transition metals.
(Use a periodic table to help if you need it.)

nickel magnesium sulfur chromium tin iodine
calcium potassium titanium aluminium cobalt silver silicon

1 Four examples of the uses of transition metals and their compounds are listed below. For each example, give **one** common property of transition metals that makes the material suitable for that use. Grade 4-6

a) Tantalum is used to make parts for high-temperature furnaces.

....

[1]

b) Tungsten can be used to make weights for fishing hooks.

....

[1]

c) Oxides of iron can be used to make stained glass for windows.

....

[1]

d) Copper can be used to make pipes to carry water.

....

[1]

[Total 4 marks]

2 Vanadium is a transition metal with atomic number 23.
Several different oxides of vanadium exist, for example VO_2 and V_2O_5. Grade 6-7

a) The Contact Process is used to produce sulfuric acid from sulfur, oxygen and water. Vanadium pentoxide, V_2O_5, is added to the reaction vessel during the process. This increases the rate of the reaction. Suggest what role vanadium pentoxide is playing in this process.

....

[1]

b) Carys has samples of vanadium(IV) oxide, VO_2, and sodium oxide, Na_2O.
One sample is a deep blue powder and the other is a white powder.
Which one would you expect to be the vanadium(IV) oxide? Explain your answer.

....

....

[1]

[Total 2 marks]

Alloys

1 Metals are able to be bent and shaped. Grade 6-7

a) Explain how the structure and bonding in metals means they are able to be bent and shaped.

....

.... [2]

b) An alloy is a mixture of a metal and at least one other element.
Explain why it is usually harder to change the shape of an alloy than a pure metal.

....

....

....

.... [3]

[Total 5 marks]

2 This question is about different alloys and their uses.
Figure 1 shows some data about the properties of four alloys. Grade 6-7

Figure 1

Alloy	Carbon Composition (%)	Strength (MPa)	Density (g cm^{-3})
Alloy 1 (stainless steel)	0.07	200	8.1
Alloy 2 (low carbon steel)	0.1	250	7.6
Alloy 3 (high carbon steel)	1.6	350	7.9
Alloy 4 (aluminium alloy)	0	115	2.6

a) Use the data in **Figure 1** to state the effect on strength of increasing the carbon content in steel.

.... [1]

b) A vice is used to hold an object in place while work is carried out on it.
The material a vice is made from needs to be strong and heavy to hold objects in place.
Suggest which alloy, from **Figure 1**, would be the **most suitable** for this purpose.

.... [1]

c) Alloy 4 has the lowest strength value of all the metals shown in the table and yet it is used to make many parts of commercial aircraft. Using the data in **Figure 1**, explain why this is.

.... [1]

[Total 3 marks]

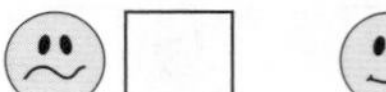

Corrosion

1 Electroplating is a method used to coat a metal object with another metal using electrolysis. (Grade 4-6)

Give **two** reasons why objects are electroplated.

....

....

[Total 2 marks]

2 Martha and Joe both own bikes with iron bike chains. Martha leaves her bike outside and, after a week, discovers that the chain has started to rust. (Grade 6-7)

a) Joe keeps his bike inside. Is his bike more or less likely to rust than Martha's? Explain your answer.

....

....

[2]

b) Martha buys a new iron bike chain. She decides to oil the chain to prevent it from rusting. Explain why oiling is a suitable method for protecting a bike chain from rusting.

....

....

[2]

[Total 4 marks]

3 There are several methods that can be used to prevent the corrosion of metals and alloys. (Grade 6-7)

a) A ship manufacturer wants to prevent the corrosion of a steel ship using sacrificial protection. Describe what is meant by sacrificial protection and explain how it protects the ship.

....

....

....

....

[3]

b) A roofing company coats an iron roof with a layer of zinc to protect it from rusting. After a while, the zinc layer becomes scratched. Would you expect the iron roofing to begin to rust? Explain your answer.

....

....

[2]

[Total 5 marks]

Titrations

1 A student carried out a titration where 0.165 mol dm^{-3} hydrochloric acid was used to neutralise 22.0 cm^3 of magnesium hydroxide solution. He repeated the titration three times.

a) Calculate the mean titre of hydrochloric acid using the results in **Figure 1**.
Ignore any anomalous results.

	Titration			
	1	2	3	4
Titre (cm^3)	35.10	33.30	33.40	33.35

Figure 1

Mean = ... cm^3
[2]

b) Using your result from part a), calculate the number of moles of hydrochloric acid that were needed to neutralise the solution of magnesium hydroxide. Give your answer to 3 significant figures.

Moles = ... mol
[2]
[Total 4 marks]

2 Annalise carried out four repeats of a titration. She calculated the mean titre and found that 40.0 cm^3 of 0.100 mol dm^{-3} sodium hydroxide was used to neutralise 20.0 cm^3 of hydrochloric acid. The equation for the reaction is: $NaOH + HCl \rightarrow NaCl + H_2O$

a) Calculate the concentration of the hydrochloric acid in mol dm^{-3}.

Concentration = ... mol dm^{-3}
[3]

b) Convert the concentration of the hydrochloric acid to g dm^{-3}.
(Relative atomic masses: H = 1, Cl = 35.5)

Concentration = ... g dm^{-3}
[2]
[Total 5 marks]

Target AO3

3 Two students conducted titrations to find the concentration of a solution of sulfuric acid. Both of the students used calcium hydroxide solution of a known concentration as the base.

a) Student **A**'s titration results are shown in **Figure 2** and Student **B**'s results are shown in **Figure 3**.

Figure 2

Repeat	1	2	3	4	Mean
Volume of calcium hydroxide (cm^3)	32.6	34.0	33.4	32.8	33.2

Figure 3

Repeat	1	2	3	4	Mean
Volume of calcium hydroxide (cm^3)	28.1	28.9	29.3	27.7	28.5

i) Which student's results are more **precise**? Explain your answer.

....

....

[2]

ii) Each student calculated the concentration of the sulfuric acid using their own data. Student **A** calculated a concentration of 0.518 mol dm^{-3}. Student **B** calculated a concentration of 0.421 mol dm^{-3}. The actual concentration of the sulfuric acid was 0.400 mol dm^{-3}. Which student's results are more **accurate**? Explain your answer.

....

....

[2]

b) Predict how the volume of calcium hydroxide solution required to neutralise the sulfuric acid would change if the concentration of the calcium hydroxide solution was doubled.

....

[1]

c) The end-point of this titration occurs at around pH 7.2.
Use the information in **Figure 4** to choose the most appropriate indicator for this experiment.

Figure 4

Indicator	Transition Range
bromocresol purple	5.2 - 6.8
phenolphthalein	8.2 - 10.0
phenol red	6.8 - 8.2

....

[Total 6 ma

Exam Tip

It's really important to know the differences between the meanings of scientific terms such as precision and accur
Make sure you pay attention to exactly what the question is asking about before you start writing your answer.

4 A chemist completes a titration where 0.00850 moles of potassium hydroxide are neutralised by 0.0250 dm^3 of sulfuric acid. The equation for the reaction is:

$$2KOH + H_2SO_4 \rightarrow K_2SO_4 + 2H_2O$$

Grade 7-9

What is the concentration of the sulfuric acid in g dm^{-3}? (Relative formula mass of H_2SO_4 = 98)

....

....

....

....

[Total 3 marks]

5 Amy has a sodium hydroxide solution of an unknown concentration. She plans to find the concentration of the solution by titrating it with a 0.200 mol dm^{-3} solution of sulfuric acid.

Grade 7-9 **PRACTICAL**

a)* Describe how to carry out a titration, with reference to the equipment used.

....

....

....

....

....

....

....

....

....

....

....

[6]

took 22.5 cm^3 of the 0.200 mol dm^{-3} solution of sulfuric acid to neutralise 25.0 cm^3 of lium hydroxide solution. The equation for the reaction is: $2NaOH + H_2SO_4 \rightarrow Na_2SO_4 + 2H_2O$ culate the concentration of the sodium hydroxide. Give your answer to 3 significant figures.

Concentration = ... mol dm^{-3}

[4]

[Total 10 marks]

Percentage Yield

1 Kezia and Steven are reacting some lithium with water to form lithium hydroxide and hydrogen gas. From the mass of reactants, they calculate the theoretical yield of lithium hydroxide to be 25 g.

Grade 4-6

a) Kezia finds that 17 g of lithium hydroxide is produced.
What is the percentage yield of lithium hydroxide? Tick **one** box.

- [ ] **A** 63%
- [ ] **B** 72%
- [ ] **C** 68%
- [ ] **D** 54%

[1]

b) Steven's experiment produces 22 g of lithium hydroxide.
Calculate the percentage yield of lithium hydroxide in his reaction.

Percentage yield = ... %

[3]

[Total 4 marks]

2 In a precipitation reaction, copper sulfate solution reacts with sodium hydroxide solution. The equation for the reaction is:

$$CuSO_4 + 2NaOH \rightarrow Cu(OH)_2 + Na_2SO_4$$

Grade 6-7

a) If 39.75 g of copper sulfate reacts with an excess of sodium hydroxide, calculate the theoretical yield of the copper hydroxide. Give your answer to 3 significant figures.
(Relative atomic masses: Cu = 63.5, S = 32, O = 16, H = 1)

Theoretical yield = ... g

[3]

b) A student carries out this reaction and produces 16.5 g of copper hydroxide. Use your answer in part a) to calculate the percentage yield of the reaction to 3 significant figures.

Percentage yield = ... %

[3]

[Total 6 marks]

3 When heated, magnesium carbonate decomposes to form magnesium oxide and carbon dioxide.
The equation for the reaction is: $MgCO_3 \rightarrow MgO + CO_2$

In an industrial reaction, 44.10 kg of magnesium carbonate decomposed to form 15.75 kg of magnesium oxide, MgO. Calculate the percentage yield of magnesium oxide.
(Relative atomic masses: Mg = 24, C = 12, O = 16)

Percentage yield = ... %

[Total 6 marks]

4 Ammonia is produced in the Haber process by reacting nitrogen gas with hydrogen gas.
The equation for this reaction is: $N_2 + 3H_2 \rightleftharpoons 2NH_3$

a) A factory used 14 kg of nitrogen gas to produce 4.5 kg of ammonia.
Calculate the percentage yield for the reaction.
(Relative atomic masses: N = 14, H = 1)

Percentage yield = ... %

[6]

b) Suggest **two** reasons why the percentage yield was less than 100%.

....

....

[2]

c) Give **two** reasons why it is desirable for a factory to obtain as high a percentage yield as possible.

....

....

[2]

[Total 10 marks]

Exam Tip

Don't forget that percentage yield is just one factor that businesses consider when they're choosing a process to make chemicals in industry. You might get an exam question where you have to think about why a company might use a reaction to make a chemical by thinking about factors like atom economy and rate of reaction as well as percentage yield.

Atom Economy

Warm-Up

Complete the table by calculating the atom economy for the two reactions.

Reaction	M_r of desired product	Total M_r of all products	Atom Economy (%)
$NaOH + HCl \rightarrow NaCl + H_2O$	58.5	76.5	....
$2Cu + O_2 \rightarrow 2CuO$	159	159	....

1 Some chemicals can be made by several different reactions. Industrial companies need to take different factors into consideration before deciding which reaction pathway is the most profitable and environmentally friendly. **Figure 1** shows data for three different reactions that each produce the same desired product.

Figure 1

Reaction	Atom economy (%)	Percentage yield (%)	Rate	Any useful by-products?
A	100	84	Medium	N/A (no by-products)
B	?	64	Slow	Yes
C	73.5	53	Fast	No

a) i) Give the definition of atom economy.

....

....

[1]

ii) In reaction **B**, the relative formula mass of all the products is 141 and the relative formula mass of the desired product is 111. Use this data to calculate the atom economy of the reaction. Give your answer to 3 significant figures.

Atom economy = ... %

[3]

b) Use the table and your answer to part a) ii) to suggest which reaction pathway would be the most suitable to be carried out in industry. Explain your answer.

....

....

....

....

....

[3]

[Total 7 marks]

2 Magnesium chloride has a variety of applications, including use in fertilisers, waste water treatment and medicine. It can be produced by several different reactions. Three reactions are shown below.

X $Mg + 2HCl \rightarrow MgCl_2 + H_2$

Y $MgCO_3 + 2HCl \rightarrow MgCl_2 + H_2O + CO_2$

Z $MgO + 2HCl \rightarrow MgCl_2 + H_2O$

(Relative atomic masses: Mg = 24, Cl = 35.5, O = 16, C = 12, H = 1)

a) i) Calculate the relative molecular mass of magnesium chloride.

relative molecular mass = ...

[1]

ii) Calculate the atom economy reaction X. Give your answer to 2 significant figures.

Atom economy = ... %

[4]

iii)Calculate the atom economy reaction Y. Give your answer to 2 significant figures.

Atom economy = ... %

[4]

iv) Calculate the atom economy reaction Z. Give your answer to 2 significant figures.

Atom economy = ... %

[4]

b) A company is looking at the cost implications of using each of the reactions. Explain how the atom economy of a reaction can affect:

i) the amount of raw materials needed to make a certain amount of product.

....

....

[1]

ii) the cost associated with disposing of chemical waste.

....

....

[2]

c) Using your answers to part a), suggest which of the three reactions, **X**, **Y** or **Z**, would be the **least** profitable method for making magnesium chloride in industry.

....

[1]

[Total 17 marks]

Target AO3

3 The Solvay process is used to produce sodium carbonate.
The overall equation for the process is: $CaCO_3 + 2NaCl \rightarrow Na_2CO_3 + CaCl_2$

Grade 7-9

a) The reactions used in the Solvay process are:

$$\text{Step 1: } CaCO_3 \rightarrow CaO + CO_2$$

$$\text{Step 2: } NaCl + NH_3 + H_2O + CO_2 \rightarrow NH_4Cl + NaHCO_3$$

$$\text{Step 3: } 2NaHCO_3 \rightarrow Na_2CO_3 + CO_2 + H_2O$$

$$\text{Step 4: } CaO + 2NH_4Cl \rightarrow CaCl_2 + 2NH_3 + H_2O$$

The desired product, sodium carbonate, is formed in the third step.
Explain how the final step improves the overall atom economy of the process.

....

....

....

....

[3]

b) The first step of the Solvay process is the thermal decomposition of calcium carbonate, which is obtained from limestone.
A student carried out an experiment to decompose calcium carbonate by strongly heating 10.0 g of limestone chips in a crucible over a Bunsen burner. The student's actual yield was much lower than the theoretical yield. Suggest two reasons their method did not produce the theoretical yield.

....

....

....

....

[2]

c) The Leblanc process can also be used to produce sodium carbonate.
The overall reaction is: $2NaCl + H_2SO_4 + 2C + CaCO_3 \rightarrow 2HCl + 2CO_2 + Na_2CO_3 + CaS$.
The atom economy for the Leblanc process is 31.3%, compared to 48.8% for the Solvay process.
Evaluate why the Solvay process is preferable in terms of the reaction and the atom economy.

....

....

....

....

....

....

[3]

[Total 8 marks]

The Haber Process

1 The Haber process uses the following exothermic reaction: $N_{2\,(g)} + 3H_{2\,(g)} \rightleftharpoons 2NH_{3\,(g)}$ Grade 4-6
The conditions used for the reaction affect how quickly it reaches equilibrium.

In terms of how quickly equilibrium is reached, what is the effect of:

a) increasing the pressure? ....

[1]

b) decreasing the temperature? ....

[1]

[Total 2 marks]

2 The Haber process makes ammonia, NH_3, in an exothermic reaction between hydrogen and nitrogen. The reaction is carried out at a pressure of 200 atm and a temperature of 450 °C. Grade 7-9

a) i) A company increases the temperature in the reaction vessel for the Haber process to 580 °C. Which of the following is the result of this change in temperature? Tick **one** box.

- [ ] **A** Higher rate of reaction.
- [ ] **B** Lower rate of reaction.
- [ ] **C** No change in the rate of reaction.
- [ ] **D** Rate of reaction is halved.

[1]

ii) The company thinks the increase in temperature will increase the yield of product from the Haber process. Do you agree or disagree with the company? Explain your answer.

....

....

....

[2]

b) In a bid to make the process cheaper, the company decides to reduce the pressure at which they carry out the Haber process. Give **two** disadvantages of using a low pressure to carry out the Haber process.

....

....

[2]

c) The Haber process uses an iron catalyst. How does the iron catalyst affect:

i) the rate of the reaction? ....

[1]

ii) the yield? ....

[1]

[Total 7 marks]

Target AO3

3 The Haber process is an important process in the chemical industry.
Figure 1 shows a graph of the amount of product formed versus time.
Each line on the graph represents a reaction conducted at a different temperature.
All the other variables in this reaction were kept the same.

Figure 1

Amount of product evolved

A

B

C

Time

a) Which line in **Figure 1** represents the reaction that was run at the highest temperature? Explain your answer.

....

....

....

[2]

b) The reaction shown by line **B** is the closest to the temperature used in industry. Use **Figure 1** to suggest why this temperature is preferred to those used in reactions **A** and **C**.

....

....

....

....

[4]

c) The unused reactants in the Haber process are recycled back into the reaction. Without this recycling, the yield would only be about 10%. Explain why recycling the reactants is an important part of the process.

....

....

[2]

[Total 8 marks]

Exam Tip

You will recognise the Haber process, but you will also come across reactions in the exam that you haven't seen before. Just use the knowledge that you do have about the topic to answer any questions with unfamiliar contexts.

Fertilisers

Warm-Up

Use the words below to complete the sentences about fertilisers.
You don't have to use every word, but each word can only be used once.

nitrogen hydrogen ammonium potassium phosphorus nitric acid

Fertilisers are made from compounds containing the elements nitrogen, ...
and .... , which are essential for plant growth. The salt ....
nitrate is a fertiliser which can be made by reacting ammonia with ....

1 A student is making a sample of ammonium sulfate crystals using a titration method.
She adds an indicator to dilute sulfuric acid, then adds ammonia until she sees a colour change.
The student then crystallises the solution and is left with impure ammonium sulfate crystals.

Grade 6-7

a) i) Suggest a piece of equipment that she could use to add the ammonia solution to the acid.

....

[1]

ii) Suggest an indicator that she could use to show when the reaction is complete.

....

[1]

b) What should the student have done to produce pure ammonium sulfate crystals?

....

....

....

[2]

c) In industry, the same reaction is used to make ammonium sulfate, but the method is different.
Give **one** reason why factories do **not** use this laboratory method to produce ammonium sulfate.

....

....

[1]

[Total 5 marks]

2 The Haber process is used to produce ammonia.
It is said that without the Haber process, it would be impossible to grow enough food to feed the population of the world. Suggest why this is true.

Grade 7-9

....

....

....

[Total 3 marks]

Calculations with Gases

For the questions on these pages, you may need the following information:
One mole of any gas occupies 24 dm^3 at room temperature and pressure.

1 Hydrogen, H_2, and sulfur dioxide, SO_2, are both gases at room temperature and pressure. 

a) Calculate the volume of 23.0 moles of H_2 at room temperature and pressure.

Volume = ... dm^3
[1]

b) Calculate the volume of 96 g of SO_2, at room temperature and pressure.
(Relative formula mass of SO_2 = 64)

Volume = ... dm^3
[2]
[Total 3 marks]

2 A student burned 7.5 g of ethane, C_2H_6, in an excess of oxygen.
The reaction produced water and carbon dioxide. 

$$C_2H_{6(g)} + 3\frac{1}{2}O_{2(g)} \rightarrow 2CO_{2(g)} + 3H_2O_{(l)}$$

a) Calculate the volume of ethane used in the reaction, at room temperature and pressure.
(Relative atomic masses: C = 12, H = 1, O = 16)

Volume = ... dm^3
[3]

b) Using the reaction equation and the amount of ethane burned,
calculate the volume of CO_2 produced at room temperature and pressure.

Volume = ... dm^3
[2]
[Total 5 marks]

3 A student took some calcium carbonate, in the form of marble chips, and added hydrochloric acid. The equation for the reaction is:

$$CaCO_{3(s)} + 2HCl_{(aq)} \rightarrow CaCl_{2(aq)} + CO_{2(g)} + H_2O_{(l)}$$

a) 920 cm^3 of carbon dioxide, CO_2, was produced during the reaction. This had a mass of 1.76 g. Calculate the molar volume of the carbon dioxide. (Relative atomic masses: C = 12, O = 16)

Molar volume = ... dm^3 mol^{-1}

[2]

b) The student repeated the experiment under a different set of conditions. This time, 175 cm^3 of carbon dioxide with a molar volume of 25.0 dm^3 mol^{-1} was produced. Calculate the mass of carbon dioxide produced in this reaction.

Mass = ... g

[2]

[Total 4 marks]

4 Carbon dioxide can be produced by reacting oxygen with carbon monoxide.

$$2CO_{(g)} + O_{2(g)} \rightarrow 2CO_{2(g)}$$

a) A student reacted 28 g of carbon monoxide with oxygen at room temperature and pressure. Calculate the volume of oxygen involved in the reaction. (Relative atomic masses: C = 12, O = 16)

Volume of oxygen = ... dm^3

[4]

b) Calculate the volume of carbon dioxide produced in the reaction in part a).

Volume of carbon dioxide = ... dm^3

[1]

[Total 5 marks]

Fuel Cells

1 Fuel cells are an alternative way of producing energy, instead of burning crude oil. Grade 4-6

a) Give the definition of a fuel cell.

....

....

[2]

b) Which of the following statements about fuel cells is **correct**? Tick **one** box.

☐ **A** Fuel cells produce a voltage indefinitely.

☐ **B** Fuel cells produce a voltage until one of the reactants is completely used up.

☐ **C** Fuel cells start to produce a voltage once all the reactants are used up.

☐ **D** Fuel cells produce a voltage until the reactants are partly used up.

[1]

[Total 3 marks]

2 Most cars on the road today are powered by internal combustion engines. Hydrogen-oxygen fuel cells could replace internal combustion engines in the future. Grade 6-7

a) Explain why hydrogen-oxygen fuel cells are considered 'cleaner' than internal combustion engines.

....

....

....

[2]

b) Explain why using hydrogen as a fuel instead of petrol might still require the use of fossil fuels.

....

....

....

[2]

c) Give **one** other disadvantage of using hydrogen-oxygen fuel cells to power cars.

....

....

[1]

[Total 5 marks]

Exam Tip

You might get an exam question about the advantages and disadvantages of using fuel cells for a particular purpose. Make sure you think carefully about your answer — some advantages and disadvantages only apply to certain uses.

 ☐  ☐  ☐

Group 1 — Alkali Metals

1 The alkali metals are found in Group 1 of the periodic table. Grade 4-6

a) Which of the following statements is the **best** description of the alkali metals? Tick **one** box.

☐ **A** Soft metals with relatively high melting points.

☐ **B** Soft metals with relatively low melting points.

☐ **C** Hard metals with relatively high melting points.

☐ **D** Hard metals with relatively low melting points.

[1]

b) The alkali metals readily react to form ionic compounds.
Explain why their ions usually have a charge of +1.

....

....

[2]

[Total 3 marks]

2 A teacher is demonstrating the reactions between water and some alkali metals to her class. In one reaction, she adds a small piece of potassium to cold water. Grade 6-7

a) Name the **two** products of this reaction.

....

[2]

b) Describe what you would expect to see if a small piece of potassium was added to cold water.

....

....

....

....

[2]

c) It is **not** safe to carry out the reaction between rubidium and water in the laboratory.
Explain why this is the case, using ideas about the electronic configurations of Group 1 metals.

....

....

....

....

....

[3]

[Total 7 marks]

 ☐  ☐  ☐

Group 7 — Halogens

Warm-Up

Which of the following statements about the halogens is **true**? Tick **one** box.

- [ ] They are non-metals that exist as single atoms.
- [ ] They are metals that exist as single atoms.
- [ ] They are non-metals that exist as molecules of two atoms.
- [ ] They are metals that exist as molecules of two atoms.

1 Amelia is testing gases. Grade 4-6

Figure 1 shows a gas being tested.

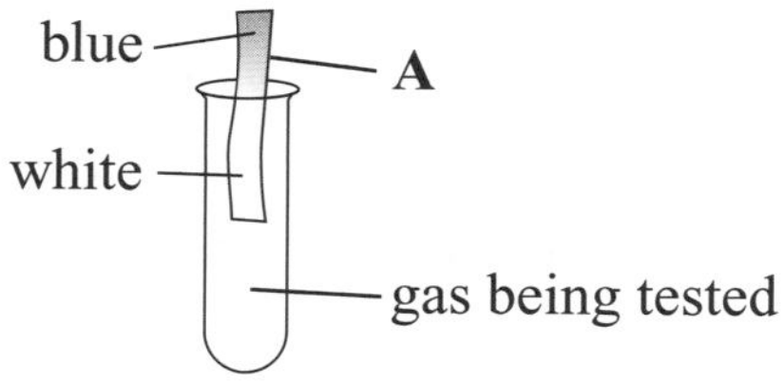

Figure 1

a) Identify the item labelled **A** in **Figure 1**.

....

[1]

b) Suggest which gas was present in the test tube.

....

[1]

[Total 2 marks]

2 The halogens can react with alkali metals to form metal halide salts. Grade 4-6

a) Name the metal halide salt that will be formed when the following pairs of elements react.

i) Bromine and sodium.

....

[1]

ii) Iodine and potassium.

....

[1]

b) When chlorine gas reacts with lithium, the salt lithium chloride, LiCl, is formed.
Write the balanced symbol equation for this reaction.

....

[2]

[Total 4 marks]

3 A chemist is carrying out some reactions involving halogens. Grade 6-7

a) i) In his first experiment he reacts hydrogen gas with chlorine gas.
Write a balanced chemical equation for this reaction.

....

[2]

ii) The chemist dissolves the product of this reaction in water and adds universal indicator.
What colour will the solution turn? Explain your answer.

....

....

[2]

b) The chemist carries out another reaction at room temperature and pressure, using a different gaseous halogen. Determine which of the halogens he must be using. Explain your answer.

....

....

[2]

c) Describe the appearance of bromine at room temperature.

....

[2]

[Total 8 marks]

4 The reactivity of halogens is dependent on their electronic configuration. Grade 7-9

a) Describe the electronic configuration of the halogens and how it changes down Group 7.

....

....

....

[2]

b) Sodium reacts violently with fluorine, at room temperature, to form sodium fluoride.
Predict how astatine might react with sodium at room temperature. Explain your answer.

....

....

....

....

....

[3]

[Total 5 marks]

Exam Tip

One of the most important things to learn about Group 7 elements is the trend you find in reactivity as you go down or up the group. And you need to be able to explain this trend using the electronic structure of the halogens. Smashing.

Halogen Displacement Reactions

1 Josie investigated the reactions that occur when chlorine, bromine or iodine are added to different sodium halide solutions. **Figure 1** shows her results.

	Sodium chloride solution ($NaCl_{(aq)}$, colourless)	Sodium bromide solution ($NaBr_{(aq)}$, colourless)	Sodium iodide solution ($NaI_{(aq)}$, colourless)
Add chlorine water ($Cl_{2\,(aq)}$, colourless)	no reaction	solution turns orange	....
Add bromine water ($Br_{2\,(aq)}$, orange)	no reaction	....	solution turns brown
Add iodine water ($I_{2\,(aq)}$, brown)	no reaction	no reaction	no reaction

Figure 1

a) Use your knowledge of the reactivity trend of the halogens to fill in the missing results in **Figure 1**.

[2]

b) Explain why there was no reaction when Josie added iodine water to sodium bromide solution.

....

....

[2]

c) i) Construct a balanced symbol equation for the reaction that happened when Josie added chlorine water to sodium bromide solution.

....

[2]

ii) Explain, in terms of electrons, why the reaction between chlorine water and sodium bromide solution can be described as a redox reaction.

....

....

....

[2]

d) Astatine is below iodine in Group 7. Predict whether chlorine water would react with sodium astatide solution. Explain your answer.

....

....

[2]

[Total 10 marks]

Group 0 — Noble Gases

1 Old-style filament light bulbs contain a thin metal filament. If these light bulbs were filled with air, oxygen would react with the filament causing it to burn away. To avoid this, the light bulbs are filled with argon. Grade 6-7

Explain why argon is suitable for this use, including ideas about electronic structure.

....

....

....

....

[Total 3 marks]

2 The noble gases are inert gases that make up Group 0 of the periodic table. Grade 6-7

Figure 1 shows some information about the first four noble gases.

Element	Symbol	Boiling point (°C)	Density (kg m^{-3})
Helium	He	–269	0.18
Neon	Ne	–246	0.90
Argon	Ar	–186	?
Krypton	Kr	–153	3.7

Figure 1

a) i) The element below krypton in Group 0 is xenon.
Use the information in **Figure 1** to predict what the boiling point of xenon will be.

boiling point = ... °C
[1]

ii) Use the information in **Figure 1** to predict the density of argon.

density = ... kg m^{-3}
[1]

b) Would you expect the boiling point of radon to be higher or lower than the boiling point of xenon? Explain your answer.

....

....

[1]
[Total 3 marks]

Exam Tip

Make sure you get lots of practice at questions like Q2, where you're given information about some of the elements in a group and asked to use it to predict something about another element in the group. They need careful thinking through.

Reaction Rate Experiments

1 A scientist reacts hydrochloric acid with marble chips to form calcium chloride, water and carbon dioxide gas.

PRACTICAL

a) He decides to measure the volume of carbon dioxide formed to work out the rate of the reaction. Outline a method the scientist could follow to monitor the volume of gas produced over the course of the reaction.

....

....

....

....

[3]

b) **Figure 1** shows a graph of his results. On **Figure 1**, sketch a curve that shows how the volume of gas produced would change over time if the experiment was carried out at a higher temperature.

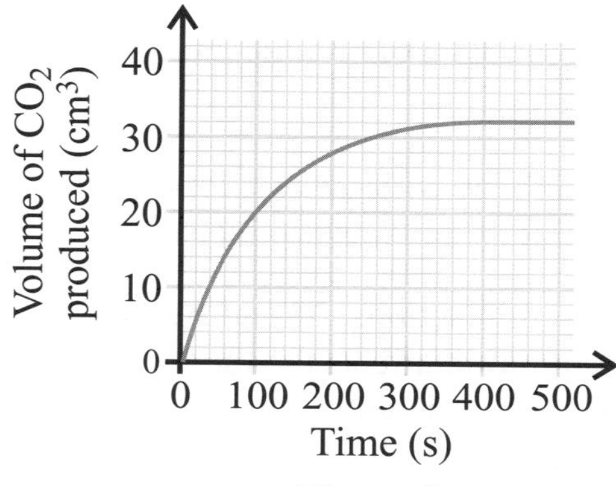

Figure 1

[2]

c) The scientist repeated the reaction using different quantities of reactants. Reaction **X** used 0.500 g of marble chips and an excess of 0.100 mol dm^{-3} hydrochloric acid. Using **Figure 2**, determine which of the following sets of conditions could have resulted in reaction **Y**. Tick **one** box.

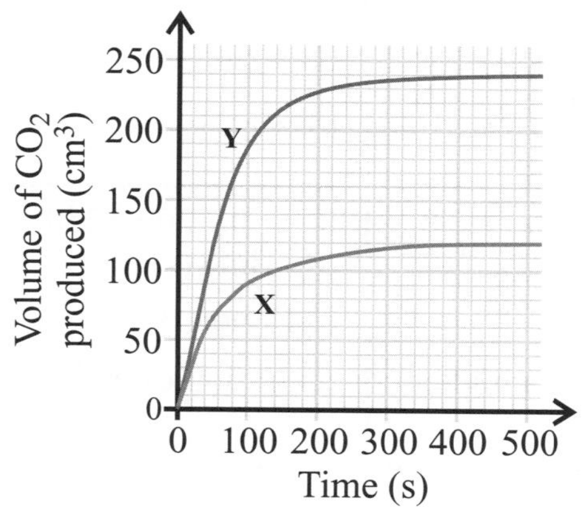

Figure 2

☐ **A** 0.250 g of marble chips and an excess of 0.100 mol dm^{-3} hydrochloric acid.

☐ **B** 1.00 g of marble chips and an excess of 0.100 mol dm^{-3} hydrochloric acid.

☐ **C** 0.250 g of marble chips and an excess of 0.200 mol dm^{-3} hydrochloric acid.

☐ **D** 1.00 g of marble chips and an excess of 0.200 mol dm^{-3} hydrochloric acid.

[1]

[Total 6 marks]

2 Laiza is investigating the effect of temperature on the rate of the reaction between sodium thiosulfate and hydrochloric acid. The reaction forms a cloudy, yellow precipitate of sulfur.

Grade 6-7

PRACTICAL

a) She measures out volumes of both reactants and gently heats each of the solutions in a water bath to 50 °C. Outline a method that Laiza could follow to monitor the rate of this reaction.

....

....

....

[3]

b) Laiza repeats the experiment but instead heats both reactant solutions to 30 °C.

i) How would you expect the rate of this reaction to compare to the rate of the reaction at 50 °C?

....

[1]

ii) Name **one** factor Laiza would have to keep the same for both reactions to make it a fair test.

....

[1]

[Total 5 marks]

3 Shabnam reacted magnesium ribbons with hydrochloric acid. As the reaction proceeded, hydrogen gas was produced.

Grade 6-7

Shabnam carried out two different reactions, **M** and **N**, using two different concentrations of acid in order to see how concentration affects the rate of reaction. All of the other variables were kept the same during both of the experiments. A graph of her results is shown in **Figure 3**.

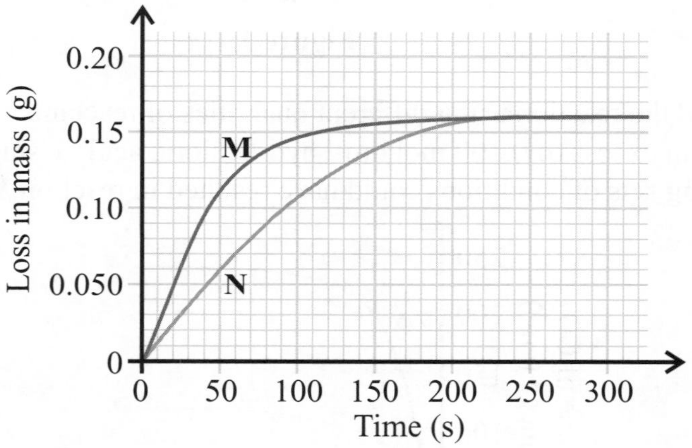

Figure 3

a) Which reaction, **M** or **N**, used a higher concentration of hydrochloric acid? Explain your answer.

....

....

[2]

b) Using the graph, calculate the rate of reaction **N** between 0 and 50 seconds.

rate = ... g s^{-1}

[2]

[Total 4 marks]

4 A student wanted to calculate the rate of reaction between nitric acid and zinc. He carried out two experiments under the same conditions, but in one he used zinc ribbons and in the other he used zinc powder.

The graph in **Figure 4** shows the rate of reaction for both experiments, labelled **Q** and **R**.

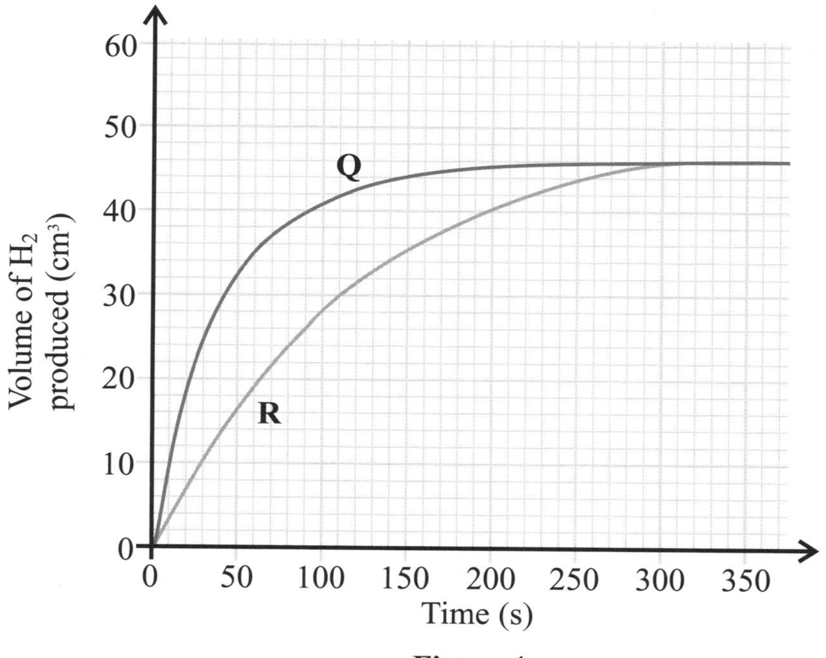

Figure 4

a) i) Calculate the rate of reaction **Q** at 50 seconds. Give your answer to 2 significant figures.

rate = ... $cm^3\ s^{-1}$
[3]

ii) Calculate the rate of reaction **R** at 120 seconds. Give your answer to 2 significant figures.

rate = ... $cm^3\ s^{-1}$
[3]

b) State which reaction, **Q** or **R**, used the powdered zinc. Explain your answer.

....

....

....
[3]

[Total 9 marks]

Exam Tip

Drawing a tangent at a specific point on a curve can be quite tricky. You need to make sure that it has the same gradient as the curve at that specific point. Drawing a tangent too different from the correct gradient could make a big difference to your final answer, so take your time and try moving your ruler around a bit first to find the best position.

Collision Theory

Warm-Up

A student is investigating the reaction between nitric acid and calcium carbonate under three different conditions, **A**, **B** and **C**. All other variables are kept the same. Circle the condition that will result in the greatest rate of reaction.

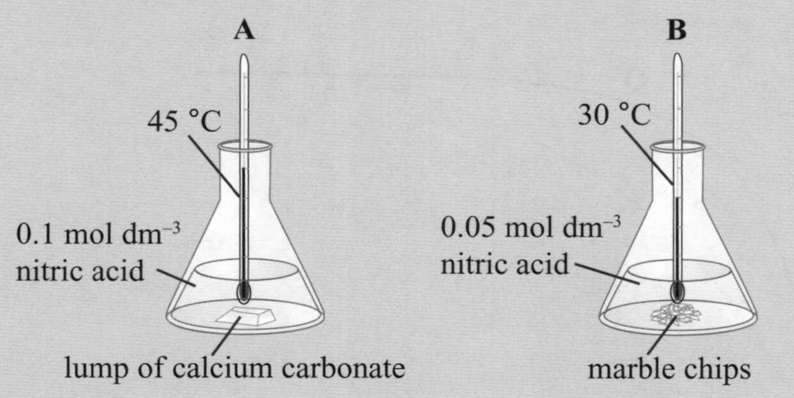

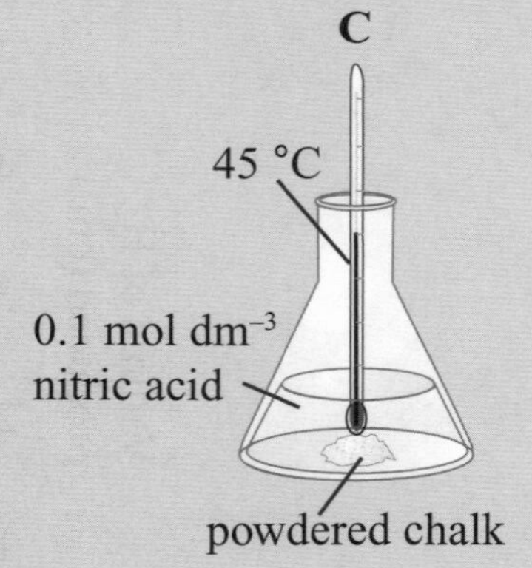

1 This question is about the rate of a chemical reaction between two reactants, one of which is in solution, and one of which is a solid.

a) Which of the following changes would **not** cause the rate of the chemical reaction to increase? Tick **one** box.

- ☐ **A** Increasing the concentration of the solution.
- ☐ **B** Heating the reaction mixture to a higher temperature.
- ☐ **C** Using a larger volume of the solution, but keeping the concentration the same.
- ☐ **D** Grinding the solid reactant so that it forms a fine powder.

[1]

b) What is the name given to the minimum amount of energy which particles must have if they are to react when they collide?

....

[1]

[Total 2 marks]

2 This question is about the rate of the reaction between magnesium and hydrochloric acid. The chemical equation for the reaction is:

$$Mg_{(s)} + 2HCl_{(aq)} \rightarrow MgCl_{2(aq)} + H_{2(g)}$$

Using collision theory, explain why cutting the magnesium into smaller pieces affects the rate of this reaction.

....

....

....

[Total 2 marks]

3 The Sabatier reaction can be used industrially to make methane from carbon dioxide and hydrogen in the following reaction:

$$CO_{2(g)} + 4H_{2(g)} \rightarrow CH_{4(g)} + 2H_2O_{(g)}$$

Grade 6-7

a) How could the pressure be altered to **increase** the rate of the reaction?

....

[1]

b) Use the collision theory to explain how this pressure change causes the rate to increase.

....

....

....

[2]

[Total 3 marks]

4 Horatio and Sharon are carrying out an experiment. They each react 50 cm^3 of 0.300 mol dm^{-3} sodium thiosulfate with 5.0 cm^3 of 2.000 mol dm^{-3} hydrochloric acid.

Grade 6-7

a) Horatio carries out his reaction at room temperature. Sharon heats her reactants to 45 °C and carries out the reaction in a 45 °C water bath. Horatio thinks that his reaction will have taken place much more quickly than Sharon's reaction. Is Horatio correct? Explain your answer using collision theory.

....

....

....

....

....

[3]

b) i) Sharon repeats her experiment using different concentrations of hydrochloric acid. Which of the following concentrations of hydrochloric acid would result in the **slowest** rate of reaction? Tick **one** box.

☐ **A** 0.350 mol dm^{-3} hydrochloric acid

☐ **B** 1.250 mol dm^{-3} hydrochloric acid

☐ **C** 2.100 mol dm^{-3} hydrochloric acid

☐ **D** 0.550 mol dm^{-3} hydrochloric acid

[1]

ii) Explain your answer.

....

....

[2]

[Total 6 marks]

Catalysts

1 Enzymes are a type of catalyst. Grade 4-6

a) Identify which of the following catalysts is an example of an enzyme. Tick **one** box.

☐ **A** Iron: a catalyst used in the Haber process.

☐ **B** Manganese(IV) oxide: a catalyst used in the decomposition of hydrogen peroxide.

☐ **C** RuBisCO: a catalyst used in photosynthesis.

☐ **D** Vanadium pentoxide: a catalyst used in the Contact process.

[1]

b) Give **one** example of when enzymes are used as catalysts in industrial processes.

....

[1]

[Total 2 marks]

2 Zola is observing the decomposition of hydrogen peroxide. The reaction is very slow. Meredith tells her to repeat the experiment with manganese(IV) oxide powder, and the rate of reaction increases. Grade 6-7

a) Zola determines that the manganese(IV) oxide must have acted as a catalyst. Explain how a catalyst works to increase the rate of reaction.

....

....

....

[2]

b) Why does Zola only need to use a small mass of manganese(IV) oxide powder to catalyse the reaction?

....

[1]

c) The reaction profiles for both the catalysed and the uncatalysed reactions are shown in **Figure 1**. Identify what each of the labels, A–D, show.

Figure 1

A: ....

B: ....

....

C: ....

....

D: ....

[4]

[Total 7 marks]

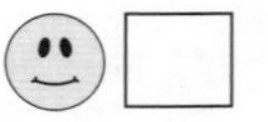

Endothermic and Exothermic Reactions

1 Which of the following energy changes describes an exothermic reaction? Tick **one** box.

		Energy of products	Temperature of surroundings
	A	Greater than reactants	Increases
	B	Less than reactants	Increases
	C	Greater than reactants	Decreases
	D	Less than reactants	Decreases

[Total 1 mark]

2 The thermal decomposition of calcium carbonate is an endothermic reaction.

Sketch and label a reaction profile for this reaction on the axes below. Label the activation energy.

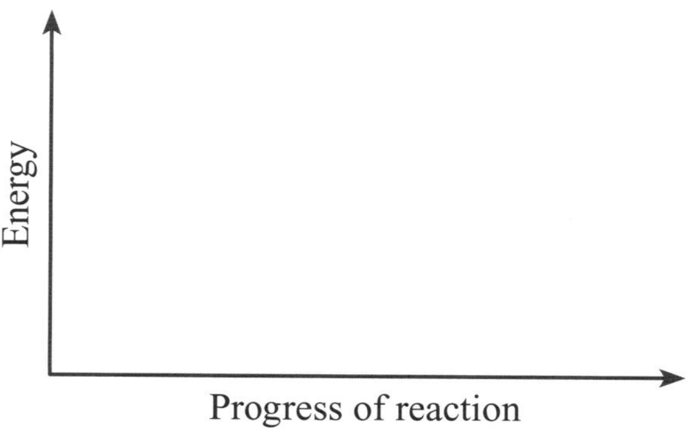

[Total 3 marks]

3 A company is looking for a reaction with a low activation energy to use in a hand warmer. The reaction profiles for the reactions being investigated are shown in **Figure 1**.

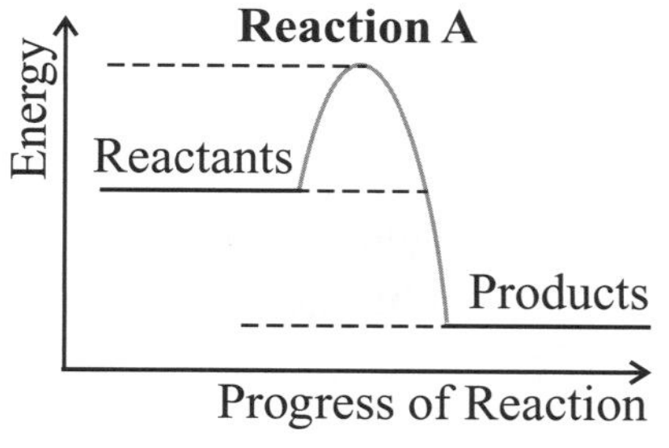

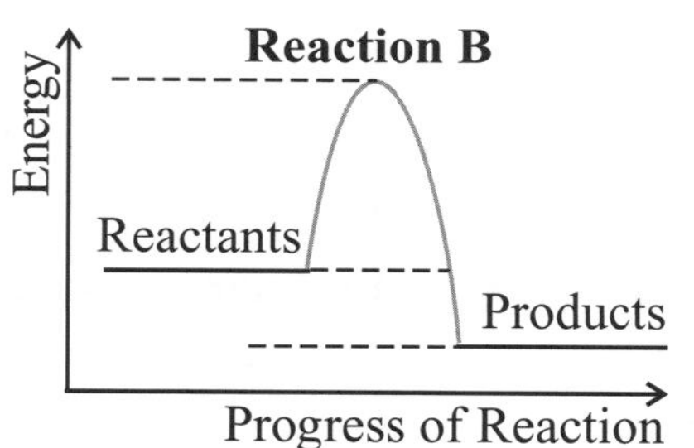

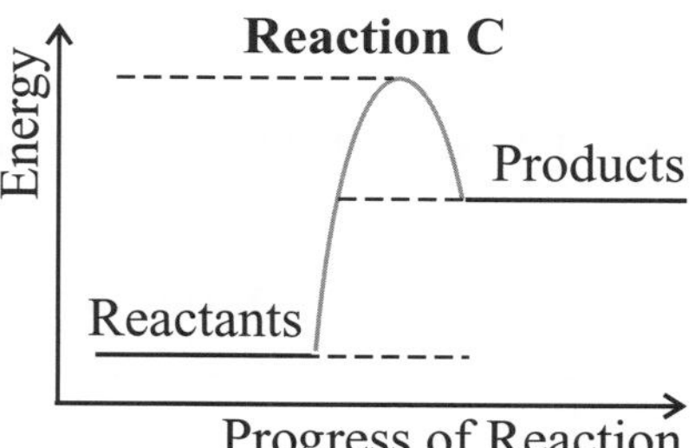

Figure 1

a) Define 'activation energy'.

....

....

[1]

b) Suggest which reaction would be **most suitable** for using in a hand warmer. Explain your answer.

....

....

....

[3]

[Total 4 marks]

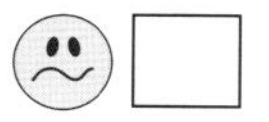  

Measuring Temperature Changes

1 A student is investigating the temperature change that occurs when he dissolves the same number of moles of two different salts, **A** and **B**, in water. Grade 6-7

a) Suggest **three** essential pieces of apparatus needed for the investigation.

....

....

[3]

b)* Describe a method that the student could use to carry out his investigation. Include details of any variables that would need to be controlled.

....

....

....

....

....

....

....

....

....

[6]

c) The student's results are shown in **Figure 1**. Complete the table.

Salt	Initial temperature (°C)	End temperature (°C)	Temperature change (°C)
A	21.0	16.0	....
B	21.0	26.5	....

Figure 1

[2]

d) Which of the statements below about the student's experiment is correct? Tick **one** box.

☐ **A** Both salts dissolved exothermically.

☐ **B** Salt A dissolved exothermically, but salt B dissolved endothermically.

☐ **C** Salt A dissolved endothermically, but salt B dissolved exothermically.

☐ **D** Both salts dissolved endothermically.

[1]

[Total 12 marks]

Bond Energies

Warm-Up

Which of the following statements is true? Tick **one** box.

- [ ] **A** During exothermic reactions, the energy taken to break the bonds in the reactants is greater than the energy released by making the bonds in the products.
- [ ] **B** During endothermic reactions, the energy released by breaking bonds in the reactants is less than the energy taken to make the bonds in the products.
- [ ] **C** During exothermic reactions, the energy taken to break the bonds in the reactants is less than the energy released by making the bonds in the products.
- [ ] **D** During endothermic reactions, the energy taken to break the bonds in the reactants is less than the energy released by making the bonds in the products.

1 Look at **Figure 1**. It shows the bond energies of some bonds.

Bond	Bond energy (kJ mol^{-1})
C — H	413
C — O	358
H — O	463
C = C	614
C — C	347

Figure 1

a) Use **Figure 1** to work out the energy change of the following reaction between ethene and water.

$$H_2C{=}CH_2 + H{-}O{-}H \rightarrow H{-}\underset{H}{\overset{H}{C}}{-}\underset{H}{\overset{H}{C}}{-}O{-}H$$

Energy change = ... kJ mol^{-1}

[3]

b) Using your answer to a), state whether the reaction between ethene and water is endothermic or exothermic. Explain your answer.

....

....

[2]

[Total 5 marks]

2 The energy change of the following reaction is –119 kJ mol^{-1}.

$$\begin{array}{c}\mathrm{H}\ \ \mathrm{H}\\ |\ \ \ |\\ \mathrm{H-C-C-H}\\ |\ \ \ |\\ \mathrm{H}\ \ \mathrm{H}\end{array} + \mathrm{Cl-Cl} \rightarrow \begin{array}{c}\mathrm{H}\ \ \mathrm{Cl}\\ |\ \ \ |\\ \mathrm{H-C-C-H}\\ |\ \ \ |\\ \mathrm{H}\ \ \mathrm{H}\end{array} + \mathrm{H-Cl}$$

a) Compare the energy released by forming bonds in the products in this reaction with the energy used to break bonds in the reactants.

....

....

[1]

b) Use this information, as well as the data in **Figure 2**, to work out the approximate bond energy of an H—Cl bond.

Figure 2

Bond	**Bond energy (kJ mol^{-1})**
C — H	413
C — C	347
C — Cl	339
Cl — Cl	239

Bond energy = ... kJ mol^{-1}

[3]

c) Use your answer from b) to rank the bonds from **Figure 2**, and the H—Cl bond in order of strength, from weakest to strongest.

....

[1]

[Total 5 marks]

Exam Tip

In questions involving calculating energy changes from bond energies (or vice versa), it can be really useful to draw out the displayed formulas of the chemicals that you're dealing with (unless you're given them in the question of course). Displayed formulas show all of the atoms in a molecule and all the bonds between them, so doing this makes it much easier to see what bonds have broken and what new bonds have been made during a chemical reaction.

Fractional Distillation and Hydrocarbons

Warm-Up

Draw a line to match each of the following fractions of crude oil with one of its main uses.

Bitumen	Fuel for aircraft
Diesel	Surfacing roads and roofs
Kerosene	Fuel for cars and trains.

1 Crude oil is a complex mixture of hydrocarbons. Grade 4-6

a) What is a hydrocarbon?

....

[2]

b) To which homologous series do most of the hydrocarbons in crude oil belong? Tick **one** box.

☐ **A** alkenes

☐ **B** alkanes

☐ **C** alcohols

☐ **D** carboxylic acids

[1]

c) Crude oil is a finite resource. What does this mean?

....

[1]

[Total 4 marks]

2 The hydrocarbons in crude oil belong to several different homologous series. Compounds in a homologous series all share the same general formula. Give **three** other characteristics of the compounds in a homologous series. Grade 6-7

....

....

....

....

....

[Total 3 marks]

3 Propane, C_3H_8, is a hydrocarbon present in the gas fraction of crude oil. Grade 6-7

a) Propane can be used as a fuel by burning it in oxygen.

i) Why do hydrocarbons make good fuels?

....

[1]

ii) Write a balanced symbol equation for the complete combustion of propane.

....

[2]

b) Propane is a very small hydrocarbon molecule. Which of the following statements about propane is **true**? Tick **one** box.

☐ **A** It has a low boiling point and is hard to ignite.

☐ **B** It has a high boiling point and is easy to ignite.

☐ **C** It has a low boiling point and is easy to ignite.

☐ **D** It has a high boiling point and is hard to ignite.

[1]

[Total 4 marks]

4 Kerosene, diesel oil and fuel oil are all fractions of crude oil that can be used as fuels. The average chain length of the hydrocarbons in kerosene is shorter than those in diesel oil. The average chain length of the hydrocarbons in diesel oil is shorter than those in fuel oil. Grade 6-7

a) State which of the three fractions named above has the highest boiling point. Explain your answer with reference to the information above.

....

....

[2]

b) Compare the viscosity of kerosene and fuel oil. Explain your answer with reference to the information above.

....

....

[2]

c) Compare the ease of ignition of kerosene and diesel oil. Explain your answer with reference to the information above.

....

....

[2]

[Total 6 marks]

5 Crude oil can be separated using the process of fractional distillation. The length of the hydrocarbon chains is fundamental to this process.

Figure 1 shows the boiling points of two molecules that are present in two of the fractions produced by the fractional distillation of crude oil.

Hydrocarbon	Chemical formula	Boiling point (°C)
Heptane	C_7H_{16}	98
Triacontane	$C_{30}H_{62}$	450

Figure 1

a) Triacontane is present in the fuel oil fraction. Give **two** uses of fuel oil.

....

....

[2]

b) i) Which of these two hydrocarbons would you expect to be collected **further down** the fractionating column?

....

[1]

ii) Explain your answer, with reference to the intermolecular forces present between the hydrocarbon molecules.

....

....

....

....

....

....

....

....

[5]

c) A scientist tests the viscosity of heptane, triacontane and a third alkane, alkane **X**. She finds that alkane **X** is more viscous than both heptane and triacontane. Suggest which fraction of crude oil alkane **X** is likely to have been taken from.

....

[1]

[Total 9 marks]

Exam Tip

Remember that if you're given one physical property of a hydrocarbon, you can use it to predict other properties of that compound. E.g., if you're told that a certain hydrocarbon has a low boiling point, you can predict that it will have low viscosity, be easy to ignite, and come from a fraction that is collected towards the top of the fractionating column.

Pollutants

1 Acid rain is formed when certain gases dissolve in rainwater to form a dilute acid. Grade 4-6

a) Which of the following gases contributes to acid rain? Tick **one** box.

☐ **A** carbon dioxide

☐ **B** methane

☐ **C** sulfur dioxide

☐ **D** carbon monoxide

[1]

b) Give **two** possible negative effects of acid rain.

....

....

[2]

[Total 3 marks]

2 Combustion of fuels, such as petrol, in cars is a major contributor to air pollution. Grade 6-7

a) Explain how cars produce nitrogen oxides.

....

....

[2]

b) Fuel combustion can produce soot. What impact can soot have on human health?

....

[1]

c) State which toxic gas is produced by incomplete fuel combustion and explain why it is toxic.

....

....

....

[3]

d) Hydrogen gas can also be used as a fuel in cars. Give **two** advantages of using hydrogen gas rather than fossil fuels as a means of powering vehicles.

....

....

....

[2]

[Total 8 marks]

 ☐  ☐  ☐

Cracking

1 Some hydrocarbons from crude oil undergo processing by the petrochemical industry. For instance, decane, $C_{10}H_{22}$, can undergo cracking as shown in the following equation:

Grade 6-7

$$C_{10}H_{22} \rightarrow C_8H_{18} + C_2H_4$$

a) C_2H_4 is an unsaturated hydrocarbon. To which homologous series does it belong? Tick **one** box.

☐ **A** alkanes ☐ **B** alkenes ☐ **C** alcohols ☐ **D** carboxylic acids

[1]

b) Explain why a petrochemical company may need to crack hydrocarbons.

....

....

[2]

c) Cracking can form a variety of products.
Write an alternative balanced equation for the cracking of decane.

....

[1]

[Total 4 marks]

2 The hydrocarbon fractions produced by the fractional distillation of crude oil are used in many industrial processes. **Figure 1** shows the approximate percentage of each fraction produced by an oil refinery and the demand for each fraction.

Grade 6-7

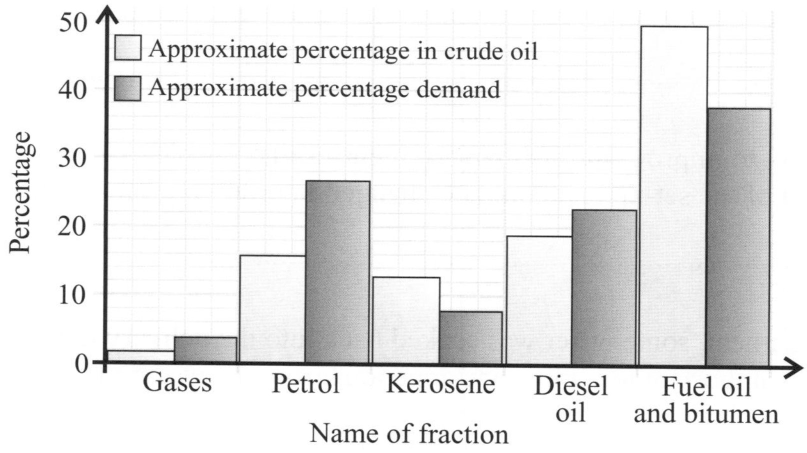

50
40
30
20
10
0
Percentage
Approximate percentage in crude oil
Approximate percentage demand
Gases
Petrol
Kerosene
Diesel oil
Fuel oil and bitumen
Name of fraction

Figure 1

a) The demand for diesel oil is greater than the supply. Using **Figure 1**, name **two** other fractions whose demand is greater than their supply.

....

[2]

b) Suggest what could be done to help match the supply of diesel oil to the demand.

....

....

[1]

[Total 3 marks]

Target AO3

3 A group of students conducted an experiment to measure the volume of gas produced when they crack a long-chain hydrocarbon. The students' set-up is shown in **Figure 2**.

Figure 2

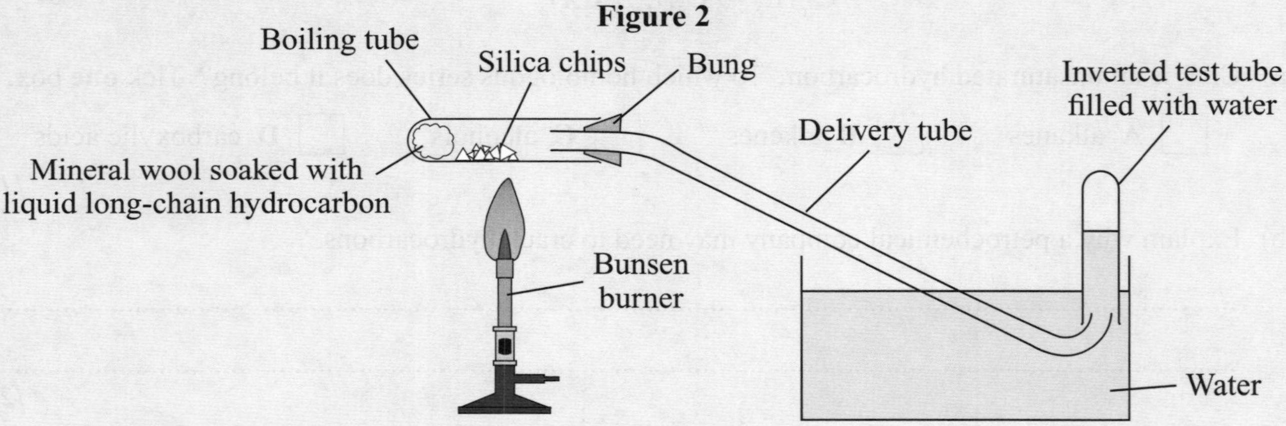

a) The bung is used to ensure that any gas produced by the reaction goes into the delivery tube. Explain why the bung is also a necessary safety precaution when using a Bunsen burner to heat the boiling tube.

....

....
[2]

b) One of the students had a lot more gas in their test tube than the others at the end of the experiment. Suggest an error that the student could have made that would cause this to occur.

....

....
[1]

c) The students want to improve the accuracy of their results. Suggest **one** part of the set-up that could be changed in order to produce more accurate results.

....
[1]

d) During the experiment, some water was sucked back into the delivery tube. Suggest why it is important to remove the apparatus from the water when this happens.

....
[1]

e) Suggest why it would not be possible to carry out this experiment in a laboratory without a catalyst.

....

....
[1]

[Total 6 marks]

Exam Tip

In the exam, you might be asked about experiments and reactions that you've never seen before. Firstly — don't panic. Secondly — think about the information you've been given and if you can link it to your existing knowledge in some way.

The Atmosphere

1 Which of these statements about Earths's early atmosphere is **correct**? Tick **one** box. Grade 4-6

☐ **A** The gases that made up Earth's early atmosphere were released by volcanic eruptions.

☐ **B** The Earth's oceans were formed when the methane in the early atmosphere condensed.

☐ **C** Earth's early atmosphere contained less carbon dioxide than the atmosphere today.

☐ **D** Earth's early atmosphere contained a lot of oxygen.

[Total 1 mark]

2 Scientists have looked at the compositions of the atmospheres of other planets to provide evidence for what the early atmosphere on Earth was like. **Figure 1** shows the current compositions of the atmospheres on Mars and Earth. Grade 6-7

	Percentage composition (%)					
	H_2O	Ne	CO_2	N_2	O_2	Ar
Mars	0.030	trace	95	2.7	0.13	1.6
Earth	0–4.0	0.0018	0.036	78	21	0.93

Figure 1

a) i) Scientists believe Earth's early atmosphere was similar to the atmosphere on Mars. Using **Figure 1**, suggest which gas made up the majority of Earth's early atmosphere.

....

[1]

ii) Explain **two** ways in which this gas was removed from Earth's atmosphere as it evolved.

....

....

[2]

b) i) Explain how oxygen built up in Earth's atmosphere and suggest why there is hardly any oxygen present in the atmosphere of Mars.

....

....

....

[2]

ii) Describe the chemical test for oxygen.

....

[1]

[Total 6 marks]

 ☐  ☐  ☐

The Greenhouse Effect and Climate Change

Warm-Up

Identify the statements below that describe things that a family can do to reduce their carbon dioxide emissions. Tick **two** boxes.

Leaving lights on all day	☐	Using a tumble drier	☐
Walking to school	☐	Turning central heating down	☐
Leaving appliances on standby	☐	Using air conditioning	☐

1 The Earth's atmosphere contains greenhouse gases which contribute to the greenhouse effect. Grade 4-6

a) Name **two** greenhouse gases.

....
[2]

b) Give **two** examples of types of human activity which are leading to an **increase** in the concentration of greenhouse gases in the atmosphere.

....

....
[2]

[Total 4 marks]

2 The Earth absorbs some electromagnetic radiation from the sun. It then radiates some of the radiation it absorbs as infrared (IR) radiation. IR radiation contributes to the greenhouse effect by interacting with greenhouse gases. Grade 6-7

a) Which of the following statements is **true**? Tick **one** box.

☐ **A** Greenhouse gases absorb all of the IR radiation that is radiated by Earth.

☐ **B** The greenhouse effect is caused by the absorption and reflection of IR radiation by greenhouse gases.

☐ **C** In general, the higher the concentration of greenhouse gases in the Earth's atmosphere, the colder the Earth becomes.

☐ **D** Greenhouse gases make up a large percentage of Earth's current atmosphere.

[1]

b) Elvis says he thinks that any amount of any greenhouse gases in the Earth's atmosphere is dangerous, as it could cause global warming. Is Elvis correct? Explain your answer.

....

....
[1]

[Total 2 marks]

3 Scientists believe that the increased burning of fossil fuels has contributed to global warming and this has caused glaciers to melt, resulting in rising sea levels.

Figure 1 shows CO_2 emissions by fossil fuels in the UK and Crown dependencies and the changes in sea levels between 1993 and 2013.

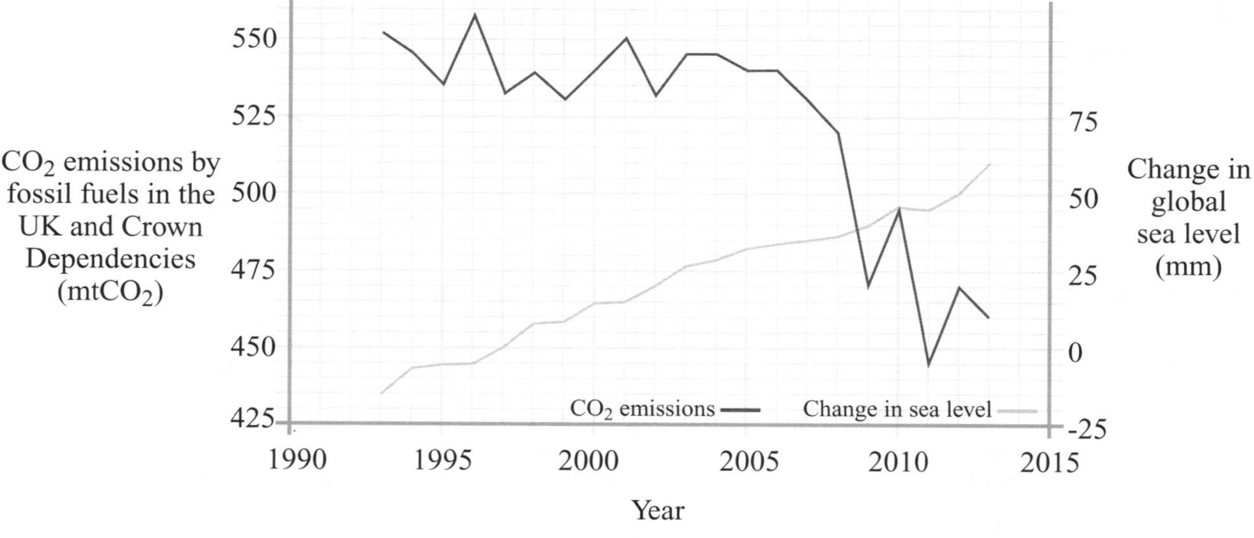

Figure 1

a)* Look at **Figure 1**. Explain whether the data shown on this graph supports a link between human activity and climate change. Discuss any problems associated with using this data to draw conclusions about the affect of carbon dioxide emissions on global sea levels.

....

....

....

....

....

....

....

....

[6]

b) Many governments are trying to decrease their country's CO_2 emissions.
Give **two** ways that the government in the UK is trying to reduce carbon dioxide emissions.

....

....

[2]

[Total 8 marks]

Exam Tip

If you're given some data about climate change to analyse, you need to think very carefully about what the data does and doesn't show, without making any assumptions. For example, if you're given some data that only relates to one country, you can't assume that the same pattern will be true for the whole world. You'd need more data to be certain.

Target AO3

4 Scientists in Antarctica use ice cores to measure how the Earth's atmosphere and temperature have changed over time. 

a) Antarctic ice contains bubbles of gas that were trapped at different points depending on when the ice first froze. Suggest how these bubbles can be used to work out how the Earth's atmosphere has changed.

....

....

[1]

b) **Figure 2** shows the carbon dioxide concentration from one Antarctic ice core, as well as the global temperature anomaly for the same period. The global temperature anomaly is the temperature difference from the average temperature for the 20th century.

Figure 2

Year	CO_2 concentration (ppm)	Global temperature anomaly (°C)
1960	319	+ 0.1
1970	324	+ 0.1
1980	340	+ 0.3
1990	355	+ 0.5
2000	374	+ 0.6

A scientist states that there is a link between carbon dioxide concentration and global temperature. Is their conclusion supported by the data in **Figure 2**? Explain your answer.

....

....

....

[2]

c) Suggest how increasing carbon dioxide levels might affect the scientists' ability to collect new ice cores in the future.

....

....

....

[2]

d) Scientists are able to collect large ice cores from deep inside ice sheets. These cores can be up to 3 km long, and can contain ice from hundreds of thousands of years ago. Collecting these cores takes a long time. Suggest **one** other limitation to collecting large ice cores.

....

....

[1]

[Total 6 marks]

Tests for Ions

PRACTICAL

1 Kelly has a small bottle of a clear solution labelled 'ammonium sulfate solution'. Her teacher asks her to perform some tests to confirm that the bottle of solution has been correctly labelled.

a) First, Kelly tests the solution for ammonium ions using the method shown in **Figure 1**.

> Method for testing for ammonium ions
> 1. Place 3 cm^3 of your test solution in a test tube.
> 2. Add 3 cm^3 of sodium hydroxide solution.
> 3. Warm the mixture gently.
> 4. Collect any gas that is given off.
> 5. Test the gas you have collected.

Figure 1

i) Name the gas that would be given off in step 4 if the solution being tested did contain ammonium ions.

....

[1]

ii) Describe how Kelly should test for this gas in step 5, and describe what a positive result would look like.

....

....

....

[2]

b) Next, Kelly tests the solution for sulfate ions using the method shown in **Figure 2**.

> Method for testing for sulfate ions
> 1. Place 3 cm^3 of your test solution in a test tube.
> 2. Add 3 cm^3 of hydrochloric acid.
> 3. Add 10 drops of Reagent **X** to the test tube and observe what happens.

Figure 2

Kelly's test solution does contain sulfate ions.
When she adds Reagent **X** to the test solution in step 3, a precipitate forms.

i) Identify Reagent **X**.

....

[1]

ii) State the colour of the precipitate that forms when Reagent **X** is added in step 3.

....

[1]

[Total 5 marks]

2 Various tests can be used to identify which metal ion is present in a compound. Grade 4-6

a) Suggest what metal ion is present in a compound that, when heated in a flame, produces a red flame.

....

[1]

b) Copper(II) nitrate is a soluble salt that contains copper(II) ions.

i) What colour flame would you expect this compound to produce during a flame test?

....

[1]

ii) If you dissolved copper(II) nitrate in water and then added a few drops of sodium hydroxide, what would you expect to observe?

....

[2]

[Total 4 marks]

3 Mark is given samples of three solutions, **A**, **B**, and **C**. Each solution contains a metal compound. He tests separate samples of each of the solutions with acidified silver nitrate solution and sodium hydroxide solution. His results are shown in **Figure 3**. Grade 6-7

Test	**Observation**		
	Solution A	**Solution B**	**Solution C**
Add acidified silver nitrate solution	yellow precipitate forms	no reaction	cream precipitate forms
Add a few drops of sodium hydroxide solution	white precipitate forms	brown precipitate forms	green precipitate forms

Figure 3

a) Suggest which metal ion solution **B** contains.

....

[1]

b) Suggest the formula of the compound in solution **C**.

....

[1]

c) i) After adding sodium hydroxide to solution **A**, Mark says "I can tell from my results that solution **A** contains aluminium ions." Explain why Mark is **wrong**.

....

....

[1]

ii) If solution **A** did contain aluminium ions, what would you expect Mark to observe if he added more sodium hydroxide solution to the test tube?

....

[1]

[Total 4 marks]

4 The compound potassium sodium carbonate has the formula $KNaCO_3$. Grade 6-7

a) Explain why it would be difficult to identify the cations in this compound using a flame test.

....

....

[1]

b) Describe how you could test a solution of this compound to show that it contained carbonate ions. You should include details of a positive result.

....

....

....

....

[3]

[Total 4 marks]

5* Oliver was asked to prepare a sample of potassium chloride. He designed a suitable method and carried it out. When he had finished, he had 5 g of the solid salt. Grade 7-9

Describe how Oliver could show that the salt he has made is potassium chloride. In your answer you should give the methods for any tests that you suggest and details of any observations you would expect to confirm the presence of the ions in the salt.

....

....

....

....

....

....

....

....

....

....

....

....

[Total 6 marks]

Exam Tip

The examiner might ask you to identify a salt in solution by looking at the results of different tests. Remember, a salt will contain both an anion and a cation, so if your answer only has ions with the same charge, you've made a mistake.

Target AO3

6 Two students were given an unknown ionic compound in solution. 

Here is the method the students used to identify the compound:

1. Add approximately 5 cm^3 of the unknown solution to two separate test tubes.
2. Add a few drops of dilute hydrochloric acid to one test tube.
3. Add a few drops of sodium hydroxide solution to the other test tube.
4. Connect a delivery tube from the test tube with the unknown solution and hydrochloric acid to a test tube of limewater, allowing any gas produced to bubble through the limewater.
5. Record any observations.

a) Suggest one change that the students should make to their method to accurately test for carbonate ions. Give a reason for your suggested change.

....

....

....

....

[2]

b) When the students carry out the test for carbonate ions correctly, no carbon dioxide is formed. In the test tube containing sodium hydroxide solution, a white precipitate forms.

Student A concludes that the compound must contain calcium ions.
Student B says that the compound must contain aluminium ions.

Suggest how the two students could carry out tests to find evidence to support or disprove their conclusions.

....

....

....

....

....

....

....

....

[4]

[Total 6 marks]

Exam Tip

If in the exam you're asked to evaluate a method and suggest improvements, you need to think critically about all the steps listed, the order that they're in, and whether any steps are missing. If a question asks you to explain why your suggestion would improve the method, make sure you include a clear reason — not just "because it's better".

Flame Photometry

1 Flame photometry is an example of an instrumental method of analysis.
Which of the following statements about instrumental methods is **false**? Tick **one** box.

☐ **A** Instrumental methods are very slow.

☐ **B** Instrumental methods are sensitive, so only a small amount of a sample is needed.

☐ **C** Instrumental methods can be more accurate than using standard laboratory tests.

☐ **D** Instrumental methods are reliant on machinery.

[Total 1 mark]

2 A chemist has a dilute solution, **M**, containing metal ions.
She tests the solution using flame photometry. **Figure 1** shows the line spectra for metal **A**, metal **B**, metal **C** and the solution, **M**.

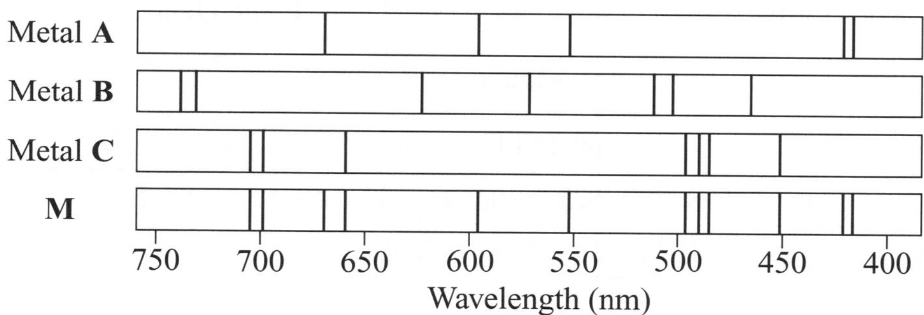

Figure 1

a) Which metal ion(s) are in the solution, **M**?

.... *[1]*

b) The chemist produces a calibration curve for an ion present in solution **M**.
The ion emits a certain wavelength of light with a relative emission intensity of 3.6.
Use the calibration curve in **Figure 2** to work out the concentration of the ion in solution **M**.

Figure 2

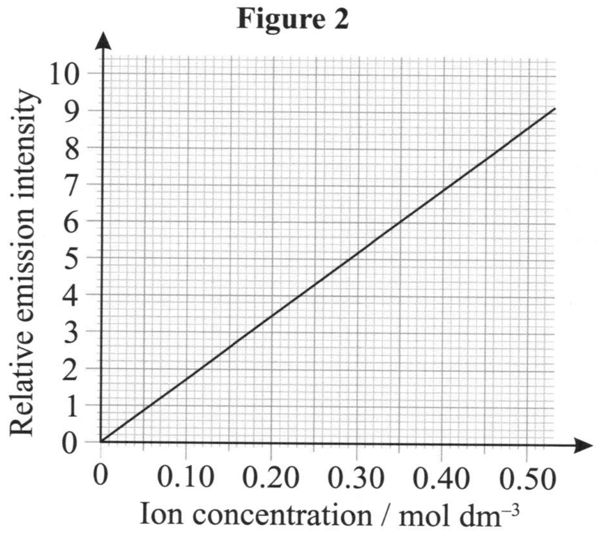

Concentration = ... mol dm^{-3}
[1]

[Total 2 marks]

Target AO3

3 Spectral line wavelength values taken from flame photometry spectra can be used to identify metal ions. **Figure 3** shows reference spectral line wavelength values for ions **W**, **X**, **Y** and **Z** in the region between 500 and 600 nm.

Figure 3

Ion	Spectral Line Wavelengths (nm)
W	527, 548
X	515, 552, 564, 570
Y	506, 518, 530, 531, 577
Z	506, 527, 559, 561, 585, 586, 597

The wavelength values for two different mixtures of metal ions, **P** and **Q**, are shown in **Figure 4**.

Figure 4

Mixture	Spectral Line Wavelengths (nm)
P	506, 518, 522, 527, 530, 531, 537, 548, 552, 557, 577, 587
Q	506, 527, 548, 559, 561, 585, 586, 597

a) Determine which ions from **Figure 3** could be present in mixture **Q**.

....

[2]

b) State which metal ions from **Figure 3** could be present in mixture **P**, and explain why the exact number of ions in this mixture cannot be determined using the data provided.

....

....

....

[2]

c) A student suggests using a flame test to help confirm which ions are present in mixture **P**. Comment on whether or not this will be useful.

....

....

....

[2]

[Total 6 marks]

Exam Tip

Don't be put off in the exam if they give you some data shown in a slightly different way to the way you are used to. Even though the "spectra" above don't look like the ones on the previous page, the information they contain is the same — it's just a case of comparing all the numbers you've been given in the same way you'd compare the lines on a chart.

Alkanes and Alkenes

Warm-Up

Circle the organic compounds below which are **unsaturated**.

```
   H          H     H        H  H  H           H  H  H                  H   H
   |           \   /         |  |  |           |  |  |                   \ /
 H-C-H          C=C        H-C--C--C-H       H-C--C--C-O-H          H     C    H
   |           /   \         |  |  |           |  |  |               \   / \
   H          H     H        H  H  H           H  H  H                C=C   H
                                                                     /   \
                                                                    H     H
```

1 Alkanes and alkenes can take part in complete combustion reactions.

Which of the following shows the **correct** word equation for the complete combustion of ethene? Tick **one** box.

☐ **A** ethene + oxygen → carbon monoxide + water

☐ **B** ethene + carbon dioxide → oxygen + water

☐ **C** ethene + oxygen → carbon dioxide + water

☐ **D** ethene + water → carbon dioxide + oxygen

[Total 1 mark]

2 Alkanes are a homologous series of hydrocarbons.

a) i) Name the alkane that contains **two** carbon atoms.

....

[1]

ii) State the number of hydrogen atoms that this alkane contains.

....

[1]

b) Draw the displayed formula of butane.

[1]

c) Alkanes can be described as '**saturated**'. What does the term **saturated** mean?

....

....

[1]

[Total 4 marks]

3 A student is investigating the chemical structure of alkenes. Grade 6-7

a) Give the general formula for alkenes.

....

[1]

b) Identify the displayed formula below that shows ethene. Tick **one** box.

☐ **A**

```
   H   H
   |   |
H— C — C —H
   |   |
   H   H
```

☐ **B**

```
H       H   H
 \      |   |
  C = C — C —H
 /          |
H           H
```

☐ **C**

```
H        H
 \      /
  C = C
 /      \
H        H
```

☐ **D**

```
   H   H   H
   |   |   |
H— C — C — C —H
   |   |   |
   H   H   H
```

[1]

c) Methane is an alkane with one carbon atom. The student notices that there is not an alkene with only one carbon atom. Explain why an alkene with one carbon atom does **not** exist.

....

....

[1]

[Total 3 marks]

4 A student investigated the reactivity of some hydrocarbons. Grade 7-9

a) The student added a sample of a hydrocarbon, **A**, to bromine water. A reaction took place.

i) The chemical formula of the product formed was $C_3H_6Br_2$.
Draw the displayed formula of hydrocarbon **A**.

[1]

ii) What would the student expect to observe when hydrocarbon **A** was added to bromine water?

....

[1]

iii) Name the type of reaction that took place between the hydrocarbon and the bromine water.

....

[1]

b) The student took some bromine water and added it to a hydrocarbon with the chemical formula, C_2H_6. What would you expect the student to have observed? Explain your answer.

....

....

[3]

[Total 6 marks]

Addition Polymers

1 The following question is about addition polymers. Grade 6-7

a) Which of these homologous series can form addition polymers? Tick **one** box.

- ☐ **A** alkenes and alkanes
- ☐ **B** alkenes only
- ☐ **C** carboxylic acids only
- ☐ **D** alcohols and carboxylic acids

[1]

b) The formula of vinyl acetate is shown in **Figure 1**.
Vinyl acetate polymerises to form poly(vinyl acetate).
Draw the formula of the repeating unit of poly(vinyl acetate).

H H
| |
C=C
| |
H O
  C — CH_3
  ||
  O

Figure 1

[1]

c) The formula of the repeating unit of poly(propene) is shown in **Figure 2**. Draw the formula of its monomer.

H CH_3
| |
—C — C—
| |
H H
n

Figure 2

[1]

d) **Figure 3** shows some of the properties of three different addition polymers.

Polymer	Properties
poly(chloroethene)	rigid, tough, low cost
poly(tetrafluoroethene)	non-stick, unreactive, heat-resistance
poly(ethene)	flexible, high electrical resistivity

Figure 3

A designer is trying to decide on a material to use in the production of a frying pan. Using **Figure 3** choose the material that would be best suited for this purpose and explain your answer.

....

....

....

[3]

[Total 6 marks]

2 A class are carrying out an investigation to look at monomers and addition polymers. 

a) The students are shown the displayed formula of the monomer methyl methacrylate. This monomer is shown in **Figure 4**. Selena believes that it can form an addition polymer but Jenna disagrees. State which student you agree with and why.

H CH$_3$
| |
C=C
| |
H C=O
|
O — CH$_3$

Figure 4

....

.... *[1]*

b) The students study poly(tetrafluoroethene), PTFE.
The repeating unit of this polymer is shown in **Figure 5**.

$$\left(\begin{array}{cc} F & F \\ | & | \\ C & - C \\ | & | \\ F & F \end{array}\right)_n$$

Figure 5

Which of the monomers below forms the polymer, poly(tetrafluoroethene)? Tick **one** box.

☐ **A** H — CF$_2$ — CF$_2$ — H (each carbon bonded to two F atoms)

☐ **B** F$_2$C=CF$_2$ (F, F on each carbon of C=C)

☐ **C** FHC=CHF (F and H on each carbon of C=C)

☐ **D** H — CFH — CFH — H (F above and H below each carbon)

[1]

c) The addition polymer poly(chloroethene), PVC, can be represented by the notation $(C_2H_3Cl)_n$.
Draw the displayed formula for the monomer that polymerises to form PVC.

[1]

[Total 3 marks]

Exam Tip

The monomers of addition polymers must have a C=C bond, but when they form polymers, this double bond becomes a single bond. Carbon always has four bonds, so if you're drawing the repeating unit of a polymer, count how many bonds your carbon atoms have. This way, you can check the bonds to make sure they're all present and correct.

Condensation Polymers

1 Which of the following molecules **cannot** take part in condensation polymerisation reactions? Tick **one** box.

☐ **A**

```
H         H   H   H   H   H   H       H
 \        |   |   |   |   |   |      /
  N — C — C — C — C — C — C — N
 /        |   |   |   |   |   |      \
H         H   H   H   H   H   H       H
```

☐ **B**

```
H       H
 \      |      O
  N — C — C //
 /      |      \
H       H       OH
```

☐ **C**

```
       H   H   H   H   H   H
       |   |   |   |   |   |
HO — C — C — C — C — C — C — OH
       |   |   |   |   |   |
       H   H   H   H   H   H
```

☐ **D**

```
     H   H   H   H
     |   |   |   |
H — C — C = C — C — H
     |           |
     H           H
```

[Total 1 mark]

2 Which of the following is **true** regarding the formation of condensation polymers? Tick **one** box.

☐ **A** A small molecule is lost when condensation polymers form.

☐ **B** Each monomer contains only one functional group.

☐ **C** The monomers must have a carbon-carbon double bond.

☐ **D** The functional groups contained in each monomer must be different.

[Total 1 mark]

3 Some condensation polymers occur naturally and are essential to our growth and survival.

a) Complete the table in **Figure 1** with the names of the types of monomer that form protein and starch polymers.

Polymer	Protein	Starch
Monomer	....	....

Figure 1

[2]

b) i) Nucleotides are a type of monomer that produce another naturally occurring polymer. Name the polymer that is formed from nucleotides.

....

[1]

ii) State how many different types of nucleotide make up this polymer.

....

[1]

[Total 4 marks]

4 A certain condensation polymerisation reaction involving two different monomers produces a polyester, **D**, and another product, **E**.

a) Which of the following sets of molecules would react to form a polyester? Tick **one** box.

☐ **A** n
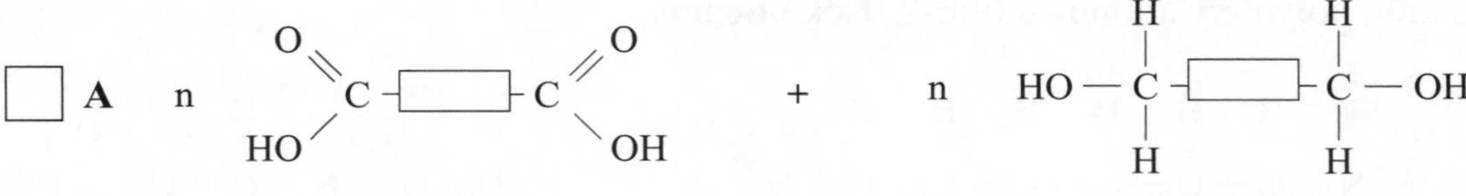

☐ **B** n HOOC–[ ]–COOH + n H_2N–[ ]–NH_2

☐ **C** n H_2N–[ ]–NH_2 + n HO–CH_2–[ ]–CH_2–OH

☐ **D** n HOOC–[ ]–COOH + n HOOC–[ ]–COOH

[1]

b) What is the name for the link that is formed between two monomer molecules during the formation of polyesters?

....

[1]

c) Draw a block diagram showing the repeat unit of a polyester.

[2]

d) i) What is the formula of the product, **E**?

....

[1]

ii) Describe how product **E** is formed.

....

....

[2]

e) Some polyesters are carbohydrates. Name the **three** elements that are present in carbohydrates.

....

[1]

[Total 8 marks]

Disposing of Polymers

1 The following question is about recycling polymers. Grade 6-7

a) Which of the following statements about the recycling of polymers is **false**? Tick **one** box.

☐ **A** Increasing the amount of polymers that are recycled can create more jobs.

☐ **B** Recycling polymers means that less polymers need to be disposed of in landfill.

☐ **C** Recycling polymers is generally cheaper than making polymers from scratch.

☐ **D** Polymers can be recycled an infinite number of times.

[1]

b) If we don't recycle polymers, the production of new polymers in the future could be limited. Explain why this is the case.

....

....

[1]

c) Some polymers with particularly high strengths are used in the manufacture of bulletproof vests and prosthetic limbs. Explain why it may be better to manufacture brand new polymers for such uses, rather than using recycled polymers.

....

....

[2]

[Total 4 marks]

2 There are various ways to dispose of polymers. These include recycling, landfill and combustion. Grade 6-7

a) When polymers are recycled, they are melted down and reformed. Explain why polymers need to be separated before they're melted down and reformed.

....

....

[1]

b) Give **one** disadvantage of disposing of polymers in landfill.

....

....

[1]

c) Polymers can also be disposed of by combustion. Give **one** advantage and **one** disadvantage of burning polymers.

Advantage: ....

Disadvantage: ....

[2]

[Total 4 marks]

Alcohols and Carboxylic Acids

Warm-Up

Identify which of the following functional groups represents **alcohols**. Tick **one** box.

C = C	☐	-COO⁻	☐
$-NO_2$	☐	-OH	☐
-COOH	☐	$-NH_3$	☐

1 Three of the following structures belong to the same homologous series.
Identify the structure that belongs to a **different** homologous series. Tick **one** box.

☐ **A** $H-C(H)(H)-C(H)(H)-C(=O)-O-H$

☐ **B** $H-C(H)(H)-C(H)(H)-O-H$

☐ **C** $H-C(H)(H)-O-H$

☐ **D** $H-C(H)(H)-C(H)(O-H)-C(H)(H)-H$

[Total 1 mark]

2 Alcohols are a series of organic compounds with a wide range of industrial applications.

a) An alcohol containing three carbons is commonly used as a solvent.
What is the name given to this alcohol?

....

[1]

b) Ethanol is present in alcoholic drinks. Give the molecular formula of ethanol.

....

[1]

c) Methanol can be used as an additive to fuels to improve combustion.
Draw the displayed formula for methanol.

[1]

[Total 3 marks]

3 Under certain conditions, alcohols can be oxidised to form carboxylic acids. Grade 6-7

a) What is the functional group of a carboxylic acid?

....

[1]

b) Give the molecular formula of propanoic acid.

....

[1]

c) Name the carboxylic acid with the chemical formula CH_3COOH.

....

[1]

d) Methanol is mixed with an oxidising agent.
Draw the displayed formula of the product that is formed.

[2]

[Total 5 marks]

4 A student mixes butanoic acid with reactant **X** and forms a compound known as an ester. The student then mixes reactant **X** with other organic compounds. Grade 7-9

a) Predict which of the compounds below will also form an ester when mixed with reactant **X**. Tick **one** box.

```
       H   H   H   H
       |   |   |   |
☐ A  H—C — C — C — C —O—H
       |   |   |   |
       H   H   H   H
```

```
       H   H       O
       |   |     //
☐ B  H—C — C — C
       |   |     \
       H   H      O—H
```

```
       H   H   H   H       O
       |   |   |   |     //
☐ C  H—C — C — C — C — C
       |   |   |   |     \
       H   H   H   H      H
```

```
       H   O   H   H
       |   ||  |   |
☐ D  H—C — C — C — C —H
       |       |   |
       H       H   H
```

[1]

b) Explain your answer.

....

....

....

[2]

[Total 3 marks]

Production of Ethanol

1 Fermentation is a process that uses yeast to convert glucose to ethanol. Grade 6-7

a) Name the other product that is formed in this fermentation reaction.

....

[1]

b) A fermentation reaction produces a dilute solution of ethanol, **X**.
Name the technique that can be used to produce a more concentrated solution of ethanol from solution **X**, and outline how this process works.

....

....

....

....

....

[5]

[Total 6 marks]

2 Isla and Umar are both carrying out fermentation reactions in the lab. Grade 6-7

a) Umar carries her reaction out at 33 °C. Isla thinks that if she carries out her fermentation reaction at 50 °C, the rate of fermentation will increase. Do you agree with Isla? Explain your answer.

....

....

[2]

b) Umar carries out her reaction in a flask that is open to the air, whereas Isla carries her experiment out in **anaerobic** conditions.

i) Explain what is meant by **anaerobic** conditions.

....

[1]

ii) Predict the pH of the solution that Umar's fermentation reaction produces. Explain your answer.

....

....

[2]

c) Isla thinks that if she leaves her fermentation mixture for long enough, she can produce a solution of ethanol with a concentration of 40%. Explain why she is **incorrect**.

....

....

....

[2]

[Total 7 marks]

Combustion of Alcohols

PRACTICAL

1 Manveer is investigating the efficiency of three unknown alcohols, **X**, **Y** and **Z**, as fuels. Grade 7-9

a)* Describe a method that Manveer could use to determine which of these alcohols is the most efficient fuel. Include steps that he should take to ensure that a fair test is carried out.

....

....

....

....

....

....

....

....

....

....

....

....

....

[6]

b) Manveer measures how much of each alcohol is needed to raise the temperature of a set volume of water by 25 °C. His results are shown in **Figure 1**.

Figure 1

Alcohol	**X**	**Y**	**Z**
Mass of fuel burned (g)	1.53	2.19	1.76

i) Using **Figure 1**, determine which of the alcohols, **X**, **Y** or **Z**, was the most efficient fuel. Explain your answer.

....

....

[1]

ii) The longer the carbon chain of an alcohol, the more efficient it will be as a fuel. Manveer was told that the three alcohols were ethanol, propanol and butanol. Assuming that Manveer carried out a fair test, identify which of the alcohols, **X**, **Y** or **Z**, is butanol.

....

[1]

[Total 8 marks]

Nanoparticles

1 Which of the following statements about nanoparticles is **true**? Tick **one** box. Grade 4-6

- [ ] **A** Nanoparticles contain approximately one thousand atoms.
- [ ] **B** Nanoparticles are 1-100 nm in size.
- [ ] **C** All nanoparticles are the same size and shape.
- [ ] **D** Nanoparticles are smaller than simple molecules, such as carbon dioxide.

[Total 1 mark]

2 Nanoparticles of zinc oxide are used in some sunscreens to improve the protection of skin from exposure to sunlight. Grade 4-6

State **one** advantage and **one** disadvantage of using nanoparticles of zinc oxide in sunscreens.

Advantage: ....

Disadvantage: ....

[Total 2 marks]

3 Nanomedicine is the name given to the use of nanoparticles to treat illnesses. Grade 6-7

a) A scientist says "Nanomedicine could bring great benefits in the future."
Describe **one** example of a possible use of nanoparticles in medicine.
State what property of the nanoparticles you have named makes them suitable for that use.

....

....

....

[2]

b) Another scientist says "We should be cautious about using nanomedicine."
Suggest why this statement might be considered correct.

....

....

....

[2]

[Total 4 marks]

4 Explain how the small size of nanoparticles gives them different properties from larger particles of the same material. Grade 6-7

....

....

....

....

[Total 3 marks]

Types of Material and Their Uses

Warm-Up

Materials can be categorised into several different types.
Match each of the materials below with the group of materials that it belongs to.

Glass	Metal
Polystyrene	Polymer
Aluminium	Composite
Concrete	Ceramic

1 The uses of materials are determined by their properties. **Figure 1** shows the properties of some materials.

Material	Stiffness	Electrical Conductivity	Cost
Plasticised PVC	Low	Low	Low
Fibreglass	High	Low	Medium
High-density poly(ethene)	High	Low	Low
Aluminium	High	High	Medium

Figure 1

a) Which material from **Figure 1** is a composite material?

....

[1]

b) Which material from the table in **Figure 1** would be the **most** suitable for covering electrical wires to insulate them? Explain your answer.

....

....

....

....

[4]

c) Low-density poly(ethene) is a low cost material with low stiffness and low electrical conductivity. Suggest whether high-density poly(ethene) or low-density poly(ethene) would be more suitable for making a squeezy ketchup bottle. Explain your answer.

....

....

[1]

[Total 6 marks]

2 **Figure 2** shows the properties of several different materials.

Material	Density (g cm^{-3})	Strength (MPa)	Resistance to Corrosion	Cost
PVC	1.3	52	Good	Low
Carbon fibre	1.5	4100	Good	High
Copper	8.9	220	Poor	Medium
Steel	7.8	780	Poor, but easy to protect	Low
Lead	11.3	12	Good	Low

Figure 2

a) A sports company is choosing a material for a professional hockey stick. Which material from the table would be the **most** suitable? Use data from **Figure 2** to explain your answer.

....

....

....

....

....

[4]

b) Determine which material from the table is the **most** suitable for building bridges. Explain your answer using information from **Figure 2**.

....

....

....

....

....

[4]

c) Determine which material from the table would be the **most** suitable material to make drain pipes. Explain your answer using information from **Figure 2**.

....

....

....

....

....

[4]

[Total 12 marks]

Exam Tip

You may need to decide, out of a choice of materials, which one is the most suitable for making something. Although physical properties are important, don't forget to look at cost. For example, carbon fibre is very strong but also very expensive — if you need to use a lot of it, like for building bridges, it'll cost a lot and this can sometimes be a problem.

Mixed Questions

1 Fractional distillation separates crude oil into fractions. Grade 4-6

a) In a fractionating column, gaseous molecules turn into liquids at certain points in the column, where they can be siphoned off. What is the name given to the change of state when gases turn to liquids?

....

[1]

b) Which of the following fractions is extracted **above** petrol in the fractionating column? Tick **one** box.

☐ **A** Kerosene ☐ **B** Gases ☐ **C** Diesel Oil ☐ **D** Fuel Oil

[1]

[Total 2 marks]

2 Look at **Figure 1**. It shows the displayed formula of an organic compound. Grade 4-6

```
     H   H   H
     |   |   |      O
H—C—C—C—C//
     |   |   |      \
     H   H   H       O—H
```

Figure 1

a) Which homologous series does this compound belong to?

....

[1]

b) What is the name of this compound?

....

[1]

c) Find the relative formula mass of this compound.
(relative atomic masses: C = 12, H = 1, O = 16)

relative formula mass = ...

[1]

d) What is the empirical formula of this compound?

....

[2]

[Total 5 marks]

3 Calcium, Ca, and sulfuric acid, H_2SO_4, react together in a chemical reaction. Grade 4-6

a) Write a word equation for this reaction.

....

[2]

b) What is the chemical formula of the salt formed by this reaction?

....

[1]

c) Predict whether the salt formed will be soluble or insoluble.

....

[2]

d) The reaction of sulfuric acid with calcium is less violent than its reaction with sodium.
What does this tell you about the position of sodium, relative to calcium, in the reactivity series?

....

[1]

[Total 6 marks]

4 Chlorine is a Group 7 element that exists as molecules of Cl_2. Grade 4-6

a) Complete **Figure 2** to give a dot-and-cross diagram that shows the bonding in Cl_2.
You only need to show the outer electron shells.

Cl Cl

Figure 2

[2]

b) Which of the following **best** describes the structure of chlorine?
Tick **one** box.

☐ **A** Giant ionic lattice

☐ **B** Giant covalent structure

☐ **C** Simple molecular substance

☐ **D** Fullerene

[1]

c) Describe a test you could carry out for chlorine. Include any observations you would expect.

....

....

....

[2]

d) Chlorine has a melting point of –102 °C and a boiling point of –34 °C.
Predict what state chlorine would be in at –50 °C.

....

[1]

[Total 6 marks]

5 Ellie is using paper chromatography experiment to analyse the components in a sample. **Figure 3** shows the chromatogram produced by the experiment.

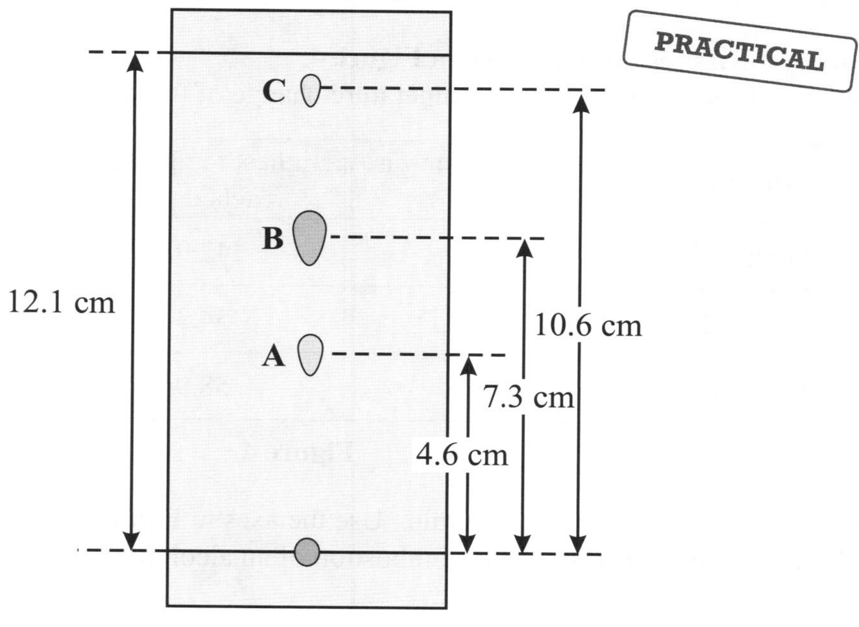

Figure 3

a) Identify the **stationary phase** in Ellie's experiment.

....

[1]

b) Use **Figure 3** to calculate the R_f values for spots **A**, **B**, and **C**.

$$R_f = \frac{\text{distance travelled by solute}}{\text{distance travelled by solvent}}$$

R_f of **A** = ...

R_f of **B** = ...

R_f of **C** = ...

[3]

c) From **Figure 3**, how can you tell that Ellie's sample contains a substance that is insoluble in the mobile phase?

....

[1]

d) Use **Figure 3** to identify the **minimum** number of components in Ellie's sample. Tick **one** box.

☐ **A** 1 ☐ **B** 2 ☐ **C** 3 ☐ **D** 4

[1]

e) Ellie concludes that her sample is a mixture. Explain what is meant by the term 'mixture'.

....

....

[1]

f) The mixture contains some liquid components with similar boiling points.
Name a technique that Ellie could use to separate the different components in the mixture.

....

[1]

[Total 8 marks]

6 Zayn carries out an experiment to investigate using alcohols as fuels. During his experiment, he heats a set volume of water by combusting equal masses of some alcohols. He measures the change in temperature of the water.

a) Some of Zayn's results are shown in **Figure 4**.
Complete **Figure 4** to show the temperature change of the water for each reaction.

Alcohol	Starting temperature (°C)	Highest temperature reached (°C)	Temperature change (°C)
Methanol	25.7	42.9	....
Ethanol	25.9	54.3	....
Propanol	26.4	58.9	....

Figure 4

[2]

b) Combustion reactions are exothermic. Use the axes in **Figure 5** to draw a reaction profile for the combustion of an alcohol in oxygen.

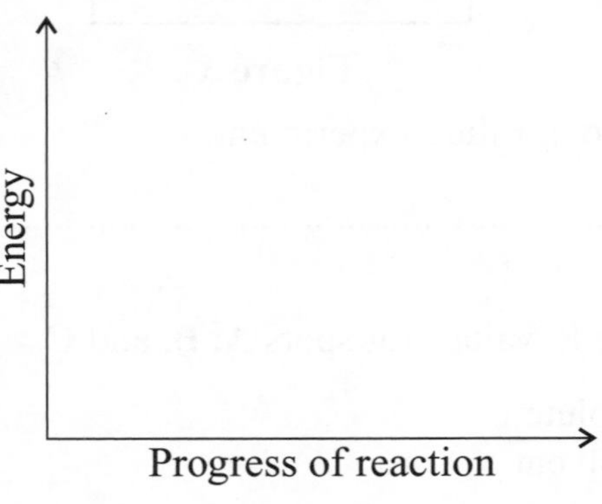

Figure 5

[2]

c) The combustion of alcohols can produce the toxic gas carbon monoxide.
Explain why carbon monoxide is toxic.

....

....

[2]

[Total 6 marks]

7 Cracking is an important industrial process. During a certain reaction, one molecule of $C_{25}H_{52}$ was cracked. One of the products was $C_{20}H_{42}$.

Grade 6-7

a) Write the chemical formula of the other product.

....

[1]

b) The mixture of products produced when $C_{25}H_{52}$ was cracked reaction was shaken with bromine water. Predict what you would observe. Explain your answer.

....

....

[2]

[Total 3 marks]

8 **Figure 6** lists some properties of four materials. 

Material	Density (g cm^{-3})	Brittleness	Corrosion resistance	Cost
Titanium	4.5	Low	High	Very high
Aluminium alloy	2.8	Low	Low	Moderate
Melamine resin	1.5	Moderate	High	Low
Glass	2.5	Very high	High	Low

Figure 6

a) Titanium and the aluminium alloy both have a metallic structure.
Suggest **one** similarity you would expect in the physical properties of titanium and the aluminium alloy, other than the properties mentioned in the table.
Explain your answer in terms of their structure and bonding.

....

....

....

[2]

b) Titanium is a transition metal.
Give **two** typical properties of transition metals which are **not** common to all metals.

1. ....

2. ....

[2]

c) A camping supplies company wants to make low-cost cups for people to use on camping holidays.
Suggest which of the materials listed in **Figure 6** would be **most** suitable for this purpose.
Explain your answer.

....

....

....

....

....

....

....

....

....

[4]

[Total 8 marks]

9 Rubidium is an element from Group 1 of the periodic table.
Fluorine is an element from Group 7.
Rubidium metal, Rb, and fluorine gas, F_2, react violently to produce a single product.

Grade 6-7

a) Write a balanced symbol equation for the reaction of rubidium metal and fluorine gas.

....

[2]

b) What type of bonding exists in the product of this reaction?

....

[1]

c) Would you expect the product of this reaction to have a high or low melting point?
Explain your answer in terms of the forces within the compound.

....

....

....

....

[2]

[Total 5 marks]

10 A student reacts chlorine water reacts with potassium iodide solution according to the following reaction.

Grade 6-7

$$Cl_{2\,(aq)} + 2KI_{(aq)} \rightarrow 2KCl_{(aq)} + I_{2\,(aq)}$$

a) Chlorine water is corrosive.
State **one** safety precaution that the student should take when carrying out the reaction.

....

[1]

b) Describe what the student would observe when he added chlorine water to potassium iodide solution.

....

[1]

c) Explain why this reaction takes place.
Give your answer in terms of the reactivity of the elements involved.

....

....

[2]

d) Write a balanced ionic equation for the reaction between chlorine and potassium iodide.

....

[2]

[Total 6 marks]

11 Some elements have several different isotopes. Look at **Figure 7**.
It shows the percentage of the atoms of some elements that exist as each of their isotopes.

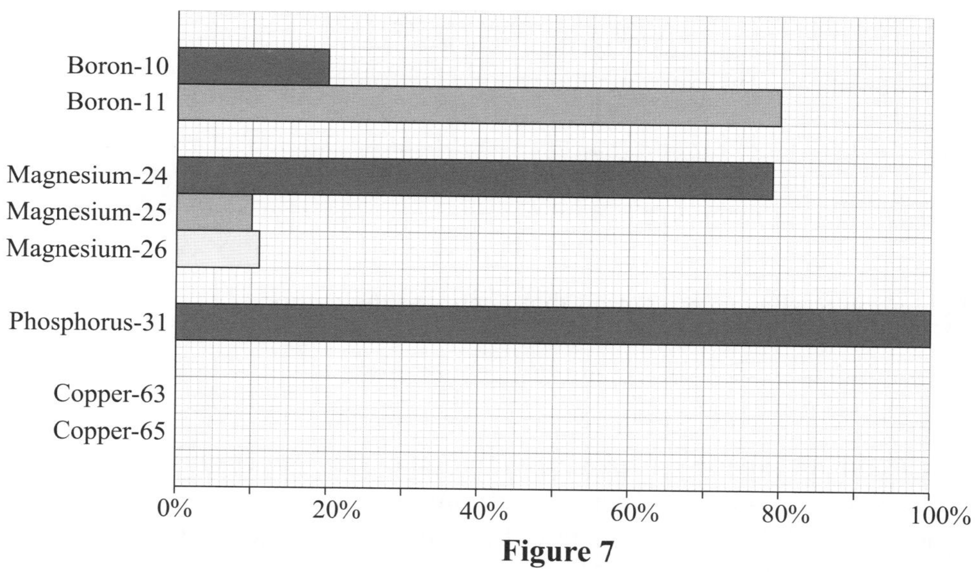

Figure 7

a) 69% of copper atoms are copper-63 and the rest are copper-65.
Complete **Figure 7** by adding bars for the two isotopes of copper.

[2]

b) Explain why the relative atomic mass of phosphorus is a whole number, while the relative atomic masses of boron, magnesium and copper are not.

....

....

....

....

....

....

[3]

c) Use **Figure 7** to calculate the relative atomic mass of magnesium.
Give your answer to three significant figures.

relative atomic mass = ...

[4]

[Total 9 marks]

12 A student has a sample of sodium sulfate, Na_2SO_4, with a mass of 34.08 g. How many oxygen atoms are in the sample, to 4 significant figures?

Grade 6-7

(relative atomic masses: Na = 23, S = 32, O = 16)

☐ **A** 1.442×10^{23} atoms

☐ **B** 5.779×10^{23} atoms

☐ **C** 1.015×10^{24} atoms

☐ **D** 1.442×10^{24} atoms

[Total 1 mark]

13 Aluminium can be obtained by electrolysis of the ore bauxite, Al_2O_3.

The overall equation for this reaction is:

$$2Al_2O_{3\,(l)} \rightarrow 4Al_{\,(l)} + 3O_{2\,(g)}$$

a) Explain why this reaction is an example of a redox reaction.

....

....

[1]

b) Write a half equation to show the reaction that occurs at the cathode.

....

[2]

c) A scientist carries out an experiment where aluminium oxide is electrolysed.
The scientist starts off with 40.8 g of pure aluminium oxide.
Predict the mass of aluminium she can extract from this mass of electrolyte.
(relative atomic masses: Al = 27, O = 16)

mass = ... g

[4]

d) Iron can be extracted from its ores by heating with carbon.
Explain why this method is **not** suitable for the extraction of aluminium from its ore.

....

....

....

[2]

e) In the UK, some metals are widely recycled. Give **two** advantages of recycling metals.

....

....

[2]

[Total 11 marks]

14 A scientist wants to produce a batch of aluminium sulfate for an experiment.
She plans to do this by reacting aluminium with an excess of sulfuric acid.
A chemical supplier offers three options to provide the quantity of aluminium she needs.

Which of these options will allow the scientist to complete her reaction in the **shortest** time?

☐ **A** 1 aluminium cube with side length 8 cm.

☐ **B** 8 aluminium cubes, each with side length 4 cm.

☐ **C** 64 aluminium cubes, each with side length 2 cm.

☐ **D** They will all take the same length of time.

[Total 1 mark]

15 The equation for the Haber process is: $N_2 + 3H_2 \rightleftharpoons 2NH_3$
In the Haber Process, the forwards reaction is exothermic. Which of the following will result in an **increase** in the yield of ammonia during the Haber process? Tick **one** box.

Grade 6–7

- ☐ **A** Decreasing the pressure.
- ☐ **C** Increasing the temperature.
- ☐ **B** Adding a catalyst.
- ☐ **D** Removing ammonia from the reaction chamber.

[Total 1 mark]

16 Andre wants to prepare a sample of copper carbonate, $CuCO_3$.
To do this, he mixes solutions of sodium carbonate, Na_2CO_3, and copper chloride, $CuCl_2$.

Grade 6–7

a) Complete the following equation for Andre's reaction by adding state symbols.

Na_2CO_3 (...........) + $CuCl_2$ (...........) $\rightarrow$ $CuCO_3$ (...........) + 2NaCl (...........)

[1]

b) When the reaction is complete, Andre wants to obtain a pure sample of copper carbonate.

i) Andre suggests using crystallisation to separate copper carbonate from the reaction mixture. Explain why this would be an **unsuitable** method.

....

....

....

[2]

ii) Suggest a suitable method Andre could use to obtain a pure sample of copper carbonate from the reaction mixture.

....

[1]

c) Calculate the atom economy of Andre's reaction to make copper carbonate.
Give your answer to two significant figures.
(relative atomic masses: Na = 23, C = 12, O = 16, Cu = 63.5, Cl = 35.5)

atom economy = ... %

[5]

d) By using a suitable method to separate the mixture, Andre obtains 21.51 g of copper carbonate. Using the masses of reactants, Andre calculated that should have produced 28.68 g of copper carbonate. Calculate his percentage yield of copper carbonate.

percentage yield = ... %

[3]

[Total 12 marks]

17 A hydrogen-oxygen fuel cell is a type of electrical cell. 

a) Hydrogen is the fuel used in the hydrogen-oxygen fuel cell.

i) Suggest **two** advantages associated with using hydrogen as a fuel instead of fossil fuels.

....

....

[2]

ii) Suggest **two** disadvantages of using hydrogen as a fuel instead of fossil fuels.

....

....

[2]

b) The reaction that occurs in a hydrogen-oxygen fuel cell is shown below.

$$2H_2 + O_2 \rightarrow 2H_2O$$

Figure 8 shows the energy of the bonds involved in this reaction.

Bond	Bond Energy (kJ mol^{-1})
O=O	498
H–H	436
O–H	463

Figure 8

Calculate the energy change for the reaction which takes place in the hydrogen-oxygen fuel cell.

energy change = ... kJ mol^{-1}

[3]

c) A scientist recorded the amount of oxygen used by a fuel cell over a certain period of time. The quantity of oxygen used occupied 156 dm^3 at room temperature and pressure. Calculate the mass of water produced if all of the oxygen reacted.

1 mole of gas occupies 24 dm^3 at room temperature and pressure.
(relative atomic masses: H = 1, O = 16)

mass = ... g

[4]

[Total 11 marks]

18 Many different chemical substances are carbon based. Grade 7-9

a) Carbon nanotubes are a type of nanoparticle. Explain what a nanoparticle is.
Explain why carbon nanotubes have different properties to bulk carbon.

....

....

[2]

b) Graphite is a material made of carbon that has applications as a lubricant.
Explain how the structure of graphite makes it suitable for this use.

....

....

....

[3]

c) i) Put the carbon-based substances butane, diamond and poly(propene) in order of melting point, from **highest** to **lowest**. Explain your answer.

Order: ....

Explanation: ....

....

....

....

[5]

ii) Which of the substances from c) i) would be most suitable for using in drill bits?
Explain your answer with reference to the bonding in your chosen material.

....

....

....

[3]

[Total 13 marks]

19 Hydrochloric acid, HCl, reacts with aluminium.
The reaction produces aluminium chloride, $AlCl_3$, and hydrogen gas. Grade 7-9

$$6HCl_{(aq)} + 2Al_{(s)} \rightarrow 2AlCl_{3\,(aq)} + 3H_{2\,(g)}$$

Calculate the volume of hydrogen gas produced when 162 g of aluminium is added to an excess of hydrochloric acid. Assume the reaction takes place at room temperature and pressure.
1 mole of gas occupies 24 dm^3 at room temperature and pressure.
(relative atomic masses: H = 1, Al = 27)

volume = ... dm^3

[Total 3 marks]

Answers

Topic 1 — Key Concepts in Chemistry

Pages 1-2 — Chemical Equations

1 C *[1 mark]*

2 $CaCO_3$**(s)** + $2HNO_3$**(aq)** → $Ca(NO_3)_2$**(aq)** + H_2O**(l)** + CO_2**(g)**
[1 mark for correct left-hand side, 1 mark for correct right-hand side.]

3 $4Na + O_2 \rightarrow 2Na_2O$
[2 marks for all formulas correct and a correctly-balanced equation, otherwise 1 mark for correct formulas in an unbalanced equation.]

For any question that involves balancing an equation, you should also get the mark if you gave matching multiples of the correct numbers.

4 a) That the substance is dissolved in water / aqueous *[1 mark]*.
b) $\mathbf{2}Al_{(s)} + \mathbf{3}H_2SO_{4\,(aq)} \rightarrow Al_2(SO_4)_{3\,(aq)} + \mathbf{3}H_{2\,(g)}$ *[1 mark]*

5 a) $\mathbf{4}NH_3 + \mathbf{5}O_2 \rightarrow \mathbf{4}NO + \mathbf{6}H_2O$ *[1 mark]*
b) There are 7 oxygen atoms on the left hand side of the equation and only 6 on the right hand side *[1 mark]*.

6 a) A solid precipitate of AgCl is formed *[1 mark]*.
b) $Ag^+_{(aq)} + Cl^-_{(aq)} \rightarrow AgCl_{(s)}$
[1 mark for left side correct, 1 mark for right side correct.]

7 $S + \mathbf{6}HNO_3 \rightarrow H_2SO_4 + \mathbf{6}NO_2 + \mathbf{2}H_2O$ *[1 mark]*

8 $Zn_{(s)} + Sn^{2+}_{(aq)} \rightarrow Zn^{2+}_{(aq)} + Sn_{(s)}$
[1 mark for left side correct, 1 mark for right side correct.]

Remember — the overall charge on an ionic compound is zero (it's neutral). So, since the sulfate ion, SO_4^{2-}, has a charge of −2, the tin ion in $SnSO_4$ must have a charge of +2. (The same applies to the zinc ion in $ZnSO_4$.)

Page 3 — Hazards and Risk

1 a) B *[1 mark]*
b) E.g. wear safety goggles / wear a lab coat / wear gloves / use the reagent in low concentrations *[1 mark]*.

2 The label shows that the chemical is an environmental hazard *[1 mark]*. The technician needs to dispose of chemicals like this carefully as if they get into water supplies/the environment, they can damage organisms *[1 mark]*.

3 How to grade your answer:
Level 0: Nothing written worthy of credit *[No marks]*.
Level 1: Some hazards or safety precautions are given, but there is little detail and key information is missing. The points made are basic and not linked together *[1–2 marks]*.
Level 2: Some of the hazards associated with the experiment have been identified. Some explanation of the relevant safety precautions needed is given, but some detail is missing. Some of the points made are linked together *[3–4 marks]*.
Level 3: A clear and detailed description of all of the hazards associated with the experiment is given. The safety precautions needed to reduce the risks are described fully. The points made are well-linked and the answer has a clear and logical structure *[5–6 marks]*.
Here are some points your answer may include:
Harmful chemicals can cause irritation/blistering of the skin.
Corrosive chemicals destroy materials, including skin/eyes.
The gas produced by the experiment may be harmful/toxic.
The student should wear safety goggles, a lab coat and gloves when handling the chemicals.
The student should carry out the reaction in a fume hood to avoid releasing the gas into the air.
The student should use small quantities of the harmful and corrosive chemicals where possible.
The student should use the harmful and corrosive chemicals in low concentrations.

Page 4 — The History of the Atom

Warm-up
Plum pudding model — A positively charged 'ball' with negatively charged electrons in it.
Bohr's model — Electrons in fixed orbits surrounding a small, positively charged nucleus.
Rutherford's nuclear model — A small, positively charged nucleus surrounded by a 'cloud' of negative electrons.

1 A *[1 mark]*

2 a) During the gold foil experiment, most of the particles did pass straight through the foil *[1 mark]* as most of the atom is 'empty' space *[1 mark]*. However, a small number of particles were deflected backwards *[1 mark]* because they hit the nucleus *[1 mark]*.
b) Niels Bohr *[1 mark]*.

Page 5 — The Atom

1 a) nucleus *[1 mark]*
b) electron *[1 mark]*
c) Neutrons and protons *[1 mark]*.
d) Protons have a relative charge of +1 *[1 mark]* and electrons have a relative charge of –1 *[1 mark]*. Because there is an equal number of protons and electrons in an atom, the positive charges on the protons cancel out the negative charges on the electrons *[1 mark]*.

Neutrons have a relative charge of zero, which means that they don't affect the overall charge of the atom (so you don't need to mention them here).

e) C *[1 mark]*

2 a) mass number = 39 *[1 mark]*
b) atomic number = 19 *[1 mark]*
c) protons = 19 *[1 mark]*
neutrons = mass number – atomic number
= 39 – 19 = **20** *[1 mark]*
electrons = 19 *[1 mark]*

Pages 6-7 — Isotopes and Relative Atomic Mass

1 a)

Isotope	No. of Protons	No. of Neutrons	No. of Electrons
^{32}S	16	16	16
^{33}S	16	17	16
^{34}S	16	18	16
^{36}S	16	20	16

[3 marks for all rows correct, otherwise 2 marks for 3 rows correct, and 1 mark for 1 or 2 rows correct.]

b) X and Z are isotopes *[1 mark]*. They have the same atomic number / same number of protons *[1 mark]* but different mass numbers / number of neutrons *[1 mark]*.

2 a) 29 – 14 = **15** *[1 mark]*
b) relative atomic mass = (28 × 92.2) + (29 × 4.70) + (30 × 3.10) ÷ 100 = (2581.6 + 136.3 + 93) ÷ 100 = 2810.9 ÷ 100 = **28.1**
[2 marks for correct answer, otherwise 1 mark for correctly substituting in values for abundances and atomic masses.]

If you're dealing with isotopic abundances which are given to you as percentages, they will always add up to 100.

3 a) Isotopes are atoms of the same element that have the same number of protons but a different number of neutrons *[1 mark]*.
b) Br-79: Number of neutrons = 79 – 35 = **44**
Br-81: Number of neutrons = 81 – 35 = **46**
[1 mark for both correct]
c) relative atomic mass = (79 × 12.67) + (81 × 12.32) ÷ (12.67 + 12.32) = (1000.93 + 997.92) ÷ 24.99 = 1998.85 ÷ 24.99 = 79.98... = **80**
[2 marks for a correct answer given to 2 significant figures, otherwise 1 mark for correctly substituting in values for abundances and atomic masses.]

4 a) The relative atomic mass of an element is the average mass of one atom of the element ***[1 mark]***, compared to 1/12th of the mass of one atom of carbon-12 ***[1 mark]***.

b) Relative atomic mass is an average of the mass numbers of all the different isotopes of an element, taking into account the abundance of each one ***[1 mark]***.

5 % isotopic abundance of Ga-71 = 100 – 60.1 = 39.9
relative atomic mass = (69 × 60.1) + (71 × 39.9) ÷ 100
= (4146.9 + 2832.9) ÷ 100 = **69.8**
[3 marks for correct answer, otherwise 1 mark for working out % abundance of Ga-71, 1 mark for correctly substituting in values for abundances and atomic masses.]

Page 8 — The Periodic Table

1 a) By atomic number ***[1 mark]***.
b) B ***[1 mark]***

2 a) Mendeleev left some gaps in order to keep elements with similar properties in the same group ***[1 mark]***.
b) i) Any value between 2.4 and 7.2 g/cm^3 ***[1 mark]***.
ii) $EkCl_4$ ***[1 mark]***
iii) Very slow ***[1 mark]***.

Page 9 — Electronic Configurations

1 C ***[1 mark]***

The electronic structure of neon is 2.8, so has 8 electrons in its outer shell.

2 a) 2.8.6 ***[1 mark]***
b)

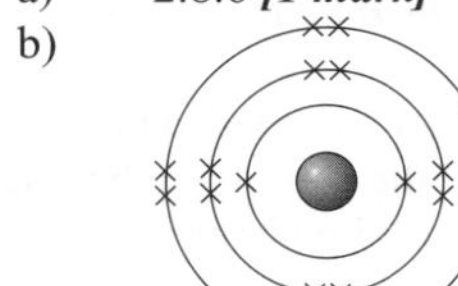

[1 mark]

3 a) The group number tells you how many electrons are in the outer shell, so magnesium has 2 outer shell electrons ***[1 mark]***. The period number tells you how many electron shells the atom has in total, so magnesium has three shells ***[1 mark]***. All the shells apart from the outer shell will be filled (the first holds 2 electrons and the second holds 8) ***[1 mark]***.
b) 2.8.2 ***[1 mark]***

Page 10 — Ions

Warm-up

A^+ — A metal from Group 1. D^- — A non-metal from Group 7.
X^{2+} — A metal from Group 2. Z^{2-} — A non-metal from Group 6.

1 a) The atom gains one or more electrons ***[1 mark]***.
b) i) +2 ***[1 mark]***
ii) Number of electrons = 12 – 2 = **10** ***[1 mark]***

2 a) C ***[1 mark]***
b) protons = 8 ***[1 mark]***, electrons = 8 – (–2) = 10 ***[1 mark]***, neutrons = 16 – 8 = 8 ***[1 mark]***

The number of protons is equal to the atomic number. The number of electrons is equal to the atomic number minus the charge (and since oxygen is in Group 6 of the periodic table, its ions will have a charge of –2). The number of neutrons is equal to the mass number minus the atomic number.

Page 11 — Ionic Bonding

1 a) calcium chloride ***[1 mark]***

Ionic compounds are made up of a metal bonded to a non-metal. All the other options only contain non-metals, so they can't be ionic.

b)

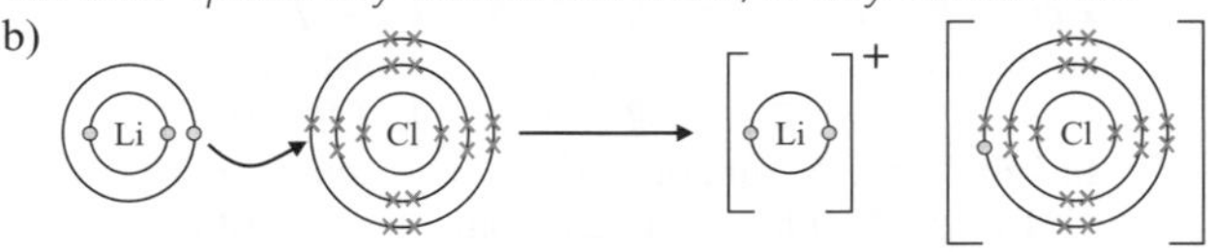

[1 mark for arrow showing electron transfer from Li to Cl, 1 mark for adding seven crosses and one dot to outer shell of the chloride ion, 1 mark for correct charges on both ions.]

c) electrostatic attraction / electrostatic force ***[1 mark]***
d) E.g. the particles in the compound are oppositely charged ions / have opposite charges / the bond is formed by electrons being transferred from one atom to another ***[1 mark]***.

2

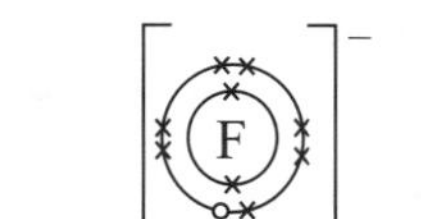
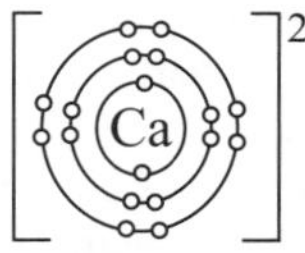

[1 mark for correct electronic structure of fluoride ions, 1 mark for correct electronic structure of calcium ion, 1 mark for correct charge on calcium ion, 1 mark for correct charge on fluoride ions.]

Pages 12-13 — Ionic Compounds

Warm-up

In an ionic compound, the particles are held together by **strong** forces of attraction. These forces act **in all directions** which results in the particles bonding together to form **giant lattices**.

1 a) D ***[1 mark]***
b) giant ionic lattice ***[1 mark]***

2 a) Sodium chloride contains positive sodium ions (Na^+) ***[1 mark]*** and negative chloride ions (Cl^-) ***[1 mark]*** that are arranged in a regular lattice/giant ionic lattice ***[1 mark]***. The oppositely charged ions are held together by electrostatic forces acting in all directions ***[1 mark]***.
b) To melt sodium chloride, you have to overcome the very strong electrostatic forces/ionic bonds between the ions ***[1 mark]***, which requires lots of energy ***[1 mark]***.

3 a) E.g.

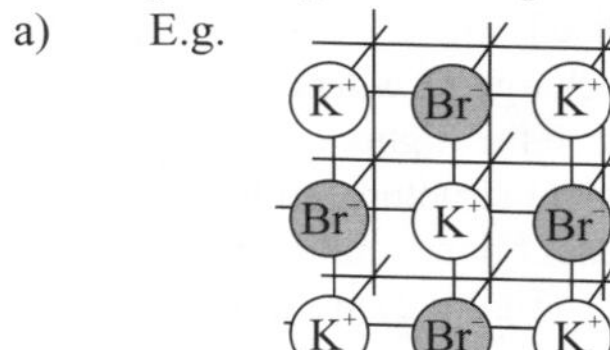

[1 mark for K+ ions, 1 mark for Br– ions, 1 mark for correct structure, with alternating ion]

You'd also get the marks if you labelled all the white circles as Br^- and all of the grey circles as K^+.

b) Advantage: e.g. the diagram shows the 3D arrangement of the ions / it suggests the structure is extended / it shows the regular (repeating) pattern of the ions ***[1 mark]***.
Disadvantage: e.g. the diagram doesn't correctly represent the sizes of ions / it shows gaps between the ions ***[1 mark]***.
c) soluble ***[1 mark]***

4 Boiling point: lithium chloride has strong ionic bonds/strong electrostatic forces of attraction between the ions ***[1 mark]***. In order to boil it, these bonds need to be broken, which takes a lot of energy ***[1 mark]***.
Electrical conductivity of solid: the ions are in fixed positions in the lattice ***[1 mark]*** and so are not able to move and carry a charge through the solid ***[1 mark]***.
Electrical conductivity of solution: in solution, the ions are free to move ***[1 mark]***, so they can carry a charge ***[1 mark]***.

Pages 14-15 — Covalent Bonding

1 a) The bonds between the atoms in a molecule are strong ***[1 mark]***, but the forces between the molecules are weak ***[1 mark]***.
b) The forces between the molecules / the intermolecular forces ***[1 mark]***.

2 A silicon atom has four outer shell electrons, so it needs another four to have a full outer shell ***[1 mark]***. So a silicon atom will form four covalent bonds ***[1 mark]***.

3 a)

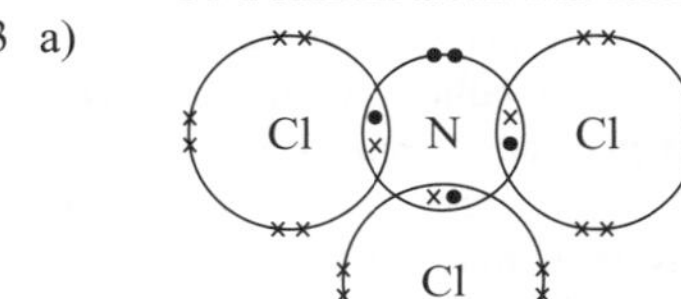

[1 mark for correctly showing three chlorine-nitrogen bonds as shared pairs of electrons, 1 mark for showing one extra electron pair on the nitrogen atom, 1 mark for showing three extra electron pairs on each chlorine atom.]

b) Nitrogen trichloride won't conduct electricity because it doesn't contain any free electrons / ions / charged particles ***[1 mark]***.

4 Hashim is wrong. Simple molecular substances have low melting and boiling points ***[1 mark]***. To melt or boil a simple molecular substance, you only need to overcome the intermolecular forces which hold the molecules together ***[1 mark]***. Intermolecular forces are weak, so they can be broken with a small amount of energy ***[1 mark]***.

5 a) Carbon needs four more electrons to get a full outer shell ***[1 mark]***, which it gains by forming four covalent bonds with hydrogen atoms ***[1 mark]***. Hydrogen only needs one more electron to complete its outer shell ***[1 mark]***, so each hydrogen atom forms one covalent bond to the carbon atom ***[1 mark]***.

b) polymer ***[1 mark]***

c) Poly(ethene) molecules are larger than methane molecules ***[1 mark]***. As molecules get bigger, the strength of the intermolecular forces between them increases ***[1 mark]***. So the forces between the molecules are stronger in poly(ethene) than they are in methane ***[1 mark]*** and more energy is needed to overcome them ***[1 mark]***.

Page 16 — Giant Covalent Structures and Fullerenes

1 a) i) graphite ***[1 mark]***

ii) fullerene / buckminster fullerene ***[1 mark]***

b) Both structures have delocalised / free electrons ***[1 mark]***, which can move and carry a charge ***[1 mark]***.

c) Graphite (figure 1) should have the higher melting point ***[1 mark]***. It has a giant covalent structure, so to melt it you need to break the strong covalent bonds holding the atoms together ***[1 mark]***. Fullerenes (figure 2) are molecular, so to melt them you only need to break the weak intermolecular forces holding the molecules together ***[1 mark]***.

d) E.g. diamond: OR graphene:

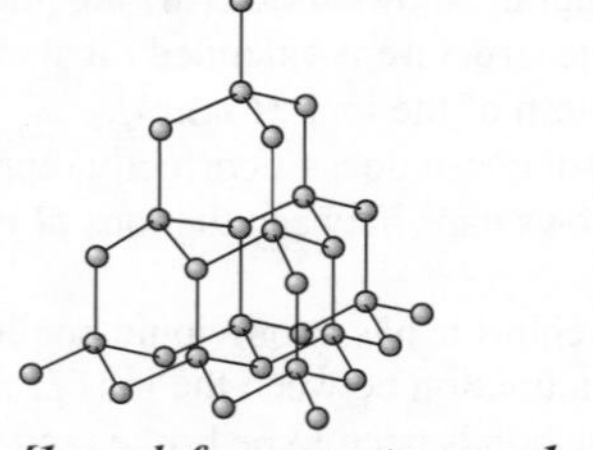

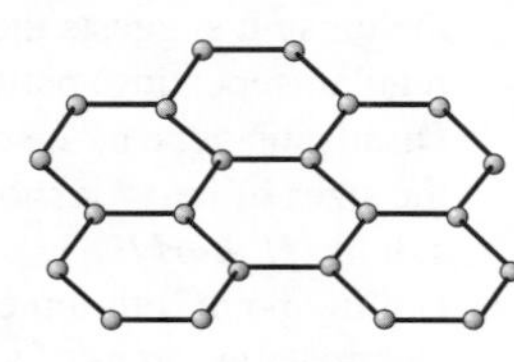

[1 mark for correct name, 1 mark for correct structure]

Page 17 — Metallic Bonding

1 a)

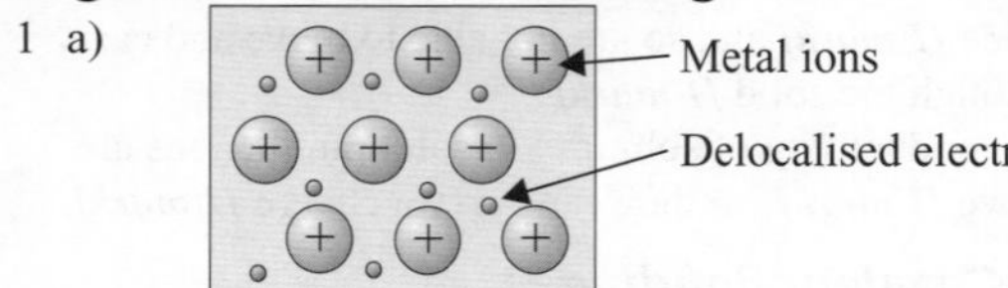

[1 mark for regular arrangement of metal ions, 1 mark for delocalised electrons, 1 mark for labels]

b) There is a strong electrostatic attraction ***[1 mark]*** between the delocalised electrons and the positive metal ions ***[1 mark]***.

c) i) Metals generally have high boiling points, because the metallic bonds / electrostatic forces between the ions and the electrons are strong ***[1 mark]*** so a lot of energy is needed to break them ***[1 mark]***.

ii) Solid B is iodine, since elements that are non-metals tend to have lower melting points than metallic elements ***[1 mark]***.

d) Metals contain delocalised electrons ***[1 mark]***, which are free to move through the structure and carry a charge ***[1 mark]***.

e) Metallic structures have layers of atoms ***[1 mark]*** that are able to slide over one another ***[1 mark]***.

Page 18 — Conservation of Mass

1 The total mass of the contents of the flask would be $3.0 + 15.8 =$ **18.8 g** ***[1 mark]***. This is because, during a reaction, mass conserved / the total mass of the system doesn't change ***[1 mark]***.

2 a) The total mass of the flask and its contents will decrease over the course of the reaction ***[1 mark]*** as one of the products is hydrogen gas, which is lost from the flask ***[1 mark]***.

b) The total mass of the flask and its contents would stay the same over the course of the reaction ***[1 mark]*** as the reaction is happening in a closed system / any hydrogen gas evolved wouldn't be able to escape, so no reactants are lost ***[1 mark]***.

Pages 19-20 — Relative Masses and Chemical Formulas

Warm-up

F_2 — 38 C_2H_6 — 30 CaO — 56 NaOH — 40

1 D ***[1 mark]***

2 The largest number that goes into both 10 and 14 exactly is 2.
B: $10 \div 2 = 5$ H: $14 \div 2 = 7$
So the empirical formula of decaborane is B_5H_7 ***[1 mark]***.

3 a) $H_2S_2O_6$ ***[1 mark]***

b) The largest number that goes into all the numbers in the molecular formula exactly is 2.
H: $2 \div 2 = 1$ S: $2 \div 2 = 1$ O: $6 \div 2 = 3$
So the empirical formula is HSO_3 ***[1 mark]***

4 M_r of $Ba(NO_3)_2$ = A_r of Ba + (2 × (A_r of N + (3 × A_r of O)))
$= 137 + (2 \times (14 + (3 \times 16))) = 137 + (2 \times (14 + 48))$
$= 137 + (2 \times 62) = 137 + 124 =$ **261**
[2 marks for correct answer, otherwise 1 mark for writing a expression that could be used to calculate the M_r of $Ba(NO_3)_2$.]

5 Emmy is incorrect, e.g. because she not has divided the numbers in the molecular formula by the largest number that will go into both exactly / she has divided both numbers in the formula by 4, but she could have divided by 8 / $8 \div 8 = 1$ and $16 \div 8 = 2$, so the empirical formula is CH_2 ***[1 mark]***.

6 M_r of X_2O_3 = (2 × A_r of X) + (3 × A_r of O)
So 160 = (2 × A_r of X) + (3 × 16)
160 = (2 × A_r of X) + 48
2 × A_r of X = 160 − 48 = 112
so A_r of X = 112 ÷ 2 = **56**
[3 marks for the correct answer, otherwise 1 mark for a correct equation for finding the M_r of X_2O_3 and 1 mark for correctly substituting in the M_r of X_2O_3 and A_r of O.]

7 Relative mass of empirical formula is
(2 × A_r of C) + (A_r of H) + (A_r of F) = (2 × 12) + 1 + 19
= 24 + 1 + 19 = 44
M_r of Q ÷ M_r of empirical formula = 132 ÷ 44 = 3
So to get the molecular formula, multiply the numbers of atoms in the empirical formula by 3:
molecular formula = $\mathbf{C_6H_3F_3}$
[3 marks for correct answer, otherwise 1 mark for finding the relative mass of the empirical formula and 1 mark for dividing the relative mass of the molecular formula by the relative mass of the empirical formula.]

Pages 21-23 — Moles and Concentration

1 D ***[1 mark]***

2 A ***[1 mark]***

3 $M_r(C_9H_8O_4) = (12 \times 9) + (1 \times 8) + (16 \times 4) = 180$
mass = moles × M_r = 12.4 × 180 = **2232 g**
[2 marks for the correct answer, otherwise 1 mark for calculating the M_r of $C_9H_8O_4$.]

4 no. molecules = moles × Avogadro's constant
$= 7 \times (6.02 \times 10^{23}) = 4.214 \times 10^{24}$
In 1 molecule of ammonia, there are 4 atoms, so in 4.214×10^{24} molecules of ammonia, there must be
$4.214 \times 10^{24} \times 4 = 1.6856 \times 10^{25} =$ **1.69×10^{25} atoms**
[2 marks for correct answer, otherwise 1 mark for correctly working out number of ammonia molecules]

5 $220 \text{ cm}^3 = (220 \div 1000) \text{ dm}^3 = 0.220 \text{ dm}^3$
mass = concentration × volume = 75.0 × 0.220
= **16.5 g** ***[1 mark]***

6 a) $400 \text{ cm}^3 = (400 \div 1000) \text{ dm}^3 = 0.4 \text{ dm}^3$
Concentration = mass ÷ volume
= 56 ÷ 0.4 = **140 g dm^{-3}** ***[1 mark]***

b) $300\ cm^3 = (300 \div 1000)\ dm^3 = 0.300\ dm^3$
Mass = concentration × volume = 140 × 0.300 = **42 g** ***[1 mark]***
If your answer to a) was incorrect, award 1 mark for correct working in b).

7 a) $600\ cm^3 = (600 \div 1000)\ dm^3 = 0.6\ dm^3$
mass of NaOH = 52 × 0.6 = 31.2 g
moles of NaOH = mass ÷ M_r = 31.2 ÷ 40.0 = **0.78 mol**
[2 marks for correct answer, otherwise 1 mark for working out the mass of NaOH]

b) i) Volume = mass ÷ concentration = 36.0 ÷ 80.0 = $0.450\ dm^3$
$0.450\ dm^3 = (0.450 \times 1000)\ cm^3$ = **$450\ cm^3$**
[2 marks for correct answer, otherwise 1 mark for calculating volume in dm³]

ii) Double the volume of water / add an extra $450\ cm^3$ of water to the solution ***[1 mark]***.

8 a) $(1.204 \times 10^{25}) \div (6.02 \times 10^{23})$ = **20 moles** ***[1 mark]***

b) A_r of element = $(9.3 \times 10^{-23}) \times (6.02 \times 10^{23})$ = 56 (2 s.f.)
So the element is **iron**.
[2 marks for correct answer, otherwise 1 mark for working out the relative atomic mass of the element].

9 a) M_r = mass ÷ moles = 343 ÷ 3.5 = **98** ***[1 mark]***

b) 65% of 98 = (98 ÷ 100) × 65 = 63.7
Moles of O in 63.7 g = 63.7 ÷ 16 = 3.98... = **4 moles**
[2 marks for correct answer, otherwise 1 mark for working out the mass of oxygen.]

c) Mass of 1 mole of S = 32 g
Mass of 4 moles of O = 16 × 4 = 64 g
Mass of H in 1 mole of acid = 98 – 64 – 32 = 2 g ***[1 mark]***
Moles of H in 2 g = 2 ÷ 1 = 2
Ratio of S : O : H = 1 : 4 : 2 ***[1 mark]***
chemical formula = **H_2SO_4**
[3 marks for correct answer, otherwise 1 mark for working out mass of S, O and H in acid and 1 mark for working out the ratio between S, O and H in the acid.]

Page 24 — Calculating Empirical Formulas

1 moles = mass ÷ A_r
moles Pb = 2.07 ÷ 207 = 0.01 moles
moles O = 0.16 ÷ 16 = 0.01 moles
ratio of Pb : O = 0.01 : 0.01
Dividing by the smallest number (0.01) gives a ratio of Pb : O of 1 : 1. The empirical formula is **PbO**.
[2 marks for correct answer, otherwise 1 mark for finding moles of Pb and O.]

2 mass of Cu = 53.66 – 10.8 = 42.86
moles = mass ÷ A_r
moles of Cu = 42.86 ÷ 63.5 = 0.6749...
moles of O = 10.8 ÷ 16 = 0.675
ratio of Cu : O = 0.6749... : 0.675
Dividing by the smallest number (0.6749...) gives a ratio of Cu : O of 1 : 1. The empirical formula is **CuO**.
[3 marks for correct answer, otherwise 1 mark for finding the mass of Cu and 1 mark for finding the moles of Cu and O.]

3 In 100 g of the hydrocarbon:
83 g is C and (100 – 83 =) 17 g is H.
moles = mass ÷ A_r
moles of C = 83 ÷ 12 = 6.916...
moles of H = 17 ÷ 1 = 17
ratio of C : H = 6.916... : 17
Dividing by the smallest number (6.916...) gives a ratio of C : H of 1 : 2.5. The smallest whole number ratio is 2 : 5, so the empirical formula must be **C_2H_5**.
[3 marks for correct answer, otherwise 1 mark for finding the mass of C and H in 100 g and 1 mark for finding the moles of C and H.]

4 a) E.g. a crucible ***[1 mark]***.

b) mass of O = 5.440 – 3.808 = 1.632 g
moles = mass ÷ A_r
moles of Fe = 3.808 ÷ 56 = 0.068
moles of O = 1.632 ÷ 16 = 0.102
ratio of Fe : O = 0.068 : 0.102.
Dividing by the smallest number (0.068) gives a ratio of Fe : O of 1 : 1.5. The smallest whole number ratio is 2 : 3, so the empirical formula must be **Fe_2O_3**.
[3 marks for correct answer, otherwise 1 mark for finding the mass of O and 1 mark for finding the moles of Fe and O.]

Pages 25-26 — Limiting Reactants

Warm-up

1) If the amount of limiting reactant in a reaction is decreased, then the amount of product made will **decrease**.
2) If the amount of limiting reactant in a reaction is increased, then the amount of product made will **increase**.
3) If the amount of an excess reactant is increased, then the amount of product made will **not change**.

1 a) magnesium ***[1 mark]***

b) The hydrochloric acid is the limiting reactant ***[1 mark]*** as there is magnesium metal left over when the reaction has finished, showing that it's in excess ***[1 mark]***.

2 $M_r(C_2H_4) = (12 \times 2) + (1 \times 4) = 28$
moles = mass ÷ M_r = 53 ÷ 28 = 1.8... moles
From the reaction equation, 1 mole of C_2H_4 produces 1 mole of CH_3CH_2OH, so 1.89... moles of C_2H_4 will produce 1.89... moles of CH_3CH_2OH.
$M_r(CH_3CH_2OH) = 12 + (1 \times 3) + 12 + (1 \times 2) + 16 + 1 = 46$
mass = moles × M_r = 1.89... × 46 = **87 g**
[2 marks for correct answer, otherwise 1 mark for working out moles of C_2H_4.]

3 a) $M_r(O_2) = 16 \times 2 = 32$
moles = mass ÷ M_r = 128 ÷ 32 = 4
From the reaction equation, 7 moles of O_2 produce 6 moles of H_2O, so 4 moles of O_2 will produce ((4 ÷ 7) × 6) = 3.42... moles of H_2O.
$M_r(H_2O) = (1 \times 2) + 16 = 18$
mass = moles × M_r = 3.42... × 18 = **61.7 g**
[3 marks for correct answer, otherwise 1 mark for working out moles of O_2 and 1 mark for multiplying the moles of O_2 by the M_r of H_2O.]

b) $M_r(CO_2) = 12 + (16 \times 2) = 44$
4.4 tonnes = 4.4 × 1 000 000 = 4 400 000 g
moles = mass ÷ M_r = 4 400 000 ÷ 44 = 100 000
For every 4 moles of CO_2 produced, 2 moles of ethane are burnt. So if 100 000 moles of CO_2 are produced, ((100 000 ÷ 4) × 2 =) 50 000 moles of ethane are burnt.
$M_r(C_2H_6) = (12 \times 2) + (1 \times 6) = 30$
mass = moles × M_r = 50 000 × 30 = 1 500 000 g
1 500 000 g = 1 500 000 ÷ 1 000 000 = **1.5 tonnes**
[3 marks for correct answer, otherwise 1 mark for finding moles of CO_2, 1 mark for finding mass of C_2H_6 in g.]

4 a) $M_r((NH_2)_2CO) = 2 \times (14 + (1 \times 2) + 12 + 16 = 60$
120.6 tonnes = 120.6 × 1 000 000 = 120 600 000 g
moles = mass ÷ M_r = 120 600 000 ÷ 60 = 2 010 000
From the reaction equation, 1 mole of $(NH_2)_2CO$ is made from 1 mole of CO_2, so making 2 010 000 moles of $(NH_2)_2CO$ will require 2 010 000 moles of CO_2.
$M_r(CO_2) = 12 + (16 \times 2) = 44$
mass = moles × M_r = 2 010 000 × 44 = 88 440 000 g
88 440 000 g = 88 440 000 ÷ 1 000 000 = **88.44 tonnes**
[3 marks for correct answer, otherwise 1 mark for finding moles of $(NH_2)_2CO$, 1 mark for finding mass of CO_2 in g.]

b) $M_r(NH_3) = 14 + (1 \times 3) = 17$
59.5 tonnes = 59.5 × 1 000 000 = 59 500 000 g
moles = mass ÷ M_r = 59 500 000 ÷ 17 = 3 500 000
From the reaction equation, 2 moles of NH_3 make 1 mole of $(NH_2)_2CO$, so 3 500 000 moles of NH_3 will make (3 500 000 ÷ 2 =) 1 750 000 moles of $(NH_2)_2CO$.

From a), $M_r((NH_2)_2CO) = 60$
mass = moles × M_r = 1 750 000 × 60 = 105 000 000 g
105 000 000 = 105 000 000 ÷ 1 000 000 = 105 tonnes
difference between masses of $(NH_2)_2CO$ = 120.6 – 105
= **15.6 tonnes**
[4 marks for correct answer, otherwise 1 mark for finding moles of (NH_3), 1 mark for finding mass of $(NH_2)_2CO$ in g, 1 mark for finding mass of $(NH_2)_2CO$ in tonnes.]

Page 27 — Balancing Equations Using Masses

1 a) 280 – 200 = **80 g** ***[1 mark]***
b) E.g. moles = mass ÷ M_r
moles of X = 200 ÷ 40 = 5 moles
moles of O_2 = 80 ÷ (2 × 16) = 2.5 moles
Since X is a metal, its formula must be just be X.
From the question, you know the reaction produced 5 moles of X oxide, so the ratio of X : O_2 : X oxide is 5 : 2.5 : 5.
Dividing all of these by 2.5 gives a ratio of 2 : 1 : 2.
$2X + O_2 \rightarrow 2(X\ oxide)$
Since X oxide is the only product, and there are two atoms of both X and O on the left-hand side of the equation, the formula of X oxide must be XO.
So, balanced equation = $2X + O_2 \rightarrow 2XO$
[4 marks for correct answer, otherwise 1 mark for calculating the moles of X and the moles of O_2 gas, 1 mark for working out the simplest ratio of X : O : X oxide, 1 mark for stating the formula of X oxide.]
You could have done some of the working for this question differently, so don't worry if you've approached it in another way. If your answer is right you'll get full marks anyway. If your answer is wrong, you should get marks for your working, as long as the method you've used is sensible.

2 E.g. moles = mass ÷ M_r
moles of Na = 1.0 ÷ 23 = 0.043
moles of Cl_2 = 1.0 ÷ 71 = 0.014
Ratio of Na: Cl_2 = (0.043 ÷ 0.014) : (0.014 ÷ 0.014) = 3.1 : 1
Ratio of Na to Cl_2 in balanced equation = 2:1
Sodium is in excess, so chlorine is the limiting reactant.
[1 mark for calculating the moles of Na present, 1 mark for calculating the moles of Cl_2 present, 1 mark for stating that chlorine is the limiting reactant.]
Don't worry if you've done the working for this question a bit differently too — as long as your method and answer are correct, you'll get all the marks.

3 E.g. mass of metal halide produced = 3.57 + 15.24 = 18.81 g
moles = mass ÷ M_r
moles of Sn = 3.57 ÷ 119 = 0.03 moles
moles of I_2 = 15.24 ÷ 254 = 0.06 moles
moles of metal halide = 18.81 ÷ 627 = 0.03
The ratio of Sn : I_2 : metal halide is 0.03 : 0.06 : 0.03.
Dividing all of these by 0.03 gives a ratio of 1 : 2 : 1.
$Sn + 2I_2 \rightarrow$ metal halide
Since all of the reactants end up in the product, and there is one atom of Sn and four atoms of I on the left-hand side of the equation, the formula of the metal halide must be SnI_4.
So, the balanced equation is: $Sn + 2I_2 \rightarrow SnI_4$
[5 marks for correct answer, otherwise 1 mark for calculating the mass of metal halide made, 1 mark for calculating the number of moles of reactants and product, 1 mark for working out the simplest ratio of Sn : I_2 : metal halide, 1 mark for stating the formula of the metal halide.]
The same goes for this question if you've approached it a different way. The correct answer gets full marks anyway, but if your answer's wrong, you should get marks for correct working that uses a correct sensible method.

Topic 2 — States of Matter and Mixtures

Page 28 — States of Matter

Warm-up
Particles in liquids are held in fixed positions by strong forces.
1 a) solid ***[1 mark]***
b) liquid ***[1 mark]***
2 When the substance is in the liquid state, the particles are constantly moving with a random motion ***[1 mark]***. In the solid state the particles can only vibrate around fixed positions ***[1 mark]***. When the substance is in the liquid state, the particles have more energy than when it is in the solid state ***[1 mark]***.

Page 29 — Changes of State

1 a) C ***[1 mark]***.
b) B and D ***[1 mark]***. In these equations new products have been formed / the atoms in the reactants have been rearranged to form different chemicals ***[1 mark]***.
2 The first change seen would be bromine freezing from a red-brown liquid to a red-brown solid ***[1 mark]***.
The next change would be mercury freezing from a silvery metallic liquid to a silvery metallic solid ***[1 mark]***.
Near the end of the experiment, the fluorine would condense from a pale yellow gas to a bright yellow liquid ***[1 mark]***.
The rubidium would start out as a silvery-white metallic solid, and remain unchanged throughout ***[1 mark]***.

Page 30 — Purity

1 The scientific definition of a pure substance is one that contains only one element or compound ***[1 mark]***. Although it is labelled 'pure', Stanley's spring water is likely to contain traces of other compounds or elements as well as water molecules ***[1 mark]***.
2 Sample A ***[1 mark]***. The purer the substance, the smaller the range of the melting point / pure substances have sharp melting points, whereas impure substances melt over a range of temperatures ***[1 mark]***.
3 a) The pure compound will have a single, sharp melting point ***[1 mark]*** whereas the mixture will melt gradually over a range of temperatures ***[1 mark]***.
b) melting point apparatus / water bath and thermometer ***[1 mark]***

Pages 31-34 — Separating Mixtures

1 a) i) A: fractionating column ***[1 mark]***
ii) B: condenser ***[1 mark]***
b) i) fractional distillation ***[1 mark]***
ii) A mixture of liquids ***[1 mark]*** with similar boiling points ***[1 mark]***.
iii) E.g. electric heater / water bath ***[1 mark]***
You don't get the mark here for naming any heating device with an open flame (like a Bunsen burner).
2 How to grade your answer:
Level 0: There is no relevant information. ***[No marks]***
Level 1: A method is described which would allow you to obtain a pure sample of only one of the components. The points made are basic and not linked together. ***[1 to 2 marks]***
Level 2: A method is described which would allow you to obtain pure samples of both components, but some details may be missing or incorrect. Some of the points made are linked together. ***[3 to 4 marks]***
Level 3: A method is described clearly and in full, which would allow you to obtain pure samples of both components. The points made are well-linked and the answer has a clear and logical structure. ***[5 to 6 marks]***
Here are some points your answer may include:
Mix the powder with water. This will dissolve the potassium iodide, but not the barium sulfate.
Filter the mixture through a filter paper in a funnel.
The potassium iodide solution will pass through the paper and can be collected in a flask.
The solid barium sulfate will be left in the filter paper.
The solid barium sulfate can be washed with water to remove any traces of potassium iodide and then dried in a drying oven / desiccator / warm place.
The remaining liquid part of the mixture will be a solution of potassium iodide.

To obtain pure potassium iodide from this solution, you can use crystallisation.
Gently heat the solution in an evaporation dish until some of the water has evaporated / until crystals start to form.
Allow the solution to cool, then filter out the crystals.
Dry the crystals by leaving them in a warm place / using a drying oven / using a desiccator.

3 a) Filtration ***[1 mark]*** would separate sodium chloride and ethanol, as the liquid ethanol would flow through the filter paper, leaving behind the solid sodium chloride ***[1 mark]***. However, a mixture of sodium chloride and water is a solution, so both the water and dissolved sodium chloride would pass through the filter paper ***[1 mark]***.

b) E.g. simple distillation ***[1 mark]***. Water and ethanol would both evaporate off and leave behind the solid sodium chloride ***[1 mark]***.

4 The difference in the boiling points of cyclohexane and cyclopentane is quite large, so you could separate them using simple distillation ***[1 mark]***. But the boiling points of cyclohexane and ethyl ethanoate are similar, so you would need to use fractional distillation to separate them ***[1 mark]***.

5 a) No, it will not work as ethanol boils at 78 °C and water boils at 100 °C, so the liquids will both evaporate before 120 °C is reached ***[1 mark]***.

b) In step 1 of the method, the student should heat the mixture to a temperature between 78 and 100 °C ***[1 mark]***. This will cause the ethanol in the mixture to evaporate, but not the water ***[1 mark]***.

c) Ethanol is a flammable solvent so the mixture could catch fire if there is a lot left in the solution ***[1 mark]***.

d) Gently heat the solution in an evaporating dish until some of the liquid has evaporated. When crystals start to form, remove the dish from the heat and leave to cool ***[1 mark]***. Filter the crystals out of the solution and leave to dry in a warm place ***[1 mark]***.

Pages 35-37 — Chromatography

1 a) ethanol ***[1 mark]***

b) The chromatogram suggests there are at least two components in the mixture ***[1 mark]***, since the mixture has separated into two spots ***[1 mark]***.

c) Distance from baseline to spot B = 0.8 cm / 8 mm ***[1 mark]***
Distance from baseline to solvent front = 4.0 cm / 40 mm ***[1 mark]***
R_f = distance travelled by solute ÷ distance travelled by solvent = 0.8 ÷ 4.0 = **0.2**
[1 mark for correctly dividing measured distance to spot B by measured distance to solvent front.]

d) Olivia could re-run the experiment with spots of the pure chemicals alongside the mixture / analyse samples of each of the pure chemicals using paper chromatography, under the same conditions as the mixture ***[1 mark]***. The R_f values of / distance travelled by each spot in the mixture will match the R_f values of / distance travelled by the pure sample of the chemical responsible for that spot ***[1 mark]***.

2 a) i) e.g. simple distillation ***[1 mark]***

ii) If he uses a thermometer in his distillation set-up, Lamar will be able to find the boiling point of the solvent, which he may be able to use to identify it ***[1 mark]***.

b) Draw a line in pencil near the bottom of a piece of chromatography paper ***[1 mark]***. Place a small spot of each ink on the line ***[1 mark]***. Pour a shallow layer of water / solvent into a beaker and place the chromatography paper in the beaker ***[1 mark]***. The water should be below the pencil line and the ink spots ***[1 mark]***. Place a lid on the beaker and leave until the solvent has risen close to the top of the paper ***[1 mark]***.

c) E.g. the ink has a spot at the same height as dye B, so dye B could be in the ink ***[1 mark]***. The ink has a spot at the same height as dyes C and E, so either (or both) of these dyes could be in the ink ***[1 mark]***. The ink has no spot at the same height as dyes A and D, so these dyes are not in the ink ***[1 mark]***. The ink has a spot with a height different to all of the dyes, so it must also contain at least one other dye ***[1 mark]***.

3 a) There are at least five compounds in the ink ***[1 mark]*** because there are 5 spots on the chromatogram ***[1 mark]***. There is at least one insoluble compound ***[1 mark]***, because there is still a spot on the baseline ***[1 mark]***.

The student can't know exactly how many compounds are in the ink, as some compounds may not be soluble in the solvent, and others may have similar R_f values so their spots will overlap.

b) The student drew line A from the baseline to the top of the spot ***[1 mark]***. They should have drawn the line to the centre of the spot ***[1 mark]***. The student drew line B from the baseline to the top of the paper ***[1 mark]***. They should have drawn line B from the baseline to the solvent front ***[1 mark]***.

Page 38 — Water Treatment

Warm-up
Potable water is the same as drinking water — true.
Potable water can only be produced from fresh water found in rivers, streams and reservoirs — false.
Ordinary tap water can be used in chemical analysis — false.

1 a) E.g. ground water / surface water / waste water / lakes / rivers / reservoirs ***[1 mark]***.

b) Distillation is expensive because it requires a lot of energy ***[1 mark]*** so it is not used in the UK as there are sufficient cheaper sources of water ***[1 mark]***.

2 a) filtration ***[1 mark]***

b) Aluminium sulfate makes fine particles in the water clump together and settle at the bottom ***[1 mark]***.

c) Chlorine gas is bubbled through the water ***[1 mark]*** to kill harmful bacteria / microbes ***[1 mark]***.

Topic 3 — Chemical Changes

Pages 39-40 — Acids and Bases

Warm-up
The following sentences should be circled:
As H^+ concentration increases, pH decreases.
Alkalis turn Universal indicator blue/purple.
Acids have pHs of less than 7.
Alkalis are soluble bases.

1 a) beer ***[1 mark]***

b) pink ***[1 mark]***

c) B ***[1 mark]***

2 A ***[1 mark]***

3 a) acid + base → salt + water ***[1 mark]***

b) $H^+_{(aq)} + OH^-_{(aq)} \rightarrow H_2O_{(l)}$ ***[1 mark]***

You still get the marks if you didn't include state symbols.

4 Solution C has the lowest concentration of hydroxide ions ***[1 mark]***, because the higher the concentration of hydroxide ions in an alkaline solution, the higher its pH will be / the lower the concentration of hydroxide ions in an alkaline solution, the lower its pH will be ***[1 mark]***.

5 a) E.g. pipette / measuring cylinder ***[1 mark]***

b) i) Red / orange / yellow ***[1 mark]***. Since all the calcium hydroxide reacted, the acid must be in excess ***[1 mark]***, so the solution is acidic ***[1 mark]***.

ii) Green ***[1 mark]***. At this point all of the acid must have reacted with / been neutralised by the base ***[1 mark]***, leaving a neutral solution ***[1 mark]***.

Page 41 — Strong and Weak Acids

1 A ***[1 mark]***

2 a) A weak acid doesn't fully ionise in solution / only a small proportion of molecules in a weak acid dissociate to release hydrogen ions ***[1 mark]***.

b) $HCOOH \rightleftharpoons HCOO^- + H^+$ ***[1 mark for correct equation, 1 mark for arrow showing reversible reaction.]***

3 a) D ***[1 mark]***

b) 1 ***[1 mark]***

An increase in the hydrogen ion concentration by a factor of 10 decreases the pH by 1. So an increase by a factor of 100 will reduce the pH by 2.

Page 42 — Reactions of Acids

1 D ***[1 mark]***

2 From top to bottom: $Zn(NO_3)_2$ ***[1 mark]***, $CaSO_4$ ***[1 mark]***, Na_2SO_4 ***[1 mark]***, KCl ***[1 mark]***

3 a) The gas produced is carbon dioxide ***[1 mark]***. If you bubble carbon dioxide through limewater ***[1 mark]***, the limewater will turn cloudy ***[1 mark]***.

b) $ZnCO_3 + 2HCl \rightarrow ZnCl_2 + H_2O + CO_2$
[2 marks for all formulas correct and a correctly-balanced equation, otherwise 1 mark for correct formulas in an unbalanced equation.]

c) zinc chloride ***[1 mark]***

Pages 43-44 — Making Insoluble Salts

1 D ***[1 mark]***

2 a) E.g. silver nitrate / $AgNO_3$ and sodium chloride / NaCl
[1 mark for any soluble silver salt, 1 mark for any soluble chloride salt.]

b) Jerry has poured too much solution into the funnel / the level of the solution goes above the filter paper ***[1 mark]***. This means that some of the solid could pass down the sides of the filter paper and into the conical flask below, reducing the amount of solid that's extracted from the solution ***[1 mark]***.

c) Deionised water doesn't contain any other ions which might contaminate the pure salt ***[1 mark]***.

3 a) C ***[1 mark]***

b) E.g. calcium chloride / $CaCl_2$ and sodium carbonate / Na_2CO_3
[1 mark for any soluble calcium salt, 1 mark for any soluble carbonate.]

4 a) $Fe(OH)_3$ ***[1 mark]***

b) i) E.g. to make sure that all of the precipitate is transferred from the beaker to the funnel / to make sure she doesn't lose any of the product ***[1 mark]***.

ii) E.g. scrape the product on to a clean piece of filter paper and dry in an oven / desiccator / warm place ***[1 mark]***.

iii) Fe^{3+}, NO_3^- and Na^+ / iron(III) ions, nitrate ions and sodium ions ***[2 marks for all three correct, otherwise 1 mark for any two correct]***.

Pages 45-46 — Making Soluble Salts

Warm-up
The following pieces of equipment should be circled:
filter funnel, fume cupboard, desiccator, water bath, conical flask, safety glasses, filter paper

1 a) C ***[1 mark]***

b) $Mg(OH)_{2\,(s)} + H_2SO_{4\,(aq)} \rightarrow MgSO_{4\,(aq)} + 2H_2O_{(l)}$
[3 marks for a correctly balanced equation with all formulas and state symbols correct, otherwise 1 mark for correct formulas in an unbalanced equation, and 1 mark for all state symbols correct.]

2 a) It dissolves in water ***[1 mark]***.

b) $2KOH + H_2SO_4 \rightarrow K_2SO_4 + 2H_2O$
[2 marks for all formulas correct and a correctly-balanced equation, otherwise 1 mark for correct formulas in an unbalanced equation.]

c) No, because the salt will be contaminated by the indicator ***[1 mark]***.

3 a) $H_2SO_4 + CuO \rightarrow CuSO_4 + H_2O$
[2 marks for all formulas correct and a correctly-balanced equation, otherwise 1 mark for correct formulas in an unbalanced equation.]

b) How to grade your answer:

Level 0: There is no relevant information. ***[No marks]***

Level 1: There is a brief explanation of how to prepare the salt but no details are given. The points made are basic and not linked together. ***[1 to 2 marks]***

Level 2: There is some explanation of to prepare the salt, including necessary equipment and how to isolate the salt, but the method is missing key details. Some of the points made are linked together. ***[3 to 4 marks]***

Level 3: There is a clear and detailed explanation of how to produce and extract a pure sample of the salt. The points made are well-linked and the answer has a clear and logical structure. ***[5 to 6 marks]***

Here are some points your answer may include:
Warm the sulfuric acid in a water bath.
Warm the acid in a fume cupboard to avoid releasing acid fumes into the room.
Add copper oxide to the acid.
When the reaction is complete and the copper oxide is in excess, the solid copper oxide will sink to the bottom.
Filter the reaction mixture to remove the excess copper oxide.
Heat the remaining solution gently (using a Bunsen burner) to evaporate off some of the water.
Leave the solution to cool and allow the salt to crystallise.
Filter off the solid salt and leave the crystals to dry.

Pages 47-49 — Electrolysis

1 a) The ions in solid potassium chloride are not free to move and so can't carry a charge ***[1 mark]***, so the potassium chloride must be molten or dissolved so that the ions are free to move and carry a charge ***[1 mark]***.

b) cathode ***[1 mark]***

2 a) B ***[1 mark]***

b) i) Bubbles of green gas would form ***[1 mark]***.

ii) Copper metal would coat the electrode ***[1 mark]***.

3 a) Inert electrodes are electrodes that do not react with the electrolyte ***[1 mark]***.

b) H^+, Cl^-, Na^+, OH^- ***[2 marks for all four correct, otherwise 1 mark for any three correct.]***

c) i) $2Cl^- \rightarrow Cl_2 + 2e^-$
[2 marks for all formulas correct and a correctly-balanced equation, otherwise 1 mark for correct formulas in an unbalanced equation.]

ii) $2H^+ + 2e^- \rightarrow H_2$
[2 marks for all formulas correct and a correctly-balanced equation, otherwise 1 mark for correct formulas in an unbalanced equation.]

4 a) A liquid or solution ***[1 mark]*** that can conduct electricity ***[1 mark]***.

b) PbI_2 ***[1 mark]***

5 How to grade your answer:

Level 0: There is no relevant information. ***[No marks]***

Level 1: The method is vague, and misses out important details. Predictions about products or observations of the electrolysis are unclear and incomplete.
The points made are basic and not linked together. ***[1 to 2 marks]***

Level 2: The method is clear, but misses out a few key details. Correct predictions of products and observations of the electrolysis are given but are missing some important details. Some of the points made are linked together. ***[3 to 4 marks]***

Level 3: There is a clear and detailed method. The products of the electrolysis are correctly predicted and the observations are described in full. The points made are well-linked and the answer has a clear and logical structure. ***[5 to 6 marks]***

Here are some points your answer may include:
Use two platinum/graphite electrodes.
Clean the electrodes using some emery paper.

Place the electrodes in a beaker filled with sodium chloride solution.
Connect the electrodes to a power supply using crocodile clips and wires.
Turn the power supply on and allow the electrolysis to occur.
Bubbles of (hydrogen) gas will be seen at the cathode.
Bubbles of green (chlorine) gas will be seen at the anode.

6 a) Sodium sulfate solution contains hydrogen ions (as well as sodium ions) ***[1 mark]***. Sodium ions are more reactive than hydrogen ions ***[1 mark]***, so hydrogen gas is discharged at the cathode ***[1 mark]***.
b) oxygen ***[1 mark]*** and water ***[1 mark]***
c) Electrolysis of e.g. molten sodium sulfate / sodium chloride ***[1 mark]*** with inert electrodes ***[1 mark]***.

You get the first mark for any named sodium salt here, as long as you also remember to say that it must be molten.

7 a) The mass of cell A would be less than the mass of cell B after 1 hour ***[1 mark]***. In both cells, at the cathode copper ions gain electrons to become copper atoms: $Cu^{2+} + 2e^- \rightarrow Cu$ ***[1 mark]***. In cell A, at the anode, oxygen gas is formed: $4OH^- \rightarrow O_2 + 2H_2O + 4e^-$ ***[1 mark]***. Mass is lost from cell A as oxygen gas escapes from the system ***[1 mark]***. In cell B, at the anode, copper atoms lose electrons to become copper ions: $Cu \rightarrow Cu^{2+} + 2e^-$ ***[1 mark]***. The copper ions stay in the cell, so the mass of cell B stays constant ***[1 mark]***.
b) Similarity: any one from: e.g. both use copper sulfate solution as an electrolyte / both involve wires and a power supply ***[1 mark]***.
Difference: e.g. in the cell used to purify copper, the anode is an impure lump of copper / in the cell used to purify copper, a sludge of impurities will gather at the bottom (which will not be present in Cell B) ***[1 mark]***.

8 Cathode: $2H^+ + 2e^- \rightarrow H_2$
Anode: $4OH^- \rightarrow O_2 + H_2O + 4e^-$
[For <u>each</u> half-equation: 2 marks for all formulas correct and a correctly-balanced equation, otherwise 1 mark for correct formulas in an unbalanced equation.]

Topic 4 — Extracting Metals and Equilibria

Pages 50-51 — Reactivity Series and Reactivity of Metals

1 Oxidation can describe the addition of oxygen ***[1 mark]***. When a metal is burnt in air, the metal gains oxygen to form a metal oxide / an oxygen-containing products ***[1 mark]***.

2 a) sodium + water → sodium hydroxide + hydrogen ***[1 mark]***
b) Iron is more resistant to oxidation than sodium / it loses (its outer) electrons and forms positive ions less easily ***[1 mark]***.

You'd also get the mark here for saying that sodium is more easily oxidised than iron / loses its outer electrons and forms positive ions more easily.

3 a) i) $Ca_{(s)} + 2H_2O_{(l)} \rightarrow Ca(OH)_{2(aq)} + H_{2(g)}$
[1 mark for each correct product]
ii) Calcium is oxidised ***[1 mark]*** because it has gained oxygen ***[1 mark]***.
iii) E.g. lithium / sodium / potassium ***[1 mark]***. As it is higher in the reactivity series than calcium / loses electrons more easily than calcium / forms positive ions more easily ***[1 mark]***.
b) potassium, sodium, zinc ***[1 mark[***

4 A ***[1 mark]***

5 a) magnesium, zinc, iron, copper ***[1 mark]***
b) i) zinc oxide ***[1 mark]***
ii) Metal X was sodium, because it reacted vigorously with cold water ***[1 mark]***.

Page 52 — Displacement Reactions

1 Magnesium is oxidised / loses electrons to form magnesium ions ***[1 mark]*** and simultaneously iron ions are reduced / gain electrons to form iron metal ***[1 mark]***.

2 a) Yes, because lead can displace silver from a salt solution / silver cannot displace lead from a salt solution ***[1 mark]***.
b) $3Mg + 2AlCl_3 \rightarrow 2Al + 3MgCl_2$
[2 marks for all formulas correct and a correctly balanced equation, otherwise 1 mark for correct formulas in an unbalanced equation]
c) The solution would change colour from colourless to green ***[1 mark]***. The piece of shiny grey nickel will be coated in dull grey lead ***[1 mark]***.

Page 53 — Extracting Metals Using Carbon

1 a) A metal ore is a rock which contains enough metal to make it economically worthwhile extracting the metal from it ***[1 mark]***.
b) Copper can be extracted from its ore by reduction with carbon ***[1 mark]***.
c) tin / zinc ***[1 mark]***

2 a) $2Fe_2O_3 + 3C \rightarrow 4Fe + 3CO_2$
[1 mark for correct equation, 1 mark for correct balancing]
b) The impurity is zinc ***[1 mark]***. Zinc is lower than carbon in the reactivity series/less reactive than carbon ***[1 mark]***, so the zinc oxide in the iron ore would also be reduced by carbon to zinc metal in the blast furnace ***[1 mark]***.

Calcium is more reactive than carbon so the calcium in calcium oxide wouldn't be reduced to calcium metal in the blast furnace.

Page 54 — Other Methods of Extracting Metals

1 a) electrolysis ***[1 mark]***
b) To lower the melting point of the electrolyte / ore ***[1 mark]***.
c) E.g. to carry out electrolysis, you need large amounts of electricity, which is expensive ***[1 mark]***. There are also costs associated with dissolving aluminium in cryolite ***[1 mark]***.

2 a) Plants are grown in soil containing metal compounds, which they absorb (via their roots) ***[1 mark]***. The plants can neither use nor dispose of the metals, so they accumulate in the leaves ***[1 mark]***. The plants are harvested, dried and burned in a furnace ***[1 mark]***. Metals can be extracted from metal compounds in the ash using electrolysis or displacement reactions ***[1 mark]***.
b) Advantage: e.g. less damaging to the environment than traditional methods ***[1 mark]***.
Disadvantage: e.g. process is very slow ***[1 mark]***.
c) E.g. bioleaching / bacterial methods ***[1 mark]***.

Page 55 — Recycling

1 a) E.g. takes up space / pollutes surroundings / doesn't preserve materials ***[1 mark]***.
b) Any two from: e.g. often uses less energy / conserves the amount of raw materials in the Earth
[1 mark for each correct answer].
c) Any two from: e.g. recycling often uses less energy than extracting materials, so it costs less / recycling creates jobs
[1 mark for each correct answer].

2 a) Material B. Only a small amount of energy is needed to recycle it whereas a lot of energy is needed to extract it ***[1 mark]***. Material B also has limited availability, so in the long term it may run out if it is not recycled ***[1 mark]***.
b) Crude oil is a non-renewable resource so it is important to conserve it ***[1 mark]***.

Pages 56-58 — Life Cycle Assessments

Warm-up
Recyclability of the product, Source of raw materials

1 a) A life cycle assessment looks at each stage of the life of a product to work out the potential environmental impact at each stage ***[1 mark]***.
b) Timber is the better choice. Timber comes from trees, which are renewable, so it is sustainable ***[1 mark]***. Polypropene comes from crude oil, which is non-renewable, and so is not sustainable ***[1 mark]***. Also, extracting timber from trees uses less energy than making polypropene, so extracting timber uses less fuel / creates less pollution ***[1 mark]***.

You don't need to consider cost when thinking about sustainability, you just need to think about how using a material might affect the environment.

c) Any two from: e.g. how much waste is produced by each process / how much pollution each process would produce / how long chairs made from each type of material would last / how much water each process uses / how easy each type of chair would be to dispose of sustainably at the end of their usable life ***[1 mark for each correct answer]***.

2 a) Any two from: e.g. extracting iron from its ore uses a lot of energy / extracting iron from its ore creates pollution / mining iron ore can damage the environment that it is taken from ***[1 mark for each correct answer]***.

b) E.g. landfill takes up limited space / generates pollution / prevents resources from being reused/recycled ***[1 mark]***.

c) E.g. by recycling it ***[1 mark]***.

3 E.g. toy A has the highest CO_2 emissions, solvent use and energy consumption, so toy A would have the highest environmental impact ***[1 mark]***. Toy B has the second lowest CO_2 emissions and the second lowest solvent use, but uses the second highest amount of energy, so it would have a medium impact / a higher impact than D, but a lower impact than A or C ***[1 mark]***. Toy C has the second highest CO_2 emissions and solvent use, but the lowest energy consumption, so would have a medium impact / a lower impact than A, but a higher impact than B or D ***[1 mark]***. Toy D has the lowest CO_2 emissions, the lowest solvent use and the second lowest energy consumption, so would have the lowest environmental impact ***[1 mark]***.

4 a) E.g. glass bottles can be reused multiple times, but cans are usually only used once ***[1 mark]***.

b) E.g. it would be more positive as the raw material would be recycled cans rather than aluminium ore ***[1 mark]***. Using recycled cans would save energy and would produce a lower amount of greenhouse gases than extracting aluminium from ore ***[1 mark]***.

You could also mention that it would preserve the supply of valuable raw materials, or that it would eliminate the environmental problems associated with mining.

c) The glass bottles have to be separated from the rest of the glass objects before they can be recycled ***[1 mark]***, which could lead to more waste if some batches are contaminated ***[1 mark]***.

d) Any one from: e.g. how likely they are to be recycled / how easy it is to recycle them / the environmental costs of disposal if they are sent to landfill / their biodegradability ***[1 mark]***

Page 59 — Dynamic Equilibrium

Warm-up

The Haber Process is **a reversible** reaction that forms **ammonia** from hydrogen and nitrogen. The nitrogen used in the process is extracted from **the air** and the hydrogen is extracted from **natural gas**.
The conditions used for the Haber Process are a temperature of **450 °C**, a pressure of **200 atm** and in the presence of an **iron** catalyst.

1 a) At dynamic equilibrium, the rates of the forward and the backward reaction are equal/the same ***[1 mark]*** and the relative concentrations of the reactants and products at equilibrium do not change ***[1 mark]***.

b) A closed system is a system where none of the reactants or products can escape ***[1 mark]***.

c) The concentration of the reactants should be increased ***[1 mark]***.

2 a) That the reaction is reversible / can go both ways ***[1 mark]***.

b) The system has reached equilibrium ***[1 mark]***. This mixture contains both blue copper(II) ions and the yellow copper compound, so the colours mix to form green ***[1 mark]***.

Pages 60-62 — Le Chatelier's Principle

1 a) The system will try to counteract that change ***[1 mark]***.

b) The temperature ***[1 mark]*** and the concentration of the reactants / products ***[1 mark]***.

2 a) The concentration of the products is greater than the concentration of the reactants ***[1 mark]***.

b) D ***[1 mark]***

c) Russell. Decreasing the pressure will move the position of equilibrium to the left / to the side with more moles of gas / favour the backward reaction ***[1 mark]***. This will decrease the yield of methanol ***[1 mark]***.

3 a) At higher temperatures there will be more ICl and less ICl_3 ***[1 mark]***. This is because the reverse reaction is endothermic, so heating the mixture moves the equilibrium to the left ***[1 mark]***.

b) There would be more ICl_3 and less ICl ***[1 mark]*** because the increase in pressure causes the equilibrium position to move to the side with the fewest molecules of gas ***[1 mark]***.

4 a) At higher temperature there's more product / (brown) NO_2 in the equilibrium mixture ***[1 mark]***. This suggests that the equilibrium has moved to the right ***[1 mark]***, so the forward reaction is endothermic ***[1 mark]***.

From Le Chatelier's principle, you know that increasing the temperature will favour the endothermic reaction (since the equilibrium position will move to oppose the change). So the forward reaction must be endothermic, as there's more NO_2 in the equilibrium mixture at higher temperatures.

b) The mixture would go a darker brown ***[1 mark]***, as the decrease in pressure causes the equilibrium to move to the side with the most molecules of gas ***[1 mark]***, meaning more NO_2 is formed ***[1 mark]***.

5 a) At time A, some of the sulfur trioxide was removed from the reaction, lowering the concentration present ***[1 mark]***. As the reaction continued, more sulfur trioxide was produced, increasing the concentration present in the reaction ***[1 mark]***.

b) The forward reaction must be exothermic ***[1 mark]***, as the equilibrium shifts to favour the reverse reaction in order to lower the temperature of the reaction ***[1 mark]***.

c) At time B, the pressure of the system was increased ***[1 mark]***. The graph shows the concentration of SO_3 increasing and the concentration of SO_2 decreasing after this point, so the equilibrium has shifted in the direction of the side with fewer gas molecules ***[1 mark]***.

d)

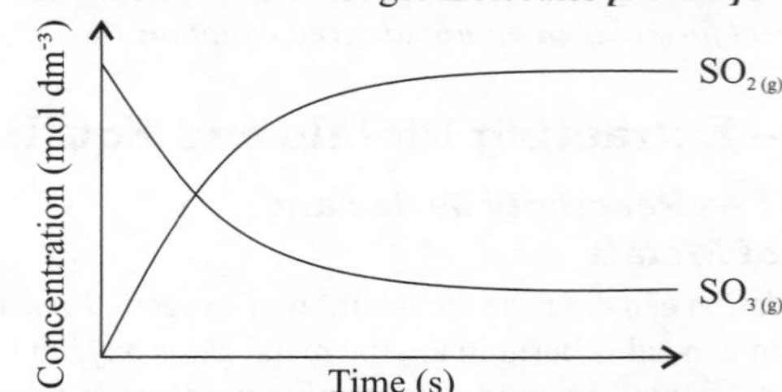

[1 mark for the correct curves, 1 mark for the correct labels]

At low pressure, the equilibrium will move towards the side of the reaction that has more molecules of gas (i.e. the products).

Topic 5 — Separate Chemistry 1

Page 63 — Transition Metals

Warm-up

The elements that should be circled are: nickel, chromium, silver, titanium and cobalt.

1 a) E.g. transition metals have high melting points ***[1 mark for any correct property related to the given use]***.

b) E.g. transition metals have high densities ***[1 mark for any correct property related to the given use]***.

c) E.g. transition metals have colourful compounds ***[1 mark for any correct property related to the given use]***.

d) E.g. transition metals are unreactive/resistant to corrosion ***[1 mark for any correct property related to the given use]***.

If you didn't give the properties shown here, you still get a mark for any property of a transition metal that's clearly connected to the use. For example, if you wrote 'malleable' for d), you'd get the mark, because you need to be able to shape a material easily if you're making it into pipes.

2 a) Vanadium is acting as a catalyst ***[1 mark]***.

b) You would expect the deep blue powder to be vanadium(IV) oxide, because transition metal compounds are usually colourful ***[1 mark]***.

Page 64 — Alloys

1 a) Metallic structures have layers of atoms/ions ***[1 mark]*** that are able to slide over one another ***[1 mark]***.

b) Atoms of different elements are different sizes ***[1 mark]***. Adding atoms of a different size to a pure metal distorts the layers ***[1 mark]*** making it harder for them to slide over one another ***[1 mark]***.

2 a) As you increase the carbon content, the strength increases ***[1 mark]***

b) Alloy 3 / high carbon steel ***[1 mark]***

c) Alloy 4 / the aluminium alloy is much less dense than the other alloys ***[1 mark]***.

Page 65 — Corrosion

1 E.g. electroplating an object protects it from corrosion / improves the appearance of the object.
[1 mark for each sensible reason.]

2 a) In order for iron to rust, both oxygen and water are needed ***[1 mark]***. If Joe's bike is kept inside, it is less likely rust as it is less likely to come into contact with water ***[1 mark]***.

b) The oil keeps oxygen and water off the chain ***[1 mark]***, but still allows the chain to run smoothly ***[1 mark]***.

3 a) Sacrificial protection involves attaching a metal that is more reactive than steel to the ship ***[1 mark]***. The more reactive metal will lose electrons/be oxidised more easily than steel ***[1 mark]***, so it will corrode instead of the steel ***[1 mark]***.

b) No, the zinc layer acts as sacrificial protection as well as a barrier / the zinc is more reactive than iron ***[1 mark]*** so it will lose electrons in preference to iron, even if it's scratched ***[1 mark]***.

Pages 66-68 — Titrations

1 a) Mean titre = (33.30 + 33.40 + 33.35) ÷ 3 = **33.35 cm^3**
[2 marks for correct answer, otherwise 1 mark for attempting to calculate mean using values 2, 3 and 4.]

Result 1 is anomalous, so you should ignore it when you calculate the mean.

b) Moles = concentration × volume
Moles of HCl = 0.165 × (33.35 ÷ 1000)
= 0.00550275 = **0.00550 mol**
[2 marks for correct answer, but deduct 1 mark if answer is not given to 3 s.f.. Otherwise 1 mark for a correct expression for finding the number of moles of HCl.]

Even if your answer to part a) was incorrect, you would still get the marks for part b) if you carried out the calculation correctly.

2 a) Moles = concentration × volume
Moles of NaOH = 0.100 × (40.0 ÷ 1000) = 0.00400 mol
1 mole of NaOH reacts with 1 mole of HCl.
So, 0.00400 mol NaOH reacts with 0.00400 mol HCl.
Concentration of HCl = 0.00400 ÷ (20 ÷ 1000)
= **0.200 mol dm^{-3}**
[3 marks for correct answer, otherwise 1 mark for a correct expression for the number of moles of NaOH and 1 mark for a correct expression for the number of moles of HCl.]

b) M_r (HCl) = 35.5 + 1 = 36.5
Concentration (g dm^{-3}) = concentration (mol dm^{-3}) × M_r
Concentration = 0.200 × 36.5 = **7.30 g dm^{-3}** ***[2 marks for correct answer, otherwise 1 mark for correct M_r of HCl.]***

If you got the wrong answer in part a) but carried out the correct calculations in part b), you'd still get the marks.

3 a) i) Student A's results are more precise ***[1 mark]*** because their data is less spread out than Student B's data ***[1 mark]***.

ii) Student B's results are more accurate ***[1 mark]*** because they produce a calculated concentration closer to the true concentration of the solution ***[1 mark]***.

b) The volume of calcium hydroxide solution required to neutralise the acid would decrease by half ***[1 mark]***.

c) phenol red ***[1 mark]***

4 From the balanced equation, 2 moles of KOH reacts with 1 mole of H_2SO_4. So, 0.00850 mol KOH must have reacted with 0.00425 mol H_2SO_4.
Concentration = moles ÷ volume
Concentration of H_2SO_4 = 0.00425 ÷ 0.0250
= 0.170 mol dm^{-3}
Concentration (g dm^{-3}) = concentration (mol dm^{-3}) × M_r
= 0.170 × 98 = 16.66 = **16.7 g dm^{-3}**
[3 marks for correct answer, otherwise 1 mark for finding the moles of H_2SO_4 and 1 mark for finding the concentration of H_2SO_4 in mol dm^{-3}.]

5 a) How to grade your answer:

Level 0: There is no relevant information. ***[No marks]***

Level 1: There is a brief explanation of how to carry a titration but it has limited detail and little technical equipment is mentioned. The points made are basic and not linked together. ***[1 to 2 marks]***

Level 2: There is an explanation of how to carry out a titration and some of the equipment required is named, but there are limited details. Some of the points made are linked together. ***[3 to 4 marks]***

Level 3: There is a clear and detailed explanation of how to carry out a titration and all the equipment needed is clearly named. The points made are well-linked and the answer has a clear and logical structure. ***[5 to 6 marks]***

Here are some points your answer may include:
Measure out a known volume of the sodium hydroxide solution using a pipette and put it in a conical flask.
Add a few drops of a suitable indicator (e.g. phenolphthalein or methyl orange) to the sodium hydroxide.
Stand the flask on a white tile, to make the colour changes easier to see.
Use a burette to add the sulfuric acid to the sodium hydroxide, swirling the conical flask regularly.
Stop the titration when the indicator changes colour — this is when the sodium hydroxide is completely neutralised.
Record the volume of sulfuric acid required to cause this colour change.
Repeat the titration with the same volume of sodium hydroxide solution, but add the acid one drop at a time, close to the end point.
Record the exact volume of sulfuric acid required to neutralise the sodium hydroxide.
Repeat the titration several times until there are at least three concordant titres.

b) Moles = concentration × volume
Moles of H_2SO_4 = 0.200 × (22.5 ÷ 1000) = 0.00450 moles
1 mole of H_2SO_4 reacts with 2 moles of NaOH.
So, 0.00450 moles of H_2SO_4 reacts with (0.00450 × 2)
= 0.00900 moles of NaOH
Concentration of NaOH = 0.00900 ÷ (25.0 ÷ 1000)
= **0.360 mol dm^{-3}**
[4 marks for correct answer, otherwise 1 mark for a correct expression for finding the number of moles of NaOH, 1 mark for a correct expression for finding the number of moles of H_2SO_4 and 1 mark for using the fact that 1 mole of H_2SO_4 reacts with 2 moles of NaOH.]

Pages 69-70 — Percentage Yield

1 a) C ***[1 mark]***

b) Percentage yield = (22 ÷ 25) × 100 = **88%**
[3 marks for correct answer, otherwise 1 mark for dividing the actual yield by the theoretical yield and 1 mark for multiplying the result by 100.]

2 a) $M_r(CuSO_4) = 63.5 + 32 + (4 \times 16) = 159.5$
$M_r(Cu(OH)_2) = 63.5 + [2 \times (16 + 1)] = 97.5$
Moles of $CuSO_4$ = mass ÷ $M_r(CuSO_4)$
= 39.75 ÷ 159.5 = 0.2492... mol
1 mole of $CuSO_4$ produces 1 mole of $Cu(OH)_2$, so 0.2492... moles of $CuSO_4$ should produce 0.2492... moles of $Cu(OH)_2$.
Theoretical yield = 0.2492... × 97.5 = 24.298... = **24.3 g**
[3 marks for correct answer, but deduct 1 mark if answer is not given to 3 s.f.. Otherwise 1 mark for correct moles of $CuSO_4$ and 1 mark for correct moles of $Cu(OH)_2$.]

b) Percentage yield = (16.5 ÷ 24.3) × 100 = 67.901... = **67.9%**
[3 marks for correct answer, but deduct 1 mark if answer is not given to 3 s.f.. Otherwise 1 mark for dividing actual yield by theoretical yield and 1 mark for multiplying by 100.]

If your answer to part a) was incorrect, you'd still get full marks in part b) if you used that answer but did everything else right.

3 $M_r(MgCO_3) = 24 + 12 + (3 \times 16) = 84$
$M_r(MgO) = 24 + 16 = 40$
Mass of $MgCO_3$ in g = 44.10 × 1000 = 44 100 g
Moles = mass ÷ M_r
Moles ($MgCO_3$) = 44 100 ÷ 84 = 525 mol
1 mole of $MgCO_3$ produces 1 mole of MgO.
So 525 moles of $MgCO_3$ should produce 525 moles of MgO.
Theoretical yield = 525 × 40 = 21 000 g = 21.00 kg
Percentage yield = (15.75 ÷ 21.00) × 100 = **75%**
[6 marks for correct answer, otherwise 1 mark for correct moles of $MgCO_3$, 1 mark for correct moles of MgO, 1 mark for finding the theoretical yield of MgO, 1 mark for dividing actual yield by theoretical yield and 1 mark for multiplying by 100.]

4 a) $M_r(N_2) = 2 \times 14 = 28$. $M_r(NH_3) = 14 + (3 \times 1) = 17$.
Mass of N_2 in g = 14 × 1000 = 14 000 g
Moles = mass ÷ M_r
Moles (N_2) = 14 000 ÷ 28 = 500 mol
1 mole of N_2 produces 2 moles of NH_3.
500 moles of N_2 should produce 2 × 500 = 1000 mol of NH_3.
Theoretical yield = moles × M_r = 1000 × 17
= 17 000 g = 17 kg
Percentage yield = (4.5 kg ÷ 17 kg) × 100 = **26%**
[6 marks for correct answer, otherwise 1 mark for correct number of moles of N_2, 1 mark for correct number of moles of NH_3, 1 mark for calculating the theoretical yield of NH_3, 1 mark for dividing actual yield by theoretical yield and 1 mark for multiplying by 100.]

b) Any two from: e.g. the reaction is reversible so may not have gone to completion / products may have been lost during the reaction / there may have been other unwanted reactions ***[1 mark for each correct answer]***.

c) Any two from: e.g. to reduce waste / increase sustainability / to reduce cost ***[1 mark for each correct answer]***.

Pages 71-73 — Atom Economy

Warm-up

Reaction	Atom economy (%)
$NaOH + HCl \rightarrow NaCl + H_2O$	**76.5**
$2Cu + O_2 \rightarrow 2CuO$	**100**

Atom economy of first reaction = (58.5 ÷ 76.5) × 100 = 76.5%
Atom economy of second reaction = (159 ÷ 159) × 100 = 100%

1 a) i) The percentage of the mass of the reactants in a reaction that gets turned into the desired product ***[1 mark]***.

ii) Atom economy = (111 ÷ 141) × 100 = **78.7%**
[3 marks for the correct answer, but deduct 1 mark if answer is not given to 3 s.f.. Otherwise 1 mark for dividing 111 by 141 and 1 mark for multiplying by 100.]

b) Reaction A. It has 100% atom economy so all of the reactants are turned into a useful product ***[1 mark]***. It also has the highest percentage yield, so it should waste the least reactants ***[1 mark]***. It has the second highest rate of reaction, so it produces the required amount of product in a sensible length of time ***[1 mark]***.

2 a) i) $M_r(MgCl_2) = [24 + (2 \times 35.5)] =$ **95** ***[1 mark]***

ii) M_r of desired product = $M_r(MgCl_2) = 95$
M_r of all products = $M_r(MgCl_2) + M_r(H_2)$
= 95 + (2 × 1) = 95 + 2 = **97**
Atom economy = (95 ÷ 97) × 100 = **98%**
[4 marks for correct answer, but deduct 1 mark if answer is not given to 2 s.f.. Otherwise 1 mark for correct M_r of all products, 1 mark for dividing M_r of desired product by M_r of all products and 1 mark for multiplying by 100.]

iii) M_r of desired product = $M_r(MgCl_2) = 95$
M_r of all products = $M_r(MgCl_2) + M_r(H_2O) + M_r(CO_2)$
= 95 + [(2 × 1) + 16] + [12 + (2 × 16)]
= 95 + 18 + 44 = **157**
Atom economy = (95 ÷ 157) × 100 = **61%**
[4 marks for correct answer, but deduct 1 mark if answer is not given to 2 s.f.. Otherwise 1 mark for correct M_r of all products, 1 mark for dividing M_r of desired product by M_r of all products and 1 mark for multiplying by 100.]

iv) M_r of desired product = $M_r(MgCl_2) = 95$
M_r of all products = $M_r(MgCl_2) + M_r(H_2O)$
= 95 + [(2 × 1) + 16] = 95 + 18 = **113**
Atom economy = (95 ÷ 113) × 100 = **84%**
[4 marks for correct answer, but deduct 1 mark if answer is not given to 2 s.f.. Otherwise 1 mark for correct M_r of all products, 1 mark for dividing M_r of desired product by M_r of all products and 1 mark for multiplying by 100.]

b) i) Reactions with low atom economies use more raw materials to produce a certain amount of product, as less of the reactants are converted to useful products ***[1 mark]***.

ii) Reactions with low atom economies produce more waste materials as more reactants are converted into by-products ***[1 mark]***. The more waste products you need to dispose of, the higher the cost will be ***[1 mark]***.

c) reaction Y ***[1 mark]***

3 a) The final step re-uses products from earlier steps ***[1 mark]*** to re-form some of the reactants from the second step in the process ***[1 mark]***. This eliminates reactants and undesired products from the overall equation, so a higher proportion of atoms in the reactants go into the product ***[1 mark]***.

b) Any two from: e.g. the limestone may not have been pure calcium carbonate / the calcium carbonate in the middle of larger chips may not have decomposed / the student may not have heated the limestone to a high enough temperature / the student may not have heated the limestone for a long enough time ***[2 marks — 1 mark for each correct answer]***.

c) E.g. the Solvay process has a higher atom economy than the Leblanc process, which means that the Solvay process is greener as a higher proportion of the reactants are converted into products. / The Solvay process requires fewer reactants, which makes it cheaper and easier to run. / The Solvay process only produces one by-product compared to three from the Leblanc process, which means that the waste is likely easier to deal with. / The Leblanc process uses sulfuric acid, which is corrosive, compared to the reactants of the Solvay process which are less dangerous
[3 marks — 1 mark for each correct point].

Pages 74-75 — The Haber Process

1 a) Equilibrium will be reached more quickly ***[1 mark]***.

b) Equilibrium will be reached more slowly ***[1 mark]***.

2 a) i) A ***[1 mark]***

ii) Disagree. The forward reaction is exothermic, so increasing the temperature moves the equilibrium position towards the reactants ***[1 mark]***. This reduces the yield of ammonia ***[1 mark]***.

b) E.g. using a low pressure will decrease the rate of reaction. / Using a low pressure will reduce the yield of ammonia.
[1 mark for each correct reason]

c) i) The catalyst increases the rate of reaction ***[1 mark]***.

ii) The catalyst has no effect on the yield ***[1 mark]***.

3 a) Line C *[1 mark]*. E.g. the initial slope of the graph is steeper because increasing the temperature will increase the rate of reaction *[1 mark]*.

You could also give the reason that the Haber Process has a low yield at higher temperatures.

b) E.g. the initial slope of line A is shallower than line B *[1 mark]*, which shows that reaction A reaches equilibrium more slowly than reaction B *[1 mark]*. The height of line C is lower than line B *[1 mark]*, which shows that reaction C produces less product than reaction B *[1 mark]*.

c) E.g. recycling the reactants means that eventually all of the reactants will be converted into ammonia *[1 mark]*. This means that unused reactants aren't wasted *[1 mark]*.

Page 76 — Fertilisers

Warm-up

Fertilisers are made from compounds containing the elements nitrogen, **potassium** and **phosphorus**, which are essential for plant growth. The salt **ammonium** nitrate is a fertiliser which can be made by reacting ammonia with **nitric acid**.

If you put potassium and phosphorus the other way round, your answer would still be correct.

1 a) i) burette *[1 mark]*

ii) e.g. methyl orange *[1 mark]*

b) The student should have noted exactly how much ammonia it took to neutralise the sulfuric acid *[1 mark]*, then repeated the titration with the same volume of acid and alkali but without adding indicator *[1 mark]*.

c) Any one from: e.g. it is not practical to use the titration method for large, industrial quantities / crystallisation is a slow process *[1 mark]*.

2 Ammonia produced using the Haber process is used to make many fertilisers *[1 mark]*. Fertilisers allow farmers to increase crop yields by helping plants to grow bigger and faster *[1 mark]*. Without the Haber process we wouldn't have enough ammonia to make the fertilisers that allow farms to produce enough food to feed everyone *[1 mark]*.

Pages 77-78 — Calculations with Gases

1 a) 1 mole occupies 24 dm^3 at room temperature and pressure, so volume of 23.0 moles = 23.0 × 24 = **552 dm^3** *[1 mark]*

b) Moles of SO_2 = 96 ÷ 64 = 1.5 mol

Volume of SO_2 = 1.5 × 24 = **36 dm^3**

[2 marks for correct answer, otherwise 1 mark for using the correct formula to calculate volume.]

2 a) $M_r(C_2H_6)$ = (2 × 12) + (6 × 1) = 24 + 6 = 30

Moles of ethane = 7.5 ÷ 30 = 0.25 mol

Volume of ethane = 0.25 × 24 = **6 dm^3**

[3 marks for correct answer, otherwise 1 mark for M_r of ethane, 1 mark for using the correct formula to calculate the volume.]

b) Molar ratio of ethane : carbon dioxide = 1:2

Volume of carbon dioxide = 6 × 2 = **12 dm^3** ***[2 marks for correct answer, otherwise 1 mark for 1:2 molar ratio.]***

3 a) $M_r(CO_2)$ = 12 + (2 × 16) = 44

Moles = mass ÷ M_r = 1.76 ÷ 44 = 0.040 mol

920 cm^3 = (920 ÷ 1000) dm^3 = 0.92 dm^3

Molar volume = volume ÷ moles = 0.92 ÷ 0.040 = **23 dm^3 mol^{-1}**

[2 marks for correct answer, otherwise 1 mark for correct moles of CO_2.]

b) 175 cm^3 = (175 ÷ 1000) dm^3 = 0.175 dm^3

Moles = volume ÷ molar volume = 0.175 ÷ 25.0 = 0.00700 mol

From a), $M_r(CO_2)$ = 44

Mass = M_r × moles = 44 × 0.00700 = **0.31 g**

[2 marks for correct answer, otherwise 1 mark for correct moles of CO_2.]

4 a) $M_r(CO)$ = 12 + 16 = 28

Volume of carbon monoxide = (28 ÷ 28) × 24 = 24 dm^3

Molar ratio of carbon monoxide : oxygen = 2:1

So volume of oxygen = 24 ÷ 2 = **12 dm^3**

[4 marks for correct answer, otherwise 1 mark for using the correct formula to calculate the volume, 1 mark for correct volume of carbon monoxide and 1 mark for 2:1 molar ratio.]

b) 24 dm^3 *[1 mark]*

This is a classic example of a question that's simpler than it first looks — the molar ratio of CO : O_2 : CO_2 in the equation is 1 : 2 : 1, so you must have the same volume of CO_2 as CO (or twice the volume of O_2, if you prefer).

Page 79 — Fuel Cells

1 a) A fuel cell is an electrical cell that is supplied with a fuel and oxygen *[1 mark]* and uses energy from the reaction between them to produce electrical energy *[1 mark]*.

b) B *[1 mark]*

2 a) Internal combustion engines produce pollutants (e.g. carbon dioxide, sulfur dioxide, nitrogen oxides, carbon monoxide) *[1 mark]* but hydrogen-oxygen fuel cells only produce water *[1 mark]*.

b) The hydrogen used in fuel cells is usually produced either from hydrocarbons which come from fossil fuels *[1 mark]*, or from electrolysis of water, which uses electricity that is often generated by burning fossil fuels *[1 mark]*.

c) E.g. hydrogen is a gas, so it takes more space to store than petrol. / Hydrogen is explosive so it's difficult to store safely *[1 mark for any sensible disadvantage]*.

Topic 6 — Groups in the Periodic Table

Page 80 — Group 1 — Alkali Metals

1 a) B *[1 mark]*

b) The alkali metals all have one outer electron *[1 mark]*, so losing one electron gives them a +1 ion with a stable electronic structure/full outer shell *[1 mark]*.

2 a) potassium hydroxide *[1 mark]*, hydrogen *[1 mark]*

b) Any two from: it would float around on the surface of the water / vigorous fizzing / it would decrease in size (as it melts and dissolves) / hydrogen gas produced by the reaction will ignite *[1 mark for each correct answer]*.

c) Rubidium is more reactive than potassium *[1 mark]* because the outer electron is further away from the nucleus / the atomic radius is larger *[1 mark]*. So, rubidium will react more violently with water than potassium / may explode when placed in water *[1 mark]*.

Pages 81-82 — Group 7 — Halogens

Warm-up

They are non-metals that exist as molecules of two atoms.

1 a) damp blue litmus paper *[1 mark]*

b) chlorine *[1 mark]*

2 a) i) sodium bromide *[1 mark]*

ii) potassium iodide *[1 mark]*

b) $2Li + Cl_2 \rightarrow 2LiCl$

[2 marks for all formulas correct and a correctly-balanced equation, otherwise 1 mark for correct formulas in an unbalanced equation.]

3 a) i) $H_2 + Cl_2 \rightarrow 2HCl$

[2 marks for all formulas correct and a correctly-balanced equation, otherwise 1 mark for correct formulas in an unbalanced equation.]

ii) red *[1 mark]* A hydrogen halide/hydrogen chloride forms an acidic solution when dissolved in water *[1 mark]*.

b) Fluorine *[1 mark]*. It is the only other halogen that is a gas at room temperature *[1 mark]*.

c) A red-brown *[1 mark]* liquid *[1 mark]*.

4 a) The halogens have seven electrons in their outer shell *[1 mark]*. As you go further down the group additional shells are added / the outer electron is further away from the nucleus *[1 mark]*.

b) Both astatine and fluorine have 7 outer shell electrons so react in a similar way *[1 mark]*. So astatine will react with sodium to form sodium astatide *[1 mark]*. However, astatine will react more slowly than fluorine since reactivity decreases down the group *[1 mark]*.

Page 83 — Halogen Displacement Reactions

1 a) chlorine water and sodium iodide solution:
solution turns brown *[1 mark]*
bromine water and sodium bromide solution:
no reaction *[1 mark]*

b) Iodine is less reactive than bromine *[1 mark]*, so iodine cannot displace bromine from sodium bromide *[1 mark]*.

c) i) $Cl_2 + 2NaBr \rightarrow Br_2 + 2NaCl$
[1 mark for all reactants and products correct, 1 mark for equation being correctly balanced.]

ii) During the reaction, the chlorine is reduced (it gains electrons) *[1 mark]* and the bromide ions are simultaneously oxidised (they lose electrons) *[1 mark]*.

d) Yes *[1 mark]*, as chlorine is more reactive than astatine *[1 mark]*.

Page 84 — Group 0 — Noble Gases

1 Argon has a full outer shell of electrons, giving it a stable electronic structure *[1 mark]*. It won't easily give up or gain electrons, making it inert *[1 mark]*. This means that it won't react with the metal filament in the light bulb *[1 mark]*.

2 a) i) A boiling point higher than –152 °C *[1 mark]*.

ii) A density between 1.0 kg m^{-3} and 3.6 kg m^{-3} *[1 mark]*.

b) Higher, because the boiling points of the elements increase as you go down Group 0 *[1 mark]*.

Topic 7 — Rates of Reaction and Energy Changes

Pages 85–87 — Reaction Rate Experiments

1 a) Add the calcium carbonate to the hydrochloric acid in a conical flask and seal with a gas syringe *[1 mark]*. Immediately start the stopwatch and use the gas syringe to measure the volume of carbon dioxide produced *[1 mark]* at set time intervals until gas production stops *[1 mark]*.

b) E.g.

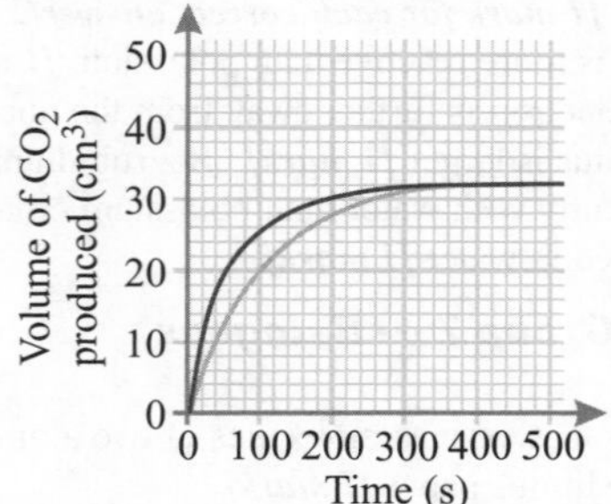

[1 mark for your curve having a steeper gradient at the start. 1 mark for your curve finishing at the same volume of CO_2 as the original curve.]

c) B *[1 mark]*

2 a) Remove the two solutions from the water bath and immediately mix the solutions in a conical flask *[1 mark]*. Place the flask over a black mark on a piece of paper *[1 mark]* and time how long it takes for the black mark to disappear through the sulfur precipitate *[1 mark]*.

b) i) The reaction will have a lower rate *[1 mark]*.

ii) E.g. the concentration of the acid/sodium thiosulfate / the volume of acid/sodium thiosulfate used / the depth of the acid/sodium thiosulfate ***[1 mark for any sensible answer]***.

3 a) The higher the concentration, the faster the rate of reaction *[1 mark]*. Reaction M has a curve of a steeper gradient / the reaction finishes sooner, which signifies a greater rate and so a higher concentration *[1 mark]*.

b)

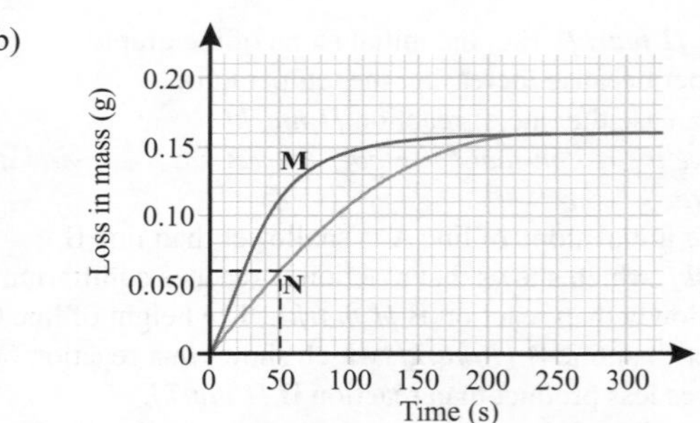

change in y = 0.060 change in x = 50
Gradient = change in y ÷ change in x
= 0.060 ÷ 50 = **0.0012 g s^{-1}**
[2 marks for correct answer, otherwise 1 mark for a correct equation to calculate the gradient.]

4 a) i) Draw a tangent to curve **Q** at 50 s, e.g.:

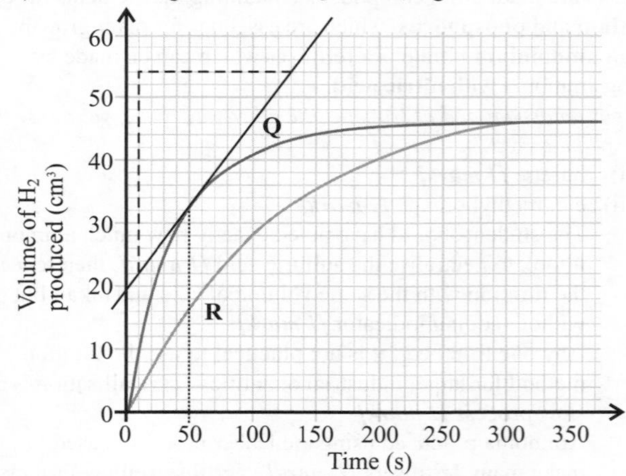

Then calculate the gradient of your tangent, e.g.:
Change in y = 54 – 22 = 32
Change in x = 130 – 10 = 120
Gradient = change in y ÷ change in x = 32 ÷ 120
= **0.27 cm^3 s^{-1}**
[Accept answers between 0.22 cm^3 s^{-1} and 0.32 cm^3 s^{-1}. 3 marks for a correct answer given to 2 significant figures, but deduct 1 mark if not given to 2 significant figures. Otherwise 1 mark for drawing a correct tangent and 1 mark for using the correct equation to calculate the gradient.]

It's OK if you've drawn your tangent slightly differently to this one, or if you've used a different bit of the tangent to calculate the gradient. As long as your tangent's sensible and your final answer is in the range given, you'll get the marks.

ii) Draw a tangent to curve **R** at 120 s, e.g.:

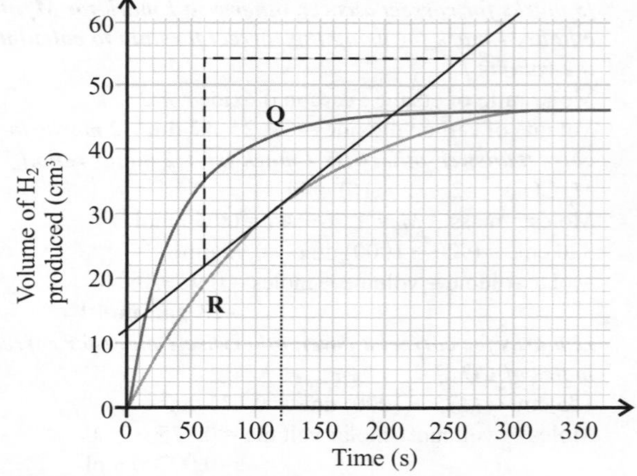

Then calculate the gradient of your tangent, e.g.:
Change in y = 54 – 22 = 32
Change in x = 260 – 60 = 200
Gradient = change in y ÷ change in x = 32 ÷ 200
= **0.16 cm^3 s^{-1}**

[Accept answers between 0.11 cm³ s⁻¹ and 0.21 cm³ s⁻¹. 3 marks for correct answer given to 2 s.f., but deduct 1 mark if not given to 2 s.f.. Otherwise 1 mark for drawing a correct tangent and 1 mark for using the correct equation to calculate the gradient.]

The same thing applies to the second tangent and calculation too...

b) Reaction Q must used powdered zinc. Powdered zinc has a larger surface area to volume ration than zinc ribbon ***[1 mark]***, so the rate of reaction would be higher for powdered zinc than for zinc ribbon ***[1 mark]***. The line for reaction Q has a steeper gradient / finishes sooner than the line for reaction R, so it must have a higher rate ***[1 mark]***.

Pages 88–89 — Collision Theory

Warm-up

C

1 a) C ***[1 mark]***

b) activation energy ***[1 mark]***

2 Smaller pieces have a higher surface area to volume ratio ***[1 mark]***. So for the same volume of metal, the particles around it will have more area to work on and collisions will be more frequent ***[1 mark]***.

3 a) Increase the pressure ***[1 mark]***.

b) Increasing the pressure means that the particles are more crowded/there are more particles in a given volume ***[1 mark]***. This will increase the frequency of successful collisions between particles, so the rate will increase too ***[1 mark]***.

4 a) Horatio is incorrect. Increasing the temperature to 45 °C will cause the particles to move faster which results in more frequent collisions ***[1 mark]***. Higher temperatures also increase the energy of collisions which means more collisions will be successful ***[1 mark]***. So, the reaction will have a higher rate at the higher temperature ***[1 mark]***.

b) i) A ***[1 mark]***

ii) It has the lowest concentration ***[1 mark]*** so there are less particles of hydrochloric acid in the same volume, so collisions are less frequent ***[1 mark]***.

Page 90 — Catalysts

1 a) C ***[1 mark]***

b) E.g. in the fermentation process that is used to produce alcoholic drinks ***[1 mark]***.

2 a) The catalyst decreases the activation energy needed for the reaction to occur ***[1 mark]*** by providing an alternative reaction pathway that has a lower activation energy ***[1 mark]***.

b) Manganese(IV) oxide powder isn't used up in the reaction ***[1 mark]***.

c) A: (energy of) reactants ***[1 mark]***
B: activation energy with a catalyst ***[1 mark]***
C: activation energy without a catalyst ***[1 mark]***
D: (energy of) products ***[1 mark]***

Page 91 — Endothermic and Exothermic Reactions

1 B ***[1 mark]***

2 E.g.

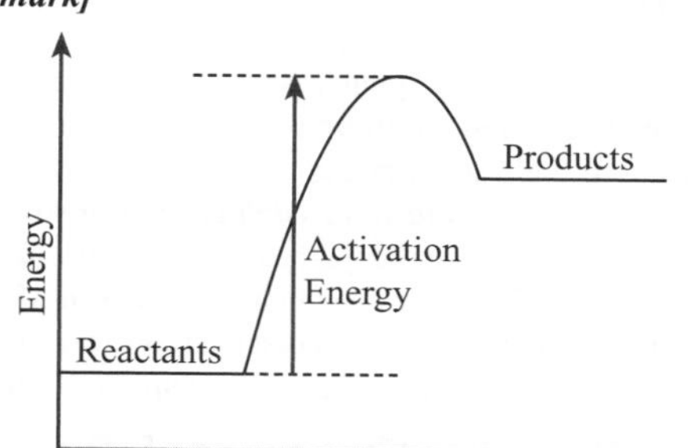

[1 mark for reactants and products correctly labelled and at appropriate energies, 1 mark for correct shape of curve, 1 mark for activation energy correctly labelled.]

3 a) The activation energy is the minimum amount of energy that is needed to start a reaction ***[1 mark]***.

b) Reaction A is the most suitable reaction ***[1 mark]***. Reaction C is endothermic / does not give out heat ***[1 mark]***. Reaction A has a lower activation energy than Reaction B / gives out more energy than Reaction B ***[1 mark]***.

Page 92 — Measuring Temperature Changes

1 a) Any three from: e.g. thermometer / polystyrene cup (and lid) / mass balance / measuring cylinder / beaker filled with cotton wool ***[1 mark for each]***.

b) How to grade your answer:

Level 0: There is no relevant information. ***[No marks]***

Level 1: The method is vague, and misses out important details about how the investigation could be carried out. The points made are basic and not linked together. ***[1 to 2 marks]***

Level 2: The method is clear, but misses out a few key details about how the investigation would be carried out or how the variables could be controlled. Some of the points made are linked together. ***[3 to 4 marks]***

Level 3: A detailed method is given that includes ways to reduce energy transfer to the surroundings, and specifies variables that should be controlled throughout the investigation. The points made are well-linked and the answer has a clear and logical structure. ***[5 to 6 marks]***

Here are some points your answer may include:
Place a polystyrene cup into a large beaker of cotton wool.
Add a measured volume of water to the polystyrene cup.
Record the initial temperature of the water.
Add a measured number of moles of salt A.
Stir the mixture.
Place a lid on the polystyrene cup to reduce the amount of energy transferred to the surroundings.
Record the maximum or minimum temperature reached by the mixture.
Repeat the experiment for salt B.
Use the same volume of water when repeating the experiment.
Use the same equipment/container/amount of insulation/ thermometer when repeating the experiment.

c)

Salt	Initial temperature / °C	End temperature / °C	Temperature change / °C
A	21.0	16.0	**–5.0**
B	21.0	26.5	**5.5**

[1 mark for each row correctly completed]

d) C ***[1 mark]***

Pages 93–94 — Bond Energies

Warm-up

C

1 a) E.g. energy change = energy required to break bonds – energy released by forming bonds

bonds broken: (1 × C=C) + (1 × H—O)
= 614 + 463 = 1077 kJ mol^{-1}

bonds made: (1 × C—C) + (1 × C—H) + (1 × C—O)
= 347 + 413 + 358 = 1118 kJ mol^{-1}

energy change = 1077 – 1118 = **–41 kJ mol^{-1}**

[3 marks for correct answer, otherwise 1 mark for calculating the energy of bonds broken and 1 mark for calculating the energy of bonds made.]

If there are any bonds that appear on both sides of the equation, you can ignore them (that's what we've done here). But if you find it easier to work out the total energy of all the bonds in the products and the total energy of all the bonds in the reactants, that's fine. You'll get the same answer.

b) The reaction is exothermic ***[1 mark]*** as the energy change of reaction is negative / energy is given out during the reaction / it takes less energy to break the bonds in the reactants than the energy given out when the bonds in the products are made ***[1 mark]***.

2 a) The energy released by forming bonds in the products is greater than the energy used to break the bonds in the reactants ***[1 mark]***.

b) E.g. bonds broken: (1 × C—H) + (1 × Cl—Cl) = 413 + 239 = 652 kJ mol^{-1}
bonds made: (1 × C—Cl) + (1 × H—Cl) = 339 + H—Cl
energy change = energy required to break bonds – energy released by forming bonds
–119 = 652 – (339 + H—Cl)
–119 = 313 – H—Cl
H—Cl = 313 + 119 = **432 kJ mol^{-1}**
[3 marks for the correct answer, otherwise 1 mark for correctly calculating energies of bonds made and broken and 1 mark for a correct expression for energy change of reaction including the H—Cl bond .]

c) Cl—Cl, C—Cl, C—C, C—H, H—Cl
[1 mark for correct order.]

Stronger bonds take more energy to break, so stronger bonds will have higher bond energies.

Topic 8 — Fuels and Earth Science

Pages 95–97 — Fractional Distillation and Hydrocarbons

Warm-up
Bitumen — Surfacing roads and roofs.
Diesel — Fuel for cars, lorries and trains.
Kerosene — Fuel for aircraft.

1 a) A compound formed from hydrogen and carbon ***[1 mark]*** only ***[1 mark]***.

b) B ***[1 mark]***

c) One day it will run out / it is being used at a much faster rate than the rate at which it is being reformed ***[1 mark]***.

2 They have molecular formulas that differ by CH_2 from neighbouring compounds ***[1 mark]***. They share similar chemical properties ***[1 mark]***. They show a gradual variation in physical properties ***[1 mark]***.

3 a) i) When they are burned, they give out lots of energy ***[1 mark]***.

ii) $C_3H_8 + 5O_2 \rightarrow 3CO_2 + 4H_2O$
[1 mark for formulas of all reactants and products correct, 1 mark for correct balancing.]

b) C ***[1 mark]***

4 a) Fuel oil has the highest boiling point ***[1 mark]***. Fuel oil has the longest / largest molecules of the three fractions, and the longer / larger the hydrocarbon, the higher its boiling point ***[1 mark]***.

b) Fuel oil is more viscous than kerosene ***[1 mark]***. Fuel oil has longer / larger molecules than kerosene, and the longer / larger the hydrocarbon, the higher the viscosity ***[1 mark]***.

It's perfectly fine if you phrased your answer the other way round here (i.e. "Kerosene will be less viscous than fuel oil, because...").

c) Kerosene is easier to ignite than diesel oil ***[1 mark]***. Kerosene has shorter / smaller molecules than diesel oil, and the shorter / smaller the hydrocarbon, the easier it is to ignite ***[1 mark]***.

Same here — it's fine if you phrased your answer the other way round (i.e. "Diesel oil will be harder to ignite than kerosene, because...").

5 a) E.g. fuel for large ships ***[1 mark]*** and in power stations ***[1 mark]***.

b) i) triacontane ***[1 mark]***

ii) E.g. the further down the column a hydrocarbon is collected, the higher its boiling point ***[1 mark]***. Long hydrocarbons, like triacontane, have higher boiling points than shorter hydrocarbons like heptane ***[1 mark]***. This is because their chains are much longer, so the intermolecular forces between the chains are stronger ***[1 mark]***. More energy is needed to overcome these forces and turn the hydrocarbon into a gas ***[1 mark]***, so triacontane will have a higher boiling point than heptane and will be collected further down the column ***[1 mark]***.

c) Bitumen / fuel oil ***[1 mark]***.

Since alkane X is more viscous than triacontane, it must be a longer molecule. So it must either be a longer hydrocarbon from the fuel oil fraction, or be in the only fraction with longer molecules (bitumen).

Page 98 — Pollutants

1 a) C ***[1 mark]***

b) Any two from: e.g. lakes could become acidic causing plants and animals to die / trees could be killed / damage to limestone buildings and stone statues / corrosion of metals ***[1 mark for each correct answer]***.

2 a) Nitrogen and oxygen from the air ***[1 mark]*** react together at the high temperatures produced by combustion in the engine ***[1 mark]***.

b) Soot can cause respiratory problems ***[1 mark]***.

c) Carbon monoxide ***[1 mark]***. It binds to red blood cells, reducing the amount of oxygen they can transport ***[1 mark]***. This can lead to fainting, coma or even death ***[1 mark]***.

d) Any two from: e.g. burning hydrogen only produces water/does not produce pollutants/carbon dioxide/carbon monoxide/soot like burning fossil fuels does. / Hydrogen is obtained from water which is a renewable source (so it won't run out, unlike fossil fuels). / More hydrogen can be made from the water produced by the fuel cell as a waste product ***[1 mark for each correct answer]***.

Pages 99-100 — Cracking

1 a) B ***[1 mark]***

b) The amount of some fractions produced does not always meet the demand for those products ***[1 mark]***. More of the product can be produced by cracking longer molecules into smaller, more useful ones ***[1 mark]***.

c) E.g. $C_{10}H_{22} \rightarrow C_7H_{16} + C_3H_6$ ***[1 mark]***

Cracking equations must always be balanced and have a shorter alkane and an alkene on the right-hand side.

2 a) Gases ***[1 mark]*** and petrol ***[1 mark]***.

b) Molecules from the fuel oil and bitumen fractions could be cracked to produce extra diesel ***[1 mark]***.

3 a) The hydrocarbon is very flammable ***[1 mark]***. The bung prevents hydrocarbon vapour from escaping the boiling tube and igniting ***[1 mark]***.

b) E.g. they didn't completely fill the test tube with water at the start of the experiment ***[1 mark]***.

c) E.g. the test tube could be replaced with a measuring cylinder ***[1 mark]***.

d) If cold water was sucked back into the hot boiling tube, it could cause the boiling tube to crack ***[1 mark]***.

e) E.g. the reaction would take too long without a catalyst. / It would not be safe/possible to reach the temperature required to conduct this reaction in a laboratory without a catalyst ***[1 mark]***.

Page 101 — The Atmosphere

1 A ***[1 mark]***

2 a) i) carbon dioxide ***[1 mark]***

ii) Any two from, e.g: plants evolved which removed carbon dioxide through photosynthesis / carbon dioxide was locked in fossil fuels/sedimentary rocks / carbon dioxide dissolved in the oceans ***[1 mark for each correct answer]***.

b) i) As green plants photosynthesised, they produced oxygen ***[1 mark]***. Hardly any oxygen is present in Mars' atmosphere as there are no plants / no discovered life on Mars ***[1 mark]***.

ii) Oxygen gas will relight a glowing splint ***[1 mark]***.

Pages 102–104 — The Greenhouse Effect and Climate Change

Warm-up
Walking to school
Turning central heating down

1 a) Any two from: e.g. carbon dioxide / methane / water vapour ***[1 mark for each correct answer]***

b) E.g. burning fossil fuels / deforestation *[1 mark for each correct answer]*

2 a) B *[1 mark]*

b) Elvis is incorrect, e.g. because greenhouse gases are responsible for the greenhouse effect, which is important as it keeps the Earth warm enough to support life *[1 mark]*.

3 a) How to grade your answer:

Level 0: There is no relevant information. *[No marks]*

Level 1: There is a brief explanation of what the data in the graph shows, but uncertainty is not discussed. The points made are basic and not linked together. *[1 to 2 marks]*

Level 2: There is an explanation of what the data in the graph shows. There is some mention of the uncertainty associated with any conclusions drawn from this data. Some of the points made are linked together. *[3 to 4 marks]*

Level 3: There is a clear and detailed conclusion of what the data in the graph shows, and the uncertainty associated with conclusions drawn from this data is thoroughly discussed. The points made are well-linked and the answer has a clear and logical structure. *[5 to 6 marks]*

Here are some points your answer may include:

The data in the graph shows that CO_2 emissions in the UK have decreased from the 1993 through to 2013.

The data shows that global sea levels have risen from the 1993 through to 2013.

The data suggests that CO_2 emissions are not the cause of rising sea levels as the CO_2 emissions in the UK decreased as the sea level rose.

The data in this graph does not support a link between human activity and climate change.

The CO_2 emissions from burning fossil fuels are only from one country and are not a global figure.

The global CO_2 emissions from burning fossil fuels may be increasing so there could be a link between CO_2 emissions and a rise in sea levels.

CO_2 emissions from other sources, not just burning fossil fuels, should be considered.

b) Any two from: e.g. encouraging energy efficiency / creating financial incentives to reduce CO_2 emissions / using more renewable energy / increasing research into new energy sources *[1 mark for each correct answer]*.

4 a) E.g. the composition of the gases in the bubbles could be analysed to find out the concentration of gases in the atmosphere at different times *[1 mark]*.

b) The data does support the scientist's conclusion *[1 mark]*. The global temperature anomaly, and therefore the global temperature, increases as the concentration of carbon dioxide increases *[1 mark]*.

c) E.g. increasing carbon dioxide levels in the atmosphere cause the global temperature to increase *[1 mark]*. Higher temperatures may cause ice caps to melt, reducing the amount of ice available for scientists to collect *[1 mark]*.

d) Any one from: e.g. collecting large ice cores is expensive / drilling so deep might disturb the local environment / scientists may require specialist equipment to collect/store large ice cores *[1 mark]*.

Topic 9 — Separate Chemistry 2

Pages 105–108 — Tests for Ions

1 a) i) ammonia *[1 mark]*

ii) Hold a piece of damp red litmus paper over the gas *[1 mark]*. If the gas is ammonia, the litmus paper will turn blue *[1 mark]*.

b) i) barium chloride solution *[1 mark]*

ii) white *[1 mark]*

2 a) lithium ion / Li^+ ion *[1 mark]*

b) i) blue-green *[1 mark]*

ii) A blue *[1 mark]* precipitate would form *[1 mark]*.

3 a) Fe^{3+} ion / iron(III) ion *[1 mark]*

b) $FeBr_2$ *[1 mark]*

The green precipitate with sodium hydroxide tells you that it contains Fe^{2+} ions. The cream precipitate with silver nitrate tells you that it contains Br^- ions. The formula of the compound must be $FeBr_2$ to balance the charges.

c) i) Other metal ions (e.g. calcium) can also react with sodium hydroxide to form a white precipitate *[1 mark]*.

ii) The white precipitate would dissolve, leaving a colourless solution *[1 mark]*.

4 a) The compound contains both sodium and potassium ions / two metal cations, so a flame test would give a mixture of colours *[1 mark]*.

b) Add dilute acid *[1 mark]*. Collect the gas produced and pass it through limewater *[1 mark]*. If carbonate ions were present in the test solution, the limewater will turn cloudy *[1 mark]*.

5 How to grade your answer:

Level 0: There is no relevant information. *[No marks]*

Level 1: There is a brief explanation of how to test the compound for either potassium ions or chloride ions. The points made are basic and not linked together. *[1 to 2 marks]*

Level 2: There is some explanation of how to test the compound for both potassium ions and chloride ions. Some of the points made are linked together. *[3 to 4 marks]*

Level 3: There is a clear and detailed explanation of how to test the compound for both potassium ions and chloride ions. The points made are well-linked and the answer has a clear and logical structure. *[5 to 6 marks]*

Here are some points your answer may include:

To test the compound for potassium ions:

Oliver could carry out a flame test to show whether or not the compound contains potassium ions.

To do this, he should clean a wire loop by dipping it into hydrochloric acid and rinsing it in distilled water.

Then he should dip the wire loop into his compound and put the loop in the clear blue part of a Bunsen flame.

If the compound contains potassium ions, Oliver should see a lilac flame.

To test the compound for chloride ions:

To test for chloride ions, Oliver will first need to dissolve a little of the solid salt in distilled water.

Next he should add a little dilute nitric acid.

Then he should add a few drops of silver nitrate solution.

If the compound contains chloride ions, a white precipitate should form.

6 a) E.g. the students should connect the test tube containing the unknown solution and the test tube containing limewater straight away after adding the hydrochloric acid to the unknown solution *[1 mark]*. This will prevent any carbon dioxide that is formed in the reaction from escaping before it is tested for with the limewater *[1 mark]*.

b) E.g. to test for calcium ions, the students can carry out a flame test *[1 mark]*. If calcium ions are present, they will see an orange-red flame *[1 mark]*. They could test for aluminium ions by adding excess sodium hydroxide solution to the test tube containing sodium hydroxide *[1 mark]*. If aluminium ions are present, the white precipitate will redissolve to form a colourless solution *[1 mark]*.

Pages 109-110 — Flame Photometry

1 A *[1 mark]*

2 a) metal A and metal C *[1 mark]*

b) 0.21 mol dm^{-3} *[1 mark]*

The relative emission intensity of the ion is 3.6, so draw a horizontal line from 3.6 on the y-axis out to the curve. Then draw a straight line down to the x-axis from this point to find the concentration.

3 a) Ions W and Z *[2 marks — 1 mark for each correct answer]*

b) Ions W and Y *[1 mark]*. Some of the wavelengths in the spectrum for mixture P are not given in Figure 3. These wavelengths could come from one or more other ions *[1 mark]*.

c) E.g. a flame test would not be useful in identifying the metal ions in the mixture, because different metal ions produce different colours *[1 mark]*. In a flame test, the colours could mix and mask each other *[1 mark]*.

Pages 111–112 — Alkanes and Alkenes

Warm-up

The following compounds should be circled:

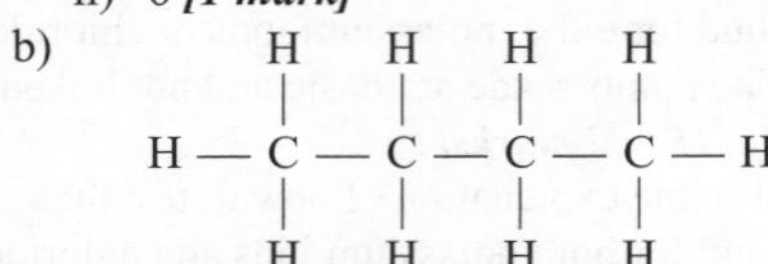

1 C *[1 mark]*

2 a) i) ethane *[1 mark]*

ii) 6 *[1 mark]*

b)

```
    H   H   H   H
    |   |   |   |
H — C — C — C — C — H
    |   |   |   |
    H   H   H   H
```

[1 mark]

c) E.g. the molecule contains no carbon-carbon double bonds / the molecule only contains carbon-carbon single bonds / all of the atoms in the molecule have formed bonds with as many other atoms as they can *[1 mark]*.

3 a) C_nH_{2n} *[1 mark]*

b) C *[1 mark]*

c) Alkenes must contain at least two carbon atoms so that a double bond can form between them *[1 mark]*.

4 a) i)

```
H       H   H
 \      |   |
  C  =  C — C — H
 /          |
H           H
```

[1 mark]

ii) The solution would turn from orange to colourless *[1 mark]*.

iii) An addition reaction *[1 mark]*.

b) Nothing would happen / the solution would stay orange *[1 mark]*. C_2H_6/ethane is a saturated hydrocarbon/an alkane/ doesn't contain a double bond *[1 mark]* so it can't react with bromine *[1 mark]*.

Pages 113–114 — Addition Polymers

1 a) B *[1 mark]*

b)

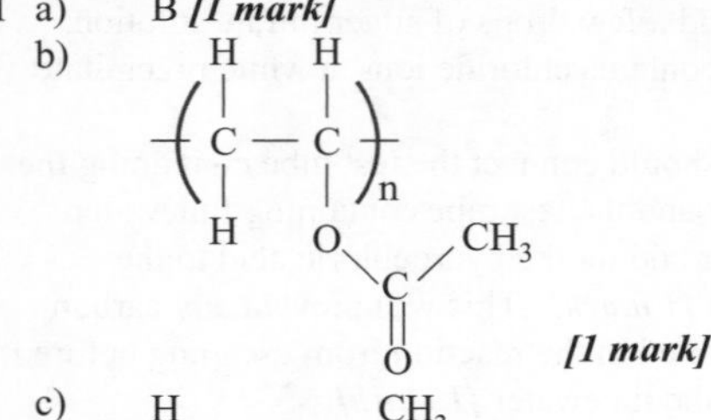

[1 mark]

c)

```
H       CH3
 \     /
  C = C
 /     \
H       H
```

[1 mark]

d) poly(tetrafluoroethene) *[1 mark]* Any two reasons from: a pan needs to be non-stick to stop food getting stuck to the surface of the pan while it cooks *[1 mark]*. / It needs to be unreactive so that food doesn't become contaminated *[1 mark]*. / It needs to be heat-resistant to stop it being damaged by heating *[1 mark]*.

2 a) Selena, as the monomer contains a double bond between two carbon atoms / the monomer contains an alkene functional group *[1 mark]*.

b) B *[1 mark]*

c)

```
H       Cl
 \     /
  C = C
 /     \
H       H
```

[1 mark]

Pages 115–116 — Condensation Polymers

1 D *[1 mark]*

2 A *[1 mark]*

3 a)

Polymer	Protein	Starch
Monomer	**amino acid**	**sugar**

[1 mark for each correct answer]

b) i) DNA *[1 mark]*

ii) four *[1 mark]*

4 a) A *[1 mark]*

b) an ester link *[1 mark]*

c)

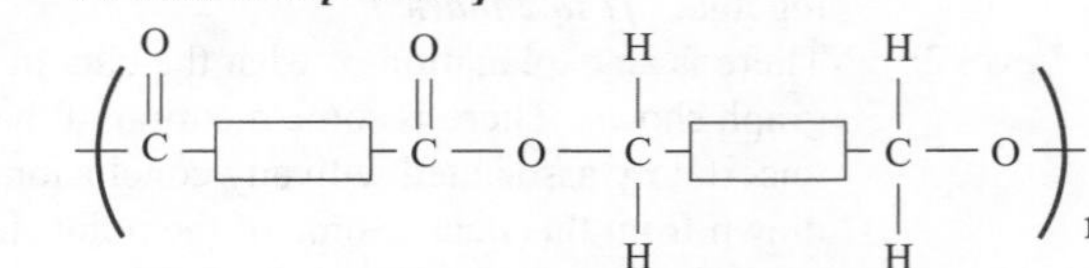

[1 mark for correct ester link connecting monomers, 1 mark for rest of the structure being correct.]

You could also draw the repeat unit with the monomers the other way round (so that the diol monomer is on the left-hand side and the dicarboxylic acid is on the right-hand side).

d) i) H_2O *[1 mark]*

ii) An -OH group from a carboxylic acid monomer *[1 mark]* combines with an H atom that is lost from an alcohol monomer *[1 mark]*.

e) carbon, hydrogen, oxygen *[1 mark]*

Page 117 — Disposing of Polymers

1 a) D *[1 mark]*

b) Most polymers are made from crude oil which is a finite resource/non-renewable *[1 mark]*.

c) E.g. the strength of polymers decreases over time *[1 mark]*. Recycled polymers will be weaker than new polymers and so less suitable for applications that require really strong polymers *[1 mark]*.

2 a) If different polymer types are mixed together, the quality/ strength of the recycled polymer product is reduced *[1 mark]*.

b) E.g. lots of valuable land gets used up as landfill sites / polymers are non-biodegradable so remain in landfill for a long time *[1 mark]*.

c) Advantage: e.g. burning polymers produces energy which can be used to generate electricity / burning polymers reduces the amount of polymers that are sent to landfill *[1 mark]*. Disadvantage: e.g. if the burning is not carefully controlled, the combustion can release toxic gases / carbon dioxide is produced when polymers are burnt which contributes to global warming *[1 mark]*.

Pages 118–119 — Alcohols and Carboxylic Acids

Warm-up

-OH

1 A *[1 mark]*

2 a) propanol *[1 mark]*

b) C_2H_5OH *[1 mark]*

c)

```
    H
    |
H — C — O — H
    |
    H
```

[1 mark]

3 a) -COOH *[1 mark]*

b) C_2H_5COOH *[1 mark]*

c) ethanoic acid *[1 mark]*

d)

```
       O
      //
H — C
      \
       O — H
```

[1 mark for –COOH functional group, 1 mark for rest of structure]

4 a) B *[1 mark]*

b) It is also a carboxylic acid / in the same homologous series as butanoic acid *[1 mark]*, so it will react in a similar way to butanoic acid / it will also react to form an ester *[1 mark]*.

Page 120 — Production of Ethanol

1 a) carbon dioxide *[1 mark]*

b) Fractional distillation *[1 mark]*. The fermentation mixture is heated *[1 mark]*. Ethanol evaporates and the vapour rises up the fractionating column, while the water stays as a liquid because it has a higher boiling point *[1 mark]*. A (Liebig) condenser condenses the ethanol vapour *[1 mark]* and the concentrated ethanol is collected in a separate flask *[1 mark]*.

2 a) No, Isla is incorrect. The enzymes in the yeast would denature *[1 mark]* so the fermentation reaction would stop *[1 mark]*.

b) i) Conditions with no oxygen *[1 mark]*.

ii) Any pH from 2-6 *[1 mark]*. Umar's fermentation mixture is open to the air, so the ethanol will react with oxygen in the air, converting it to ethanoic acid (which is acidic) *[1 mark]*.

c) When the concentration of alcohol reaches about 10–20%, the yeast get killed of by the alcohol *[1 mark]* and the fermentation reaction stops *[1 mark]*.

Page 121 — Combustion of Alcohols

1 a) How to grade your answer:

Level 0: There is no relevant information. *[No marks]*

Level 1: There is a brief explanation of how to carry the experiment but it has limited detail, little technical equipment is mentioned and no reference is made to controlling variables. The points made are basic and not linked together. *[1 to 2 marks]*

Level 2: There is some explanation of how to carry out the experiment, some description of the equipment required and reference is made to controlling variables. Some of the points made are linked together. *[3 to 4 marks]*

Level 3: There is a clear and detailed explanation of how to carry out the experiment, all the equipment needed is included and there is a full explanation of how to control variables. The points made are well-linked and the answer has a clear and logical structure. *[5 to 6 marks]*

Here are some points your answer may include:
Put a measured volume of alcohol X into a spirit burner.
Measure the mass of the burner and alcohol using a mass balance.
Measure out a volume of distilled water into a copper calorimeter and place a thermometer inside.
Insulate the calorimeter by using a draught excluder.
Cover the calorimeter with an insulating lid.
Take the initial temperature of the water.
Put the burner underneath the calorimeter and light the wick.
Stir the water throughout using the thermometer.
Blow out the spirit burner when the temperature of the water has increased by a desired amount.
Immediately reweigh the burner and fuel.
Repeat the experiment using alcohols Y and Z.
Use the same number of moles of alcohols Y and Z.
Keep the mass/volume of water, the height of the container above the wick and the length of the wick / height of the flame the same.

b) i) Alcohol X was the most efficient, since the smallest mass of alcohol X was needed to raise the temperature of the water by 25 °C *[1 mark]*.

ii) alcohol X *[1 mark]*

Page 122 — Nanoparticles

1 B *[1 mark]*

2 Advantage: e.g. sunscreens containing nanoparticles give better skin coverage / don't leave white marks on the skin *[1 mark]*.
Disadvantage: e.g. the nanoparticles in sunscreens may be harmful to human health *[1 mark]*.

3 a) Any one from: e.g. fullerenes could be used to deliver drugs directly to individual cells, because fullerenes are more easily absorbed into the body than larger particles / silver nanoparticles can be added to the fibres used to make surgical masks and wound dressings, because silver nanoparticles have antibacterial properties. ***[1 mark for a medical use of nanoparticles, 1 mark for relating the given use to properties of nanoparticles.]***

b) Nanomedicines are a new form of medicine, so they need to be tested *[1 mark]* for unexpected or harmful side effects before they can be considered safe to use *[1 mark]*.

4 E.g. the surface area to volume ratio *[1 mark]* of nanoparticles is much higher than that of larger particles *[1 mark]*. This gives nanoparticles different qualities because a much greater proportion of their atoms are available to interact with other substances *[1 mark]*.

Pages 123-124 — Types of Material and Their Uses

Warm-up

Glass — Ceramic	Polystyrene — Polymer
Aluminium — Metal	Concrete — Composite

1 a) Fibreglass *[1 mark]*

b) E.g. Plasticised PVC *[1 mark]* would be the best choice as it's an electrical insulator (it has low electrical conductivity) *[1 mark]*. It has the lowest stiffness of the four materials which allows wires to bend *[1 mark]*. It's also cheap which keeps the cost down of electrical products containing lots of wiring *[1 mark]*.

c) Low-density poly(ethene), because it is less stiff / more flexible, making the bottle easy to squeeze *[1 mark]*.

2 a) E.g. The hockey stick needs to be strong to withstand forces applied during the game. Carbon fibre and steel have the greatest strength (4100 MPa and 780 MPa, respectively). The stick needs to be lightweight. Carbon fibre has a much lower density than steel (1.5 g cm^{-3} compared to 7.8 g cm^{-3}) so would be much lighter. Carbon fibre is also resistant to corrosion which is important if used in the rain. Though carbon fibre is expensive, because the hockey stick is a professional hockey stick, the cost of the stick can be high. Carbon fibre would be the best choice because it offers the best combination of strength and low density.
[1 mark for each valid comparison between properties from the table, up to a total of 3 marks. 1 mark for choosing a material and giving suitable justification of the choice.]

b) E.g. Bridges need to be strong and steel and carbon fibre are the strongest materials in the table (780 MPa and 4100 MPa, respectively). Bridges are big structures so the cost of the material should be kept down and steel is much cheaper than carbon fibre. Bridges also need to be resistant to corrosion, and steel can be protected to prevent it corroding. Steel would be the best choice because it offers the best combination of strength, corrosion resistance and low cost.
[1 mark for each valid comparison between properties from the table, up to a total of 3 marks. 1 mark for choosing a material and giving suitable justification of the choice.]

c) Pipes need to have a good resistance to corrosion, so PVC, carbon fibre and lead would be good choices. PVC is a lot cheaper than lead and carbon fibre. PVC is also lightweight, which would allow the pipes to be mounted on houses. The strength of the material is not an important factor, so the low strength of PVC is not an issue. PVC would be the best choice because it offers the best combination of corrosion resistance, low density and low cost.
[1 mark for each valid comparison between properties from the table, up to a total of 3 marks. 1 mark for choosing a material and giving suitable justification of the choice.]

Mixed Questions

Pages 125-135 — Mixed Questions

1 a) condensation *[1 mark]*
b) B *[1 mark]*

2 a) carboxylic acids *[1 mark]*
b) butanoic acid *[1 mark]*
c) $M_r = (4 \times A_r \text{ of C}) + (8 \times A_r \text{ of H}) + (2 \times A_r \text{ of O})$
$= (4 \times 12) + (8 \times 1) + (2 \times 16)$
$= 48 + 8 + 32 =$ **88** ***[1 mark]***
d) molecular formula = $C_4H_8O_2$
The largest number that all the numbers in the molecular formula will divide by is 2:
C: $4 \div 2 = 2$ H: $8 \div 2 = 4$ O: $2 \div 2 = 1$
So the empirical formula is $\mathbf{C_2H_4O}$ ***[2 marks for correct answer, otherwise 1 mark for finding the molecular formula.]***

3 a) calcium + sulfuric acid → calcium sulfate + hydrogen
[1 mark for correct left-hand side, 1 mark for correct right-hand side.]
b) $CaSO_4$ ***[1 mark]***
Calcium is in group 2, so it forms 2+ ions. Sulfate ions have a −2 charge (this is one you just need to remember). So, for a neutral compound, you need a ratio of Ca^{2+} : SO_4^{2-} of 1 : 1.
c) insoluble ***[1 mark]***
All sulfates, except lead, barium and calcium sulfate, are soluble.
d) Sodium is above calcium in the reactivity series ***[1 mark]***.

4 a)
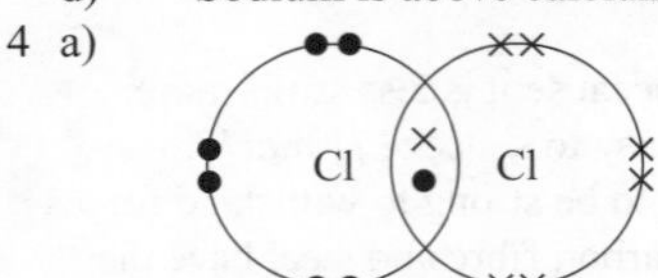

[1 mark for shared pair of electrons, 1 mark for six further electrons in the outer shell of each chlorine atom]
b) C ***[1 mark]***
c) Hold a piece of damp blue litmus paper in the gas ***[1 mark]***. It will be bleached white in the presence of chlorine ***[1 mark]***.
d) liquid ***[1 mark]***
−50 °C is between the melting and boiling points of chlorine, so chlorine would be a liquid at this temperature.

5 a) a piece of (filter) paper ***[1 mark]***
b) R_f of **A** = 4.6 ÷ 12.1 = **0.38** ***[1 mark]***
R_f of **B** = 7.3 ÷ 12.1 = **0.60** ***[1 mark]***
R_f of **C** = 10.6 ÷ 12.1 = **0.876** ***[1 mark]***
c) There is a spot of substance on the baseline / there is a substance with an R_f value of 0 ***[1 mark]***.
d) D ***[1 mark]***
e) A mixture is a substance that contains different compounds or different elements that aren't all part of a single compound ***[1 mark]***.
f) E.g. fractional distillation ***[1 mark]***

6 a) Temperature change for methanol = 42.9 – 25.7 = **17.2 °C**
Temperature change for ethanol = 54.3 – 25.9 = **28.4 °C**
Temperature change for methanol = 58.9 – 26.4 = **32.5 °C**
[2 marks for all three correct, otherwise 1 mark for any one correct.]
b)
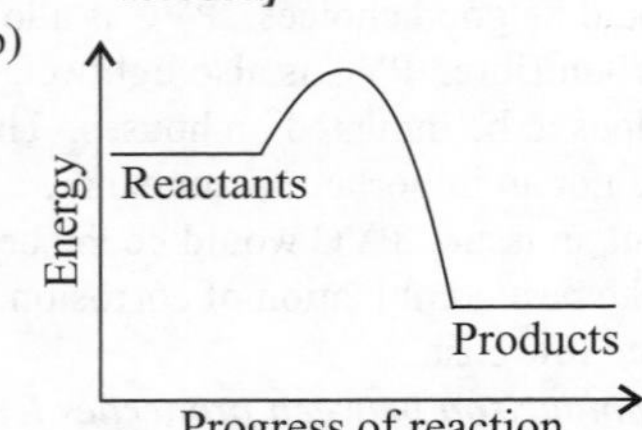

[1 mark for showing and labelling reactants and products, with products having less energy than reactants, 1 mark for a correctly-shaped curve joining reactants and products.]
c) It binds to red blood cells, reducing the amount of oxygen they can transport ***[1 mark]***. This can lead to fainting, coma or even death ***[1 mark]***.

7 a) C_5H_{10} ***[1 mark]***
b) The mixture would change from orange to colourless ***[1 mark]***. This is because the products of cracking contain alkenes/unsaturated compounds / C_5H_{10} is an alkene/unsaturated ***[1 mark]***.

8 a) E.g. both can conduct electricity as solid metals have delocalised electrons which can carry a charge.
[1 mark for any common property of metals not mentioned in the table, 1 mark for an explanation relating that property to metallic bonding].
b) Any two from e.g. transition metals and their compounds make good catalysts / they have high melting points / they have high densities / they form colourful compounds.
[1 mark for each property. No marks for properties common to metals in general, e.g. hard, strong, shiny, heat/electrical conductors.]
c) E.g. the cups need to be lightweight, as campers might want to carry them long distances in their bags, tough enough not to break easily when being packed or carried in bags, and cheap to manufacture. Glass would not be suitable, as it is very brittle, so would break easily. Titanium would be too expensive, and is the heaviest of the four materials. The aluminium alloy would be unsuitable because it corrodes and is also quite heavy. Melamine resin is more brittle than most of the others, but would be most suitable, because it's fairly tough, lightweight and cheap. ***[1 mark for each valid comparison between properties from the table, up to a total of 3 marks. 1 mark for choosing a material and giving suitable justification of the choice.]***

9 a) $2Rb + F_2 \rightarrow 2RbF$
[2 marks for all formulas correct and a correctly-balanced equation, otherwise 1 mark for correct formulas in an unbalanced equation]
b) ionic ***[1 mark]***
c) The compound will have a high melting point, because there are strong forces of electrostatic attraction between the ions ***[1 mark]*** and a large amount of energy is needed to overcome these forces and melt the solid ***[1 mark]***.

10 a) E.g. wear safety goggles / wear a lab coat / wear gloves / use dilute concentrations of chlorine water ***[1 mark]***.
b) The solution would turn from colourless to brown ***[1 mark]***.
c) Chlorine is more reactive than iodine ***[1 mark]***, so it displaces iodine from the potassium iodide solution ***[1 mark]***.
d) $Cl_2 + 2I^- \rightarrow 2Cl^- + I_2$
[1 mark for correct left-hand side, 1 mark for correct right-hand side]

11 a)
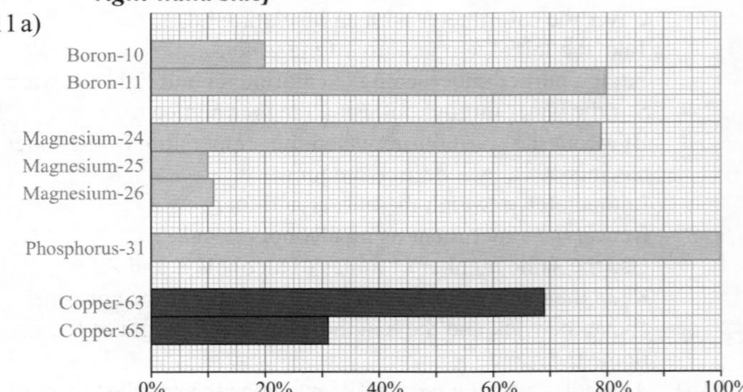

[1 mark for each correct bar]
b) The relative atomic mass of an element is the average of the mass numbers of all the atoms of that element ***[1 mark]***. Phosphorus only has one isotope, so its relative atomic mass is equal to the mass number of its atoms (31) ***[1 mark]***. Boron, magnesium and copper all have more than one isotope, which exist in different quantities, so the average of their mass numbers won't be a whole number ***[1 mark]***.

c) % Mg-24 = 79%, % Mg-25 = 10%, % Mg-26 = 11%
So, relative atomic mass of Mg =
$[(24 \times 79) + (25 \times 10) + (26 \times 11)] \div 100$
$= 2432 \div 100 =$ **24.32**
[4 marks for a correct answer, but deduct 1 mark if not correctly rounded to 3 s.f.. Otherwise 1 mark for correct % abundances of Mg isotopes and 1 mark for correctly substituting the atomic masses and abundances into an equation to work out relative atomic mass.]

12 B ***[1 mark]***
M_r of Na_2SO_4 = (2 × 23) + 32 + (4 × 16) = 142
moles of Na_2SO_4 = 34.08 ÷ 142 = 0.24 moles
In one mole of Na_2SO_4 there are 4 moles of oxygen atoms. So, in 0.24 moles of Na_2SO_4 there are (0.24 × 4 =) 0.96 moles of oxygen atoms.
number of particles in one mole = 6.02×10^{23}, so,
number of atoms in 0.96 moles = $0.96 \times 6.02 \times 10^{23} = 5.7792 \times 10^{23}$
$= 5.779 \times 10^{23}$ atoms (to 4 s.f.)

13 a) Aluminium is reduced and oxygen is oxidised / aluminium gains electrons and oxygen loses electrons ***[1 mark]***.

b) $Al^{3+} + 3e^- \rightarrow Al$ ***[1 mark for correct reactants and products, 1 mark for correct electrons]***

c) $M_r(Al_2O_3) = (2 \times 27) + (3 \times 16) = 102$
moles = mass ÷ M_r
moles of Al_2O_3 = 40.8 ÷ 102 = 0.400 moles
From the balanced equation, 2 moles of aluminium oxide produce 4 moles of aluminium.
So, 0.400 moles of aluminium oxide will produce (0.400 ÷ 2) × 4 = 0.800 moles of aluminium.
$A_r(Al) = 27$, so mass of Al = 0.800 × 27 = **21.6 g**
[4 marks for correct answer, otherwise 1 mark for correctly calculating M_r of Al_2O_3, 1 mark for working out how many moles of Al_2O_3 are in 40.8 g and 1 mark for working out how many moles of Al are made.]

d) Heating with carbon will only reduce metals that are less reactive than carbon ***[1 mark]***. Aluminium is more reactive than carbon, so heating with carbon will not extract aluminium metal from its ore ***[1 mark]***.

e) Any two from: e.g. Recycling reduces waste going to landfill. / Recycling generally requires less energy than extracting metals from their ores. / Recycling is generally cheaper than extracting metals from their ores. / Recycling reduces the need to mine ores, so it therefore reduces damage to the landscape cause by mining. / Recycling preserves natural resources, so it is more sustainable.***[1 mark for each valid advantage.]***

14 C ***[1 mark]***

15 D ***[1 mark]***

16 a) Na_2CO_3**(aq)** + $CuCl_2$**(aq)** → $CuCO_3$**(s)** + 2NaCl**(aq)**
[1 mark]

b) i) Crystallisation is used to separate soluble solids from solutions ***[1 mark]***. If Andre tried to separate the reaction mixture using crystallisation, he would end up with a mixture of solid copper carbonate and solid sodium chloride ***[1 mark]***.

ii) filtration ***[1 mark]***

c) M_r of $CuCO_3$ = A_r of Cu + A_r of C + (3 × A_r of O)
= 63.5 + 12 + (3 × 16) = 123.5
M_r of NaCl = A_r of Na + A_r of Cl = 23 + 35.5 = 58.5
Atom economy
= (M_r of desired products ÷ M_r of all products) × 100
= (M_r of $CuCO_3$) ÷ ((2 × M_r of NaCl) + (M_r of $CuCO_3$)) × 100
= (123.5) ÷ (123.5 + (2 × 58.5)) × 100
= (123.5 ÷ 240.5) × 100 = 51.35... = **51%**
[5 marks for correct answer, but deduct 1 mark if not correctly rounded to 2 s.f.. Otherwise 1 mark for calculating M_r of $CuCO_3$, 1 mark for calculating M_r of NaCl, 1 mark for dividing M_r of desired products by M_r of all products and 1 mark for multiplying by 100.]

d) percentage yield = (actual yield ÷ theoretical yield) × 100
= (21.51 ÷ 28.68) × 100 = **75%**
[3 marks for correct answer, otherwise 1 mark for a correct division and 1 mark for multiplication by 100.]

17 a) i) E.g. the only waste product made when hydrogen reacts with oxygen is water/hydrogen fuel doesn't produce pollutants (like carbon dioxide, carbon monoxide and sulfur dioxide) / hydrogen can be extracted from a renewable resource (water) / fuel cells are more efficient than conventional engines/ power stations ***[1 mark for each correct answer]***.

ii) Any two from: e.g. the extraction of hydrogen gas from raw materials often uses electricity from burning fossil fuels / hydrogen is hard to store / hydrogen fuel needs an expensive/ adapted engine ***[1 mark for each correct answer]***.

b) Bonds broken: (2 × H–H) + O=O = (2 × 436) + 498
= 872 + 498 = 1370 kJ mol^{-1}
Bonds formed: 4 × O–H = 4 × 463 = 1852 kJ mol^{-1}
Energy change = 1370 – 1852 = **–482 kJ mol^{-1}**
[3 marks for correct answer, otherwise 1 mark for correct energy value for bonds broken, 1 mark for correct energy value for bonds formed.]

c) Number of moles of O_2 = volume ÷ 24 = 156 ÷ 24 = 6.5 moles
From the reaction equation, 1 mole of O_2 reacts to form 2 moles of H_2O. So, 6.5 moles of O_2 will react to form (6.5 × 2) = 13 moles of H_2O.
M_r of H_2O = (2 × 1) + 16 = 18
moles = mass ÷ M_r
mass of H_2O formed = 13 × 18 = **234 g**
[4 marks for the correct answer, otherwise 1 mark for calculating the number of moles of O_2, 1 mark for calculating number of moles of H_2O formed and 1 mark for calculating M_r of H_2O.]

18 a) Nanoparticles are particles with a diameter between 1 nm and 100 nm / particles containing only a few hundred atoms ***[1 mark]***. Carbon nanotubes have different properties to bulk carbon because they have a very high surface area to volume ratio ***[1 mark]***.

b) Graphite contains layers of carbon atoms ***[1 mark]***. These layers are only held together by weak attractions so are able to slide over each other ***[1 mark]***. This makes graphite soft and slippery (so it can be used as a lubricant) ***[1 mark]***.

c) i) Order: diamond, poly(propene), butane ***[1 mark]***.
Explanation: Diamond is a giant covalent substance, whilst poly(propene) and butane are molecular ***[1 mark]***. Diamond has the highest melting point as you need to break the strong covalent bonds between the atoms to melt it ***[1 mark]***. Poly(propene) molecules are larger than butane molecules, so poly(propene)
has stronger intermolecular forces ***[1 mark]***, which require more energy to break ***[1 mark]***.

ii) E.g. diamond would be the best choice ***[1 mark]***. Diamond is strong and hard as it has a rigid structure, held together by strong covalent bonds ***[1 mark]***. These properties make diamond a suitable material to use in drill bits, as it would be able to withstand the forces involved in drilling ***[1 mark]***.

19 Number of moles of aluminium used
= mass of aluminium used ÷ A_r of aluminium
= 162 ÷ 27 = 6 moles
3 moles of H_2 are produced for every 2 moles of Al used, so moles of H_2 produced = (6 ÷ 2) × 3 = 9 moles
volume = number of moles × 24 = 9 × 24 = **216 dm^3**
[3 marks for correct answer, otherwise 1 mark for number of moles of aluminium used, 1 mark for number of moles of H_2 produced.]

The Periodic Table

Relative atomic mass → (top number in each box)

Atomic (proton) number → (bottom number in each box)

Periods	Group 1	Group 2											Group 3	Group 4	Group 5	Group 6	Group 7	Group 0
1								1 H Hydrogen 1										4 He Helium 2
2	7 Li Lithium 3	9 Be Beryllium 4											11 B Boron 5	12 C Carbon 6	14 N Nitrogen 7	16 O Oxygen 8	19 F Fluorine 9	20 Ne Neon 10
3	23 Na Sodium 11	24 Mg Magnesium 12											27 Al Aluminium 13	28 Si Silicon 14	31 P Phosphorus 15	32 S Sulfur 16	35.5 Cl Chlorine 17	40 Ar Argon 18
4	39 K Potassium 19	40 Ca Calcium 20	45 Sc Scandium 21	48 Ti Titanium 22	51 V Vanadium 23	52 Cr Chromium 24	55 Mn Manganese 25	56 Fe Iron 26	59 Co Cobalt 27	59 Ni Nickel 28	63.5 Cu Copper 29	65 Zn Zinc 30	70 Ga Gallium 31	73 Ge Germanium 32	75 As Arsenic 33	79 Se Selenium 34	80 Br Bromine 35	84 Kr Krypton 36
5	85 Rb Rubidium 37	88 Sr Strontium 38	89 Y Yttrium 39	91 Zr Zirconium 40	93 Nb Niobium 41	96 Mo Molybdenum 42	[98] Tc Technetium 43	101 Ru Ruthenium 44	103 Rh Rhodium 45	106 Pd Palladium 46	108 Ag Silver 47	112 Cd Cadmium 48	115 In Indium 49	119 Sn Tin 50	122 Sb Antimony 51	128 Te Tellurium 52	127 I Iodine 53	131 Xe Xenon 54
6	133 Cs Caesium 55	137 Ba Barium 56	139 La Lanthanum 57	178 Hf Hafnium 72	181 Ta Tantalum 73	184 W Tungsten 74	186 Re Rhenium 75	190 Os Osmium 76	192 Ir Iridium 77	195 Pt Platinum 78	197 Au Gold 79	201 Hg Mercury 80	204 Tl Thallium 81	207 Pb Lead 82	209 Bi Bismuth 83	[209] Po Polonium 84	[210] At Astatine 85	[222] Rn Radon 86
7	[223] Fr Francium 87	[226] Ra Radium 88	[227] Ac Actinium 89	[261] Rf Rutherfordium 104	[262] Db Dubnium 105	[266] Sg Seaborgium 106	[264] Bh Bohrium 107	[277] Hs Hassium 108	[268] Mt Meitnerium 109	[271] Ds Darmstadtium 110	[272] Rg Roentgenium 111							

The lanthanoids (atomic numbers 58-71) and the actinoids (atomic numbers 90-103) are not shown in this table.